Contents

A111 Discovering the arts and humanities

The Open University

Book 1 *Reputations*

Edited by Richard Jones

This publication forms part of the Open University module A111 *Discovering the arts and humanities*. Details of this and other Open University modules can be obtained from Student Recruitment, The Open University, PO Box 197, Milton Keynes MK7 6BJ, United Kingdom (tel. +44 (0)300 303 5303; email general-enquiries@open.ac.uk).

Alternatively, you may visit the Open University website at www.open.ac.uk where you can learn more about the wide range of modules and packs offered at all levels by The Open University.

The Open University, Walton Hall, Milton Keynes MK7 6AA

First published 2019

Edited and designed by The Open University.

Printed in the United Kingdom by Stephens & George Ltd, Dowlais, Merthyr Tydfil CF48 3TD

ISBN 978 1 4730 2462 5

1.1

Introduction

Richard Jones

Do you have a reputation? If you do, you will already know something about the subject of this book. You will know that the reputation you have acquired – for example, for making crispy roast potatoes – is not entirely justified. You have often made soggy roast potatoes. Not only that, you will know that this view of you is not widely shared. Some people have not even heard of your remarkable ability to roast potatoes. Even those who have heard about it express doubts. Once or twice, you might have been tempted to address those doubts – for example, by taking a photograph of a really crispy potato and posting it online. In doing so, you might have experienced the dizzying sense of being in control of what others think of you. It probably didn't last long though. You might have noticed that there was a growing gap between you and this so-called reputation. You might have even begun to wonder if you ever really liked potatoes in the first place.

This book is not about potatoes. But if we replace them with the different kinds of making and creating for which the people in this book are known, it perhaps comes close. The kind of questions that we might ask of our own reputations, we are going to ask here. Why are some people remembered and some forgotten? Why are people remembered for some things and not for others? What bearing does a reputation have on the person who is said to have it? What does a reputation tell us about those who are willing to believe in it? As you can tell from these questions, there is a good reason why the title of this book is *Reputations* and not just *Reputation*. None of the figures we discuss can be said to have just one of them.

What are the reputations that we are going to explore in this book? If you have already flicked through its pages, you will know that they belong to: Cleopatra, Mary (the mother of Jesus), Elizabeth I, Wolfgang Amadeus Mozart, Mary Wollstonecraft, Charles Dickens and Vincent van Gogh. It is likely that this list of names already conjures up certain ideas. If you find that it does, it is important to make a note about what they are. In studying reputations, we are not simply trying to step back in time to find the 'real' person (although, we are trying to do that in part), we are also thinking about the ways in which this person has been able to reach us today. What is it that we think we already know about them? What do we find appealing or unappealing? How has it come about that these figures can still speak to us and affect our lives?

I have been careful, so far, to say very little about the people featured in this book, because I do not want to disrupt any first impressions that you might bring. What you know or do not know about any one of these figures is already part of your study of them. This is why, before you start work on each of the chapters, you will be invited to make a note of your expectations. I will, however, make some observations about the selection of the figures. In putting together this book, the authors had to make difficult decisions about who to include and who to exclude. This means that the book itself is partly involved in perpetuating and creating certain reputations. We might ask, for example, why the artist Van Gogh is featured in the book and not some other artist? Why does Charles Dickens appear here and not some other writer? One answer is that, in putting together the book, we were thinking about the way that different figures contribute to areas of study in the arts and humanities. Mozart, for example, might be considered to be part of the canon of Western music – that is, he helps to define (or, we might say, provide the measure for) what the study of Music is about. This is not to say that studying Mozart is the only way to study Music – as later topics in the module will show. Instead, it is an aspect of the reputation of Mozart – as a canonical figure – that you are invited to consider and challenge. One person who draws attention to how canons are open to change is Mary Wollstonecraft: not that long ago, it would have been very easy to put together a book like this without Wollstonecraft in it. You may well be wondering who she is.

In this book, you will study seven different subject areas. As you explore the reputations of Cleopatra, Mary, the mother of Jesus, and Elizabeth I, you will be introduced to the methods of Classical Studies, Religious Studies and History. In the second half of the book, chapters on Mozart, Wollstonecraft, Dickens and Van Gogh introduce the approaches of Music, Philosophy, English Literature and Art History. Arranged like this, in chronological order, you will be presented with a certain version of the last 2000 years – as well as changing perspectives on how to go about studying it. Although different subject areas take different approaches, they share the common aim to build their views on evidence. You will find that in each chapter, you are working with a number of different sources in different ways. (The term 'source' is used to refer to an object of study, such as some words, a painting or a piece of music.) In doing so, you will be trying to work out whether some views about the past are more correct than others and how we know if they are.

Another word that became important to the authors as they worked on this book was 'myth'. You are probably familiar with the idea of a myth as a belief that is widely held but is ultimately false, or as a story that is perhaps told to explain some natural phenomenon or event. Even with these rudimentary definitions, it is possible to see how our notion of 'reputations' has a lot in common with the idea of myth. In asking whether we can get back to a correct view of the past, we are asking whether we can have anything more than the reputations or myths that have grown up around it. This is as much the case for Elizabeth I, for whom there is a lot of documentary evidence, as it is for Mary, the mother of Jesus, for whom there is little.

As you move through the module, you will notice some of the ways that the idea of myth is developed. In the second book, you will be able to experience the effects of storytelling first-hand, as well as study the way that Celtic myths became part of a nationalist movement in Ireland. In the third book, you will encounter the mythical figure of Antigone through both the study of ancient Greek drama and modern-day retellings of the story. In this way, the idea of reputations intersects with the other module themes of 'traditions' and 'crossing boundaries'. To study reputations is to become aware of the stories that have stuck to people, for whatever reason, and what they tell us, not only about their lives but about our own. This movement back and forth between the present and the past – or, more accurately, between our own values and the objects that we study – is what work in the arts and humanities is all about.

Chapter 1
Cleopatra

Trevor Fear

Contents

1 Introduction

In this chapter, we will start by exploring what is known about the historical figure of Cleopatra, or more properly Cleopatra VII. This will involve studying her background and political situation by looking closely at some of the material artefacts produced during her lifetime, which she most likely took an active role in designing. We will then go on to consider how Cleopatra was represented by Roman historians, since it is their image of Cleopatra that has had the most lasting impact on how she has been depicted in Western culture.

Finally, we will consider the different image of Cleopatra found in medieval Arabic culture. This work will prepare us to consider further representations of her in twentieth and twenty-first-century film and TV when we return to the module website after reading this chapter. In taking this varied approach, we will be exploring some of the different ways in which students of Classical Studies investigate the past.

2 The historical Cleopatra

You have already considered what you currently know about Cleopatra, and the associations and qualities that pop into your head when you hear her name. There is a good chance that many of the things that occurred to you have been shaped in part by the depictions of her that you have seen in films and on TV from the late twentieth and early twenty-first centuries. The historical figure of Cleopatra has been buried and obscured by the legends and stories that have accumulated around her over the last 2000 years. Let us move on now to consider some of the bare bones of the historical queen of Egypt, the starting point from which her later reputations grew.

2.1 Cleopatra: the last of the Ptolemies

Cleopatra VII was the final ruler of the last dynasty of the pharaohs of Egypt, the Ptolemies (pronounced 'tol-e-mi-z'). The Ptolemies were not native Egyptians in origin, but rather descendants of one of the generals (Ptolemy) of Alexander the Great, a Macedonian Greek, who conquered the Persian empire and its territories (including Egypt) in the fourth century BCE. They ruled over Egypt for nearly 300 years until the death of Cleopatra in 30 BCE. At its height, the kingdom of the Ptolemies consisted not only of Egypt but also territory around the Mediterranean coast (Figure 1).

The Ptolemies built their palaces not at the old sites of Egyptian rule, such as Memphis, but rather in the city that Alexander the Great had founded as a new capital for Egypt and (rather immodestly) named after himself – Alexandria. This city was a great metropolis of the ancient world. It possessed stunning architecture, such as its famous lighthouse, the tallest building in the ancient world apart from the Great Pyramid. The early Ptolemaic kings also turned the city into a leading centre of Greek intellectual activity through the establishment of the Musaeum, where they financially supported a community of scientists, mathematicians, writers and artists. In the same complex, the Ptolemies also established the Great Library of Alexandria, the largest collection of literature (primarily Greek literature) in the world at the time. In this way, Alexandria became a vibrant hub of scientific and artistic activity.

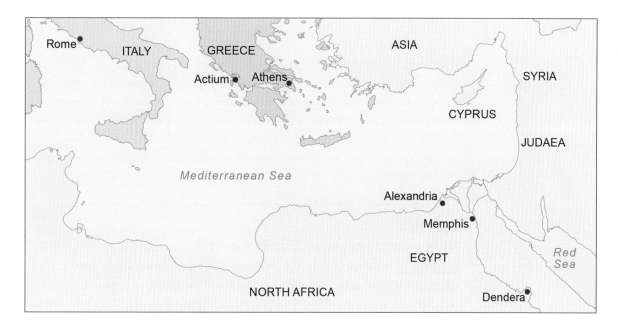

Figure 1 Map of the Mediterranean showing the principal ancient cities mentioned in this unit.

On one level, the Ptolemies can be seen as foreign colonisers of Egypt, as they built new cities in a Greek style and heavily promoted Greek culture and learning. However, as they established their rule, the Ptolemies were also very aware of the importance of maintaining ancient Egyptian practices and traditions. They understood that the new minority Greek ruling class had little chance of survival without the support of the native population of Egypt. Their success depended on maintaining a harmony between Egypt's different ethnic groups. Although the Ptolemies did bring to Egypt a new style of Greek kingdom, and along with it a new Greek social elite, they also tried to leave in place as much as possible of Egypt's old administrative structures and were duly respectful of ancient Egyptian practices. For example, they were crowned in the traditional way as pharaohs, officiated at Egyptian religious cult practices, built new temples to native Egyptian gods and renovated ancient temples.

The Ptolemies willingly took on some of the roles and responsibilities of the Egyptian pharaohs and in doing so they demonstrated at the highest level their intention to integrate their rule into the traditions of Egyptian culture. This deliberate policy of fusing together elements of Greek and Egyptian culture served to diminish any notion of the Ptolemies as simply foreign occupiers. They were not just Greeks but also Egyptians, and as rulers of the country they sought to bring together the various different peoples and cultures they reigned over.

To do this they had to be able to speak to two different audiences simultaneously: the Greek-speaking elite and the much larger body of mostly non-Greek-speaking native Egyptians. The Ptolemies learned how to be chameleons or shape shifters: kings and queens to the Greek elite and the wider Greek speaking world outside of Egypt, but at the same time the latest embodiment of the pharaohs to the native population of Egypt itself. Cleopatra, as the last of the Ptolemies, inherited these practices, and also employed these strategies to appeal to different segments of the population of Egypt.

Activity

(Allow around 15 minutes to complete this activity.)

Look back over what you have learned about the Ptolemies in this section. What challenges did they face as the rulers of Egypt and how did they go about meeting them? Try to answer this question for yourself before reading on.

Discussion

The Ptolemies were not native Egyptians and, like all invading rulers, they needed to find a way to ensure that they were accepted by the native population. To do this, the Ptolemies were respectful towards Egyptian practices and traditions and integrated themselves into them while also importing and promoting Greek culture.

2.2 A pharaoh for the people

Figure 2 shows how Cleopatra chose to depict herself and her son, Ptolemy Caesar (Ptolemy XV), the only child of Cleopatra and the Roman general Julius Caesar, to her wider Egyptian audience. These **relief sculptures** from the wall of an Egyptian temple complex use a form of stylised portraiture that was traditionally employed by the pharaohs of Egypt. Cleopatra and Ptolemy Caesar are the two figures at the far left of the wall.

Figure 2 Cleopatra and her son, Ptolemy Caesar (far left), as depicted on the southern exterior wall of the Temple of Hathor at Dendera, Egypt. Photo: © Heritage-Images/Art Media/akg-images.

Ptolemy Caesar is dressed as a traditional male pharaoh of Egypt, wearing a *shendyt* (a wrap-around skirt or kilt) and the double-crown headdress of Upper and Lower Egypt. He is also holding an offering of incense out to the Egyptian goddess Hathor opposite him, to whom the temple is dedicated. Cleopatra, on the other hand, wears the horns and solar disk associated with Hathor and carries a *sistrum* (rattle) used in the worship of the goddess. It is hard to get a sense of the grand architectural scale of the Temple of Hathor from this image, but the figures shown on the wall are around twice the size of the people they depict.

Activity

(Allow around 20 minutes to complete this activity.)

Look closely at the image of Cleopatra in Figure 2. (Remember this image can be seen in more detail on the module website.) Why do you think Cleopatra, one of the Ptolemies, might have chosen to portray herself and her son in this way to an Egyptian audience?

Discussion

Earlier you learned how the Ptolemies were respectful towards the practices and traditions of the Egyptians, and how they took on some of the roles and responsibilities of the Egyptian pharaohs who had come before them. The relief sculptures in Figure 2 show how Cleopatra also took care to present an image of herself and her family that was integrated into the belief systems of the ancient Egyptians. By depicting herself in the sort of timeless, frozen impersonality that is typical of this style of traditional Egyptian art, Cleopatra deliberately places herself and her son within an artistic tradition that stretches back thousands of years. In this way, they appear as the latest incarnations in a long list of Egyptian rulers and dutiful intermediaries between the divine and the human worlds. Through these relief sculptures, Cleopatra not only expresses her adherence to Egypt's past but also uses this past to stress both her own authority and legitimacy, as well as that of her son.

2.3 A queen for the Greek elite

Figure 3 shows Cleopatra in the different guise of a Greek queen rather than an Egyptian pharaoh. This portrait type is typical for female members of the Ptolemaic royal family. Her hairstyle, with its pulled-back braids and a bun, is usually referred to as a 'melon' hairstyle, because the braids are like the stripes on a melon. The headband, properly called a *tainia*, is a form of diadem, an emblem of royalty. The almond-shaped eyes and small mouth are also typical portrait features of Ptolemaic queens. In this way, Cleopatra also assimilates herself to the long line of queens who have gone before her. This youthful portrait serves less to individualise her and more to make her royal pedigree clear. Just as she asserts her legitimacy and authority to her wider Egyptian audience by appearing in the guise of the leading female member of the pharaonic royal family, so too she is simultaneously the latest incarnation of a **Hellenistic** queen to the ruling Greek-speaking elite.

Figure 3 Marble bust of Cleopatra, Roman, 50–30 BCE. Altes Museum, Berlin. Photo: © De Agostini/S. Vannini/Getty Images.

2.4 A power in decline

As we have just seen, Cleopatra, like all the Ptolemies who came before her, actively engaged in visual strategies to appeal to both the Egyptian and Greek elements within Egypt, appearing as both an Egyptian pharaoh and a Greek queen. The challenges she faced, however, were not limited to just being able to appeal to the different segments of the population she ruled over.

By the time Cleopatra became the ruler of Egypt after the death of her father in 51 BCE, when she was just 18 years old, the kingdom she inherited was in many ways a mere shadow of the glory days of the Ptolemaic kingdom under its early rulers in the fourth and third centuries BCE. A kingdom that had once spread around the Mediterranean was now reduced to more or less its core territory of Egypt. This situation came about due to a variety of factors: ambitious rival kingdoms progressively encroached and annexed Ptolemaic territory; the cost of foreign wars led to higher taxation, which then produced internal unrest and sporadic rebellion; and the intrigue and infighting among different members of the Ptolemaic royal family and their supporters led to the leadership of the country being frequently fragmented and uncertain. At the same time, the Ptolemies also had to come to terms with the menace posed by the rising power of Rome, which had rapidly become the pre-eminent power in the Mediterranean basin. In fact, by the time of Cleopatra, Egypt was technically already a possession of Rome, as an earlier Ptolemaic king had left his kingdom to the Roman people in his will. After this, the conquest of Egypt by Rome was a ticking time bomb that each successive Ptolemaic ruler faced.

Cleopatra's own life was also filled with uncertainty and danger: she had grown up in a political world that was turbulent and unpredictable; the urban populace of Alexandria was notoriously prone to express its discontent violently; and the upper circles of the Ptolemaic court plotted to support and depose different members of the royal family, setting sibling against sibling, parent against child, husband against wife. As a child, Cleopatra had followed her father into exile when he was forced out of Egypt (in part because of the higher taxation he imposed to cover the cost of bribing the Romans to recognise him as King of Egypt and an ally of Rome). While she was in exile, her elder sister, Berenice, was set upon the throne. When her father persuaded the Romans through further bribery to invade Egypt and restore him to the throne, Berenice was amongst those executed.

This type of violence and intrigue was common in the lives of the later Ptolemies. The urban population of Alexandria was incited to act as a kingmaker. This was a tough world in which to survive, let alone prosper. Beyond the fight to survive one's own court and family, there also lurked the ever present menace of Rome, a power that had to be appeased and carefully handled if it was to be kept at bay. Cleopatra, like her immediate Ptolemaic predecessors, lived under a constant threat of annihilation from both internal and external forces.

2.5 Cleopatra amongst the Romans

Cleopatra had good reason to be aware of the influence that the Romans exercised over Egypt. Backed by the status of being the legal heirs to the Ptolemaic kingdom, the Romans had the raw military power to intervene forcibly and settle affairs as they saw fit. Cleopatra's father had relied on the Romans to back his rule. Roman military intervention, though difficult and costly to procure, was now a virtually unstoppable force in Egyptian affairs. Egypt remained autonomous only because the leading political figures in Rome fought one another over who should oversee the permanent occupation of the Ptolemaic kingdom, and then because of Rome's descent into outright civil war. While the Romans fought each other, Egypt had a temporary respite from direct intervention, but unfortunately for the Ptolemies, the Roman civil war was to eventually come knocking on their door.

The two main rivals in the Roman civil war were the Roman generals Julius Caesar and Pompey. At the battle of Pharsalus in Greece (48 BCE) the forces of Julius Caesar gained a decisive victory. The defeated Pompey fled to Egypt, where he might have expected a little assistance since he had hosted Cleopatra's father, Ptolemy XII, in Rome and helped him secure the support he needed to forcibly restore himself to his Egyptian throne. However, Ptolemy XII was now dead, and the principal rivals for the throne were Cleopatra (who likely ruled with her father in his last years) and her younger brother Ptolemy XIII. Cleopatra was around 21 years old and her brother 14 at the time of Pompey's arrival in Egypt; the palace faction around Ptolemy XIII had gained the upper hand and Cleopatra had been forced into exile. In her absence, Ptolemy XIII was persuaded by his advisers that it would be a good idea to deliver Pompey's head in a basket to the victorious Julius Caesar. So, when Julius Caesar arrived at the city a few days later, he was promptly presented with the decapitated head of his rival. Unfortunately for Ptolemy XIII, Julius Caesar was not altogether impressed (after all, if the battle had turned out differently, it could have been his head in the basket).

After his arrival in Egypt, Julius Caesar took it upon himself to settle the dispute between Cleopatra and Ptolemy XIII, as they had been left as joint heirs to the kingdom in their father's will. It was Julius Caesar who ordered the recall of Cleopatra to Alexandria and proclaimed that the siblings should rule jointly as royal consorts. However, the faction that supported Ptolemy XIII would not accept this, and Julius Caesar and Cleopatra were besieged in Alexandria until a decisive battle was fought. In the aftermath, Ptolemy XIII was found drowned in the River Nile. Julius Caesar then arranged for Cleopatra to rule with her other younger brother, Ptolemy XIV, who in turn became her consort. During the course of these events, Julius Caesar and Cleopatra also developed a personal relationship, and when Julius Caesar departed from Egypt, he left behind Cleopatra, who was heavily pregnant with his child.

Cleopatra's relationship with Julius Caesar allowed her to come out on top in the dynastic infighting in her immediate family. It was either Ptolemy XIII or herself and she chose herself. Rome was not a force that could be ignored or resisted, but it could be accommodated. When the supporters of Ptolemy XIII resisted and fell, Cleopatra accepted the power of Rome and survived. Through the child she had with Julius Caesar, she personalised the relationship between Egypt and Rome. The Ptolemaic dynasty, in the form of her child Ptolemy Caesar XV, could now be seen as inextricably linked to Rome's most powerful figure, Julius Caesar. While Julius Caesar remained at the pinnacle of power in Rome, Cleopatra and her son could feel assured that the Ptolemaic dynasty would survive in Egypt. This was surely part of the message that was conveyed by the appearance of Cleopatra and Ptolemy Caesar on the relief sculptures on the temple walls at Dendera (Figure 4).

Cleopatra and her son were pharaohs who were now under the protection of Rome. At the same time, their appearance here perhaps also signified an acceptance that Ptolemy Caesar's place was in Egypt and not in the wider Roman world. They were not a threat to Rome but were Julius Caesar's new Ptolemaic family carrying on the Egyptian branch of the family business in his absence.

Unfortunately, the security of Cleopatra's and Ptolemy XV's position in Egypt was to be short-lived when Julius Caesar was assassinated in Rome on the Ides of March (equivalent to 15 March) in 44 BCE.

Figure 4 Cleopatra and her son, Ptolemy Caesar, on the southern exterior wall of the Temple of Hathor at Dendera in Egypt (detail of the relief sculpture shown in Figure 2). Photo: Luis Dafos/Alamy.

Activity

(Allow around 20 minutes to complete this activity.)

So far, you have been working through the twists and turns of an intricate series of events. Don't worry – you won't need to remember all the details! Before you read the next section, pause and give some thought to the following questions. Try to back up your responses by referring to what you have been reading.

1 How do you think Cleopatra must have felt on learning of the death of Julius Caesar?

2 What might she have thought were the likely consequences for herself?

Discussion

1 You might have considered that the death of Julius Caesar would have been quite a blow to Cleopatra. Aside from her personal feelings for him, there was also the question of where this now left her and her son in their attempt to establish their legitimacy as rulers of Egypt. With Julius Caesar gone, the protection of Rome for Cleopatra and Ptolemy Caesar had to be uncertain. The assassination of Julius Caesar cast a long shadow that reached all the way to Egypt.

2 Cleopatra would have been aware that the tumult that followed Julius Caesar's death would result in a power struggle in Rome that would ultimately see someone else take power. She would also have realised that sooner or later this would mean that she would need to start over and build a relationship with Rome's new power brokers, just as she had done with Julius Caesar.

After Julius Caesar's death in 44 BCE, Rome once again descended into civil war with the two principal rivals being Mark Antony (one of Julius Caesar's trusted right-hand men) and Octavian (the adopted son of Julius Caesar, named as the principal heir in his will). Mark Antony took up his power base in the eastern part of the Roman Empire and Octavian in the west. Therefore, when Rome's civil wars once more came to Egypt, it was Mark Antony whom Cleopatra found on her doorstep first in 41 BCE. The Ptolemies had a powerful navy and an abundant supply of grain, so Egypt was an obvious target for Rome's rival factions. Cleopatra would have known that it was only a matter of time before she became embroiled in this conflict and that neutrality would not be an option. She may well have already known Mark Antony, as he had served as an officer in the army that had restored her father to the throne, and she would almost certainly have come into contact with him while visiting Julius Caesar in Rome. It would also have been reasonable to think that Mark Antony, as a veteran of Rome's wars and politics, would be more likely to come out on top than Octavian, who was only 19 at the time of Julius Caesar's death.

Cleopatra and Mark Antony became allies and lovers, and once again a Roman–Egyptian alliance was cemented by a personal relationship and children (twins, a girl and a boy, and another son).

The alliance and relationship between Cleopatra and Mark Antony was more extensive and continuous than that between Cleopatra and Julius Caesar. While Julius Caesar may be thought of as an absent paternalistic figure who left Cleopatra largely to her own devices as the ruler of Egypt, Mark Antony featured more prominently and directly as the head of Rome in the east. Mark Antony's dominion stretched over the eastern portion of Rome's empire, but it appeared that he was increasingly merging his ambitions with Cleopatra's and their joint family. This vision saw Ptolemaic Egypt not so much as a subsidiary of Rome but as an active partner in a collaborative project of building an empire.

The dynastic partnership between Cleopatra and Mark Antony is depicted on coin portraits (Figure 5) issued during the 30s BCE, where their heads appear on either side of the same coin.

Figure 5 Portraits of Cleopatra (left) and Mark Antony (right) on a silver coin minted in Antioch, Syria, in 36 BCE. American Numismatic Society, ANS 1977.158.621. Courtesy of the American Numismatic Society.

Activity

(Allow around 20 minutes to complete this activity.)

Looking at the coin in Figure 5, consider the image of Cleopatra (on the left) alongside that of Mark Antony (on the right). What is your immediate impression of this image of Cleopatra? How does it compare to the image of her that you have seen in Figures 2 and 3?

Discussion

Your immediate impression might be that this is a rather different image of Cleopatra to those portrayed in Figures 2 and 3. Compared to the timeless serenity of her Egyptian style portrait on the temple walls of Dendera or her Greek style royal bust, you might think that this is a much more individualised-looking portrait. In fact, you may well have thought that this image of Cleopatra appears to be more of an unflattering caricature than a portrait: the neck is thick set; there is a roll of skin under the chin; the nose is prominent and hooked; the jaw juts out and the eyes are almost bulbous.

This is not a rogue image of Cleopatra but one that she almost certainly authorised herself. You might wonder why Cleopatra would choose to circulate such an image of herself; the answer lies again in the different audiences that she had to appeal to. Rome's increasing involvement in Egypt's affairs meant that she had to not only consider the Greek and Egyptian audiences of her own kingdom but also the wider world of the Roman Empire, particularly in the east.

These coin portraits are very much in the Roman style of portraiture of the day, known as **verism**. This was a style of sculpture that aimed at an exaggeratedly realistic depiction, often referred to as 'warts and all' portraiture. The style appears to be less about flattering the subject and assimilating it into an almost timeless continuum, as traditional Egyptian and Hellenistic representations tended to do, but rather to project powerful and striking individuality as a sign of the subject's authority.

Aside from the facial features, Cleopatra is represented very much in the manner of a Hellenistic queen. She has the same hairstyle and diadem that you saw on the bust in Figure 3. However, these standard features of a royal portrait are used here to create a more striking individualised portrait in terms of Cleopatra's features. Her accessories, an elaborate pearl necklace and a large pearl-drop earring, also serve to project her power and status (it is also possible that the ostentatious pearls that Cleopatra wears were a well-known gift from Mark Antony).

On the other side of the coin, the image of Mark Antony is similarly depicted in a veristic style. The forceful presentations of each figure and the way that they even look like each other suggests a natural symmetry and resemblance between these figures, which mirrors their political and personal alliance.

The image of Cleopatra on this particular coin was probably primarily intended for the audience of the eastern Roman Empire. She is depicted as a strong and forceful leader, a natural female counterpart to the Roman general Mark Antony, and a figure worthy of alliance with Rome and of ruling with Rome. This coin was likely circulating at the very time that a ceremony known as 'The Donations of Alexandria' took place in Alexandria in 34 BCE, where he recognised Cleopatra and Ptolemy Caesar XV as the joint rulers of Egypt and granted them additional territories. At this ceremony, Mark Antony also formally recognised Ptolemy Caesar XV as Julius Caesar's son, and proclaimed his own children with Cleopatra as the rulers of further lands in the east (some of which he had recently conquered and some of which he was yet to conquer). This was an ostentatious display whereby the eastern Roman Empire and the Ptolemaic kingdom seemingly merged into one dynastic enterprise.

Not surprisingly, Octavian in the western half of the Roman Empire could not accept this. He was the legal heir and adopted son of Julius Caesar. The recognition by Mark Antony of Ptolemy Caesar XV as Julius Caesar's son was a direct challenge to Octavian's authority and legitimacy. A showdown between the western and eastern halves of the Roman Empire and their leaders was inevitable and duly took place at the Battle of Actium in Greece in 31 BCE. There, Mark Antony and Cleopatra were defeated and they retreated to Alexandria. The forces of Octavian followed them eastwards and in the summer of 30 BCE, with no effective means of resistance left, Mark Antony and Cleopatra both took their own lives as Octavian's forces took possession of Alexandria.

Activity

(Allow around 30 minutes to complete this activity.)

Now that you have read through all the historical background on Cleopatra, this is a good opportunity to review the situation that she faced in Egypt as the last of the Ptolemaic rulers. What challenges did she face and how would you assess her responses to the various trials she encountered?

There will be no formal discussion here, as I want you to use this time to review the information that you have read up to this point independently, bringing it all together to consider your thoughts and feelings about Cleopatra so far (and whether they have changed at all).

3 Cleopatra through Roman eyes

As we have learned, Cleopatra was one of many Ptolemaic rulers of Egypt. The problems she faced as queen and pharaoh were many but not perhaps unique to her. Why, then, did Cleopatra become so special? What allowed the historical Cleopatra VII to become simply 'Cleopatra', a figure of myth and legend as well as of history? The answer to this lies in the way that her story has been told. Who tells the story, why they are telling it, and to whom, has a tremendous impact on how we receive the past and how we evaluate its participants.

Cleopatra's status as a famous historical figure in Western culture depends precisely upon her role in the bitter struggles of the Roman civil wars in the first century BCE. Without this link, Cleopatra would most likely have been just another obscure footnote in the history of the Western world. It was through her ultimately fatal interactions with the leading Romans of her day – Julius Caesar, Mark Antony and Octavian (who became Rome's first emperor under the name of Augustus) – that Cleopatra entered the mainstream of Western history. It was her various roles as the lover, ally and bitter enemy of these men that served most to define her reputation in the West. The Roman historian Cassius Dio (c.163–235 CE), summed up her life in this way: 'she captivated the two greatest Romans of her time, and because of the third, she destroyed herself' (Cassius Dio, 1987, p. 76). Here, Cleopatra is defined solely through her interactions with Roman men. This is the perspective that defined her in the Roman sources, along with, of course, ultimately being on the losing side.

The winners in conflicts are those who tend to write history and it is their representations of the losers that tend to prevail. In the current day, we are familiar with the manipulation of public opinion by the media and politicians, and with the way things can be made to look a certain way by putting a 'spin' on them. Roman political life was full of lurid accusations and vicious satirical attack, and Mark Antony's association with Cleopatra was a perfect source of ammunition for Octavian to use against him. Her historical reputation in the Western world was collateral damage in a showdown between rival Roman men.

Let us now see how Cleopatra (and Egypt in general) were used as a means to smear Mark Antony's reputation and, in the process, built up the largely negative image of Cleopatra that has since developed in Western culture.

3.1 Plutarch's Cleopatra: the shameless seducer

Plutarch's series of biographies, known as Plutarch's *Lives*, is among the principal ancient sources for the events surrounding Cleopatra and her involvement with Rome. They were written by Plutarch (b. before 50 CE and d. after 120 CE) probably in the early part of the second century CE, some 150 years or so after the events actually took place. This type of historical biography was not designed as a conventional narrative history, but rather as a series of character studies to illustrate the virtues and vices of the great figures of Greek and Roman history as a means of explaining why certain famous people did certain things in certain circumstances. To an ancient historian like Plutarch, the answer to such questions was inevitably because these figures were of a particular type of character, or because an innate tendency to behave in certain ways had been drawn out of them through their exposure to particular direct influences.

Activity

(Allow around 20 minutes to complete this activity.)

The following short passage is from Plutarch's 'Life of Caesar'. In it, Plutarch describes how Cleopatra first met Julius Caesar. Read the passage through once and then read it again whilst thinking about the following questions. Try to be clear about your own answers before moving on to the discussion.

> Cleopatra, taking only one of her friends with her (Apollodorus the Sicilian), embarked in a small boat and landed at the palace when it was already getting dark. Since there seemed to be no other way of getting in unobserved, she stretched herself out at full length inside a sleeping bag, and Apollodorus, after tying up the bag, carried it indoors to Caesar. This little trick of Cleopatra's, which showed her provocative impudence, is said to have been the first thing about her which captivated Caesar, and, as he grew to know

her better, he was overcome by her charm and arranged that she and her brother should be reconciled and should share the throne of Egypt together.

(Plutarch, 1972, p. 49)

1 How does Plutarch present Cleopatra? What does he suggest is the motivation for her actions?

2 Do you think that these events might be presented in a different light? How might Cleopatra's actions be viewed more positively?

Discussion

1 You may well have noticed the phrase 'provocative impudence' here. This suggests that the author sees Cleopatra as rather disrespectful and shameless. Perhaps he finds her scheme to enter the palace less than regal and in some way underhanded, as suggested by the words, '[t]his little trick'. The motivation for her behaviour, according to Plutarch, was that she wanted to seduce Julius Caesar.

2 Perhaps you thought that Cleopatra's night-time venture into the city held by her brother's forces with just a single companion was both a rather sensible precaution in the circumstances and also maybe a sign of courageous determination. Although Plutarch seems to characterise Cleopatra's actions as some form of shameless exhibitionism and wanton seduction, you might have considered that this is a little harsh. Cleopatra's stratagem to gain access to Julius Caesar may have been audacious, but it was born of the perilous situation in which she found herself – she was losing a civil war, Julius Caesar could help her, and she had to take the chance even though the outcome was far from certain. Her more in-depth knowledge of the Romans (through her experiences with them and her father) may well have also led her to believe that events were more likely to turn out well if she worked with the Romans rather than trying to reject them. Ultimately, her strategy was successful, with Julius Caesar moving to end the civil war and re-establish her as a co-ruler alongside her brother. Plutarch seems to assume that Cleopatra achieved her ends through underhanded means, by captivating Julius Caesar and overcoming him with 'her charm', but is it not equally plausible that Julius Caesar was impressed by her initiative, bravery and cool thinking in the most testing of conditions?

Plutarch's account of Cleopatra's actions is one of the building blocks of the rather dubious reputation that Roman authors attributed to her. Most of these authors focus on her relationships with Julius Caesar and Mark Antony.

3.2 Cassius Dio and the bewitching of Mark Antony

Another Roman source for the events surrounding Cleopatra and her involvement with Rome is Cassius Dio's *Roman History* written in the early third century CE, or about 250 years after Cleopatra's death.

Activity

(Allow around 30 minutes to complete this activity.)

Turn now to Reading 1.1 at the end of this chapter, which is a condensed version of a speech that the historian Cassius Dio says Augustus (the name later taken by Octavian) gave to his army before the Battle of Actium.

As you read through this extract, jot down some thoughts in answer to the following questions:

1   How does Augustus seek to present Mark Antony and his relationship with Cleopatra and Egypt?

2   What does this speech tell us about how ancient historians wrote history? You might consider whether you think Cassius Dio is presenting an impartial picture of the past based on a careful weighting of the evidence available to him. How does the approach of Cassius Dio differ from what we expect from historians today?

Discussion

1   Mark Antony is presented as bewitched by Cleopatra to the extent that he now fights against his own country. Any manly valour that he once possessed has been stripped away through the pursuit of a life of royal luxury at her side. The once powerful Roman general has become effeminate, his self-indulgence making him weak and no longer a threat.
    Egypt seems to symbolise a decadent and debased way of life where women are rulers and men their slaves, where animals are an object of worship, and where indulgence is rife and courage is lacking. According to Augustus, Egypt and what it stands for is contrasted sharply with Rome and its way of life. Augustus says that one only has to look at what has happened to Mark Antony to see the threat that Egypt poses to Rome and its citizens.

2 There is a lot of assertion in this speech, but no evidence and no attempt to present a balanced picture. This sounds more like a historical drama than what we might think of as history. We expect serious historians today to undertake painstaking research and back up their points with evidence and references to their source material. It is important for the modern reader to be able to see where a historian gets their information from, and to be able to judge how reliable their sources are likely to be. Cassius Dio demonstrates none of this sort of transparency of method, refers to no sources for his information, and doesn't appear to feel obliged to justify any of the assertions he puts into Augustus's mouth.

The speech is a dramatic and engaging piece of rhetoric, but when we start to think about it, we are surely justified in being a little suspicious about its authenticity. Writing about 250 years later, how did Cassius Dio know exactly what Augustus said in this speech? Did Augustus have a historian with good shorthand travelling with him? The explanation is almost certainly that Cassius Dio made up the speech himself. To us, this may seem a travesty of what history is supposed to be, but this sort of imaginative and inventive colouring of the past was not unusual in the writing of ancient history.

As we can see, Cassius Dio's account clearly represents a Roman historiographical tradition with its roots in the propaganda of Octavian's smear campaign against Mark Antony. A campaign where Cleopatra and Egypt are seen as instrumental in corrupting and debasing a once great Roman and turning Mark Antony, as Shakespeare would later famously describe in his play (written in the early years of the seventeenth century) into 'a strumpet's fool' (*Antony and Cleopatra*, Act 1, Scene 1).

3.3 Plutarch's Mark Antony: the fallen hero

Now we return to Plutarch (who we last met in Section 3.1 describing the meeting of Cleopatra with Julius Caesar) and consider his depiction of the relationship between Mark Antony and Cleopatra. As discussed previously, his *Lives* focused on Mark Antony's virtues and vices as a way of understanding his reactions to the world around him and the course his life took. (Shakespeare actually used a sixteenth-century translation of Plutarch's work when writing *Antony and Cleopatra*.)

Activity

(Allow around 15 minutes to complete this activity.)

Read the following brief extract from Plutarch's 'Life of Antony' in which he introduces Cleopatra. What does Plutarch have to say about the impact that Mark Antony's love for Cleopatra had on his character?

> [T]he love for Cleopatra which now entered his life came as the final and crowning mischief which could befall him. It excited to the point of madness many passions which had hitherto lain concealed, or at least dormant, and it stifled or corrupted all those redeeming qualities in him which were still capable of resisting temptation.

> (Plutarch, 1965, p. 292)

Discussion

As in the extract from Cassius Dio in the last activity, we can see that Cleopatra is presented as a fatal influence on Mark Antony. From Plutarch's point of view, Cleopatra brings out the worst qualities in Mark Antony and suppresses his better traits. His love for her is depicted as a madness that opened the floodgates, breaking down his capacity to resist the baser desires and passions lurking in his soul. Plutarch's account is expressly moralistic: Mark Antony's moral failings ultimately led to his destruction.

In Plutarch's account, Cleopatra represents temptation, as she incites passions in Mark Antony that break through his manly Roman defences. A little later, Plutarch goes on to describe exactly how Cleopatra achieved her hold over her audience:

> Her own beauty, so we are told, was not of that incomparable kind which instantly captivates the beholder. But the charm of her presence was irresistible, and there was an attraction in her person and her talk, together with a peculiar force of character which pervaded her every word and action, and laid all who associated with her under its spell.

> (Plutarch, 1965, p. 294)

According to Plutarch, Cleopatra's effect on Mark Antony was not due to a beauty that stopped men in their tracks. Rather, it was something that was achieved through a combination of the magnetism of her presence, voice and the sheer force of her personality. Whatever it was, Plutarch, like Cassius Dio, is clear that it was akin to a dark kind of magic that ensnared the unwary male, drove him mad and rendered him less than a man. At the same time, Plutarch also presents Cleopatra as a cunning manipulator, a master of a thousand flatteries, who shrewdly measured Mark Antony's desires and appetites and made sure to cater to them. In doing this, Plutarch notes, she turned a veteran statesman and warrior into the equivalent of a spoilt youth content to squander his precious time on idle pleasures.

Whether Mark Antony and Cleopatra actually loved each other was beside the point for Plutarch. The Roman world did not value romantic love and Mark Antony's infatuation with Cleopatra was simply another indication of effeminate indulgence and a lack of self-control. To Plutarch, romantic passion was not something to be celebrated but deplored and resisted.

The only aspect of Cleopatra's life that draws grudging admiration from Plutarch is the manner of her death. Having been captured by the Romans and placed under house arrest, Cleopatra contrived to take her own life. The manner in which she achieved this remains a mystery. Plutarch records one story that she died through the bite of a poisonous snake, an asp, which was smuggled into her house, but also another account that her demise was caused through poison that she kept in a hollow comb in her hair. When her lifeless body was found on a golden couch dressed in her royal robes, one of the tricked Roman guards asked Cleopatra's dying attendant '[I]s this well done?' She replied, 'It is well done, and fitting for a princess descended of so many royal kings' (Plutarch, 1965, p. 347).

Had she not taken her own life, the prospect that awaited Cleopatra was to be taken back to Rome and paraded in chains (as one of her sisters had been) in a ritual ceremony of Rome's triumph over its enemies. This ceremony usually culminated in the strangulation of Rome's vanquished rival. Cleopatra chose to avoid this humiliation and to end her life on her own terms. In doing this, she behaved in a way that a Roman aristocrat could relate to by choosing death over dishonour.

By looking at Plutarch and Cassius Dio's accounts, we can see that the Roman perspective on Egypt and Cleopatra drew sharp distinctions between the two sides. Rome was seen as manly, austere, disciplined and principled; Egypt as effeminate, reckless, indulgent and debauched. This provided historical authors with a moralising framework within which Cleopatra and her Egyptian ways could be blamed for the unmanning of Mark Antony.

These Roman views of Cleopatra undoubtedly have their origin in the propaganda of Octavian and his allies. Whether or not he believed his own propaganda, this sort of cultural stereotyping and vilification served a very useful function for him. Not only was it an expedient tool to discredit his most powerful enemy, but it also promoted the conflict as, at heart, one against a foreign threat rather than a fellow Roman. Thus, the defeat of Mark Antony and the acquisition of Egypt's wealth and grain could be pursued whilst avoiding the appearance of a civil war.

4 Cleopatra in medieval Arabic culture

For many people, the dominant images of Cleopatra have likely been influenced by Hollywood film and TV programmes, which in turn have been shaped by the Roman sources that we have just looked at (we will consider the images from film and TV in more detail in the online activity that follows this chapter). This leads to a tendency to identify with a reputation of Cleopatra that was originally constructed in the Roman sources before being reflected in these modern images of her. This, in turn, then leads to an assumption that this is the 'correct' portrait of this historical figure.

However, this is not the representation of Cleopatra that is found everywhere. There is a different view of Cleopatra that has its origins in the middle of the seventh century CE when Muslim armed forces conquered Egypt. From this point, Egypt became part of an Islamic caliphate rather than a portion of the eastern Roman Empire. The Arabic literature that emerged in Egypt and the wider Islamic world from this point in time, and through the next few centuries of the medieval period, painted a rather different portrait of Cleopatra. This then formed the basis of a reputation very much at odds with the one created by Roman authors.

In a recent study of medieval Arabic writing, Okasha El Daly summarises the representation of Cleopatra in the following way:

> The image of the queen in medieval Arab sources is that of a strong and able monarch who was very protective of Egypt. These sources focus on her many talents but make not one reference to sexuality or seductive power; they admire her scientific knowledge as a scholar, and her administrative ability. The most interesting aspect of her image is that of a scholar who made significant contributions in the fields of alchemy, medicine and mathematics.
>
> (El Daly, 2005, p. 131)

El Daly gives the title 'The Virtuous Scholar' to this section of his book – a phrase used to describe Cleopatra, which is common in the Arabic sources he discusses. If we contrast this way of depicting Cleopatra with how she is described by the Roman poet Propertius (who lived at the time of her conflict with Octavian) as 'meretrix regina', translated as 'the whore queen', then we can see a startling difference in attitudes. In the Arabic sources that El Daly discusses, the emphasis on Cleopatra as a ruler falls not on her relationships with Julius Caesar and Mark Antony, but rather on her activities as a builder, philosopher and scholar.

The different portrait of Cleopatra that emerges from the writings of Arabic writers in and outside Egypt most probably reflected and drew upon a strand of native Egyptian interpretation of the queen that pre-dated the Muslim annexation of Egypt. The earliest such literary source that we possess is *The Chronicles of John, Bishop of Nikiu*. This work was written towards the very end of the seventh century CE, in the generation following the Muslim conquest of Egypt. Nikiu was a province of Egypt and John was a bishop of the Coptic Orthodox Church there, which was a Christian church (Christianity was the mainstream religion of the later Roman Empire). The Coptic Orthodox Church remained in Egypt even after the country became part of an Islamic caliphate. John would almost certainly have thought of himself as a Copt (or native Egyptian) instead of an Arab.

Activity

(Allow around 20 minutes to complete this activity.)

Reading 1.2 is an extract from *The Chronicles of John, Bishop of Nikiu*. Read through the extract now and pay attention to the way that Cleopatra has been depicted. How is this different to the representations that you have encountered in Roman sources?

Discussion

The depiction of Cleopatra in this extract is entirely positive. She is described as a great leader of her country, who spent her reign improving the infrastructure of the city of Alexandria and the quality of life of those living there. The 'whore queen' of the Romans is transformed in the account of John into 'the most illustrious and wise amongst women' (1916, p. 50).

The emphasis on Cleopatra as a builder in John's passage is found in many of the later Arabic sources. John most likely represents a positive native Egyptian interpretation of Cleopatra that evolved separately from the viewpoint seen in the Roman sources. It is a little unclear in which language John's account was originally written; it may have been in Greek or in Coptic (a native Egyptian form of script adapted from Greek) but it survives in Ge'ez or Ethiopic (a north African language). This Ethiopic version, though, is apparently based on an earlier Arabic translation of John's work. Apart from giving us some idea of the often tortuous route by which literary works from the past can come to us, it also shows how John's account of Cleopatra, and the sentiments expressed in it, came to pass into medieval Arabic literature. Through being translated, John's early medieval work became part of ongoing Arabic literary activity that built on positive rather than negative depictions of Cleopatra.

For instance, another prevalent strand of Cleopatra's reputation as it is represented in medieval Arabic texts is her role, as outlined by El Daly, as 'the virtuous scholar' (2005, pp. 131–6). Her reputation here is not only as the patron and promoter of the scholarly activities of others, but also as an active participant herself. She is a scholar, a scientist and a philosopher. Tenth-century CE Arabic writer Al-Masudi writes:

> She was a sage, a philosopher who elevated the ranks of scholars and enjoyed their company. She also wrote books on medicine, charms and cosmetics in addition to many other books ascribed to her which are known to those who practice medicine.
>
> (Quoted in El Daly, 2005, pp. 132–3)

In medieval Arabic culture, Cleopatra is depicted as a woman of formidable intelligence, and it is her intellectual capacity rather than her sexuality that dominates the Arabic, as opposed to the Roman literature about her. How then do we account for these very different reputations of Cleopatra?

One possible explanation is that positive native Egyptian sources, such as John's chronicles, passed into the medieval Arabic literary world via translation, whereas the earlier accounts of the Roman authors never did. Another explanation is that the medieval Arab world was more predisposed to accept a positive portrait of a female ruler such as Cleopatra than the world of the early Roman Empire. El Daly sees the positive images of the Arabic sources as 'a reflection of the medieval Arab cultural environment which viewed powerful, intellectual women as normal, based on the well recorded history of such women from pre-Islamic Arabia and Egypt until the medieval period when many of these writers worked' (El Daly, 2005, p. 142).

The negative attitude of the Romans towards both monarchy and women in positions of public authority were not attitudes shared by those recording Cleopatra's history in the Arabic sources. This certainly is part of the reason for the differences between the Roman and Arabic sources. Another reason is that, from the perspective of medieval Arabic culture, the Roman civil wars did not comprise a prism through which Egypt and Cleopatra had to be judged. The Roman sources, and the propaganda out of which they grew, needed to vilify Cleopatra. Octavian's pursuit of a civil war against Mark Antony had to be presented as a justifiable conflict against a threatening foreign power under the leadership of a scheming and ambitious femme fatale.

It might then seem a reasonable assumption that the Arabic sources give us a more historically accurate picture of Cleopatra than their Roman counterparts. However, before concluding that these sources shine a light on the 'real' Cleopatra, as opposed to the 'distorted' image we have of her in Roman sources, we need to acknowledge that there are also some limitations with the Arabic accounts and the native Egyptian accounts that they drew upon.

First of all, *The Chronicles of John, Bishop of Nikiu* were written over 700 years after Cleopatra died. John's account is far from contemporary with Cleopatra and we have little idea about the reliability of the historical accounts that he drew upon. It is also the case that the Arabic sources span several hundred years, so it is not always very clear if the 'Cleopatra' being discussed is the right one (that is, Cleopatra VII – who we are looking at in this chapter– and not one of the six earlier Ptolemaic queens who also bore the name Cleopatra). Although El Daly says 'in general Arab writers knew that this Cleopatra was the last ruler of the Ptolemaic dynasty of Egypt' (2005, p. 131), it does seem that there are some misidentifications of Cleopatra, or confusions over her identity, in the Arabic accounts. For instance, the ninth-century CE Arab historian, Abd Al-Hakam, credited Cleopatra (using one of her Arabic names, 'Qulpatra') with building the lighthouse of Alexandria, but also remarks that some say it was built by a queen called Daluka (Abd Al-Hakam, Futuh, 40–1, as cited in El Daly, 2005, pp. 132–3).

Therefore, it seems possible that some medieval Arabic sources might be blurring together the deeds of different historical queens, or talking about the deeds of one queen under the name of another. In any event, Cleopatra was not responsible for the building of the great lighthouse of Alexandria, which was completed over 200 years before she was born. It also seems possible that part of her reputation as a scholar and polymath in medieval Arabic literature rests upon the fact that books were dedicated to her by their original authors, which led to the authorship of the same volumes becoming attributed to Cleopatra herself (El Daly, 2005, pp. 133–4).

In this manner, the reputation of Cleopatra in the Arabic world as a strong ruler, a scholar and philosopher eventually led to her being conflated with other famous female rulers and scholars. This makes it difficult to disentangle these different historical threads and to retrieve anything that we could feel represents the true historical figure of Cleopatra with any certainty. In this way, we might say that medieval Arabic culture created its own myths and legends around the historical figure of Cleopatra in much the same way that the Romans and later Western culture did. It was just that the focus of medieval Arabic culture on Cleopatra was different and so produced a contrasting reputation for the Egyptian queen.

5 Summary

In this chapter, we have taken a look at the historical figure of Cleopatra. We have seen how she was many things to many people: an Egyptian pharaoh, a Greek queen and a potential ruler of the Roman world at the side of Mark Antony. Her life was complicated, and the times she lived and ruled through were turbulent.

The way in which Cleopatra was depicted in Roman (and later in Western) culture is strikingly different to her representation in medieval Arabic culture. This gives us some notion about how the historical life and actions of a person are only a starting point as to how that figure is received in later times and cultures. The different motivations and varying cultural contexts of those looking back at a historical figure like Cleopatra have a direct impact on the reputation that they produce. This can be the case even when the commentators are likely using the same historical data.

For instance, we can perhaps see in some of Plutarch's comments the point at which Roman authors, and later medieval Arabic writers, went their separate ways in assessing Cleopatra, even as they drew on the same historical material about her. As mentioned previously, Plutarch put Cleopatra's capacity to captivate an audience down to the 'attraction in her person and her talk' and her 'peculiar force of character' instead of her stunning beauty (1965, p. 294). He also mentions that Cleopatra could converse with people from different nations without any need for an interpreter – even though the Ptolemies before her had never even bothered to learn the Egyptian language (1965, p. 294). We might suspect here that the Roman sources are drawing on the same material concerning Cleopatra's intellectual capacity and diplomatic gifts that the Arabic sources also later used. While Arabic medieval culture celebrated these qualities and used them to build a positive reputation for Cleopatra, Roman authors contrived to turn the positive of a linguistically capable and diplomatically persuasive ruler into the negative reputation of a sexually manipulative woman.

We can see quite clearly that very disparate images of Cleopatra were produced through different cultural contexts according to the contrasting pre-occupations held about her at the time. As El Daly writes:

One remarkable omission from all the medieval Arabic sources that I have studied is any reference to Cleopatra's seductive physical beauty. This absence perhaps emphasises that the fascination on the part of the Arab writers was with the conduct and achievements of the Queen rather than with her appearance.

(El Daly, 2005, p. 136)

It is not simply that the Arabic sources on Cleopatra provide a correction to a perceived bias and distortion in the reputation produced by the Romans that was then accepted into the legends of the Western world. As already mentioned, the Roman and Arabic sources most likely drew upon the same or comparable historical material about Cleopatra. What accounts for the very different reputations generated by Roman authors and medieval Arabic writers is not different source material, but how they chose to accent and interpret the same material.

Octavian's propaganda produced images of Cleopatra as a scheming seductress, whereas medieval Arabic sources focused on her role as a strong ruler and scholar, which generates a contrasting picture of her as a queen and diplomat consorting on equal terms with philosophers and scientists. We might be doubtful of the ultimate accuracy of either of these images of Cleopatra, but the medieval Arabic sources do show us that the Roman version of Cleopatra is not the only way to see her (nor indeed the only way that people do see her). What makes a difference is *how* we look at her and what we want to *find*.

You should now return to the module website to continue your study of this unit.

References

Cassius Dio (1987) *The Roman history: the reign of Augustus.* Translated by I. Scott-Kilvert. London: Penguin.

El Daly, O. (2005) *Egyptology: the missing millennium: ancient Egypt in medieval Arabic writings.* London: UCL Press.

John, Bishop of Nikiu (1916) *The chronicle of John, Bishop of Nikiu.* Translated by R.H. Charles. London and Oxford: Williams & Northgate, p. 50.

Plutarch (1972) *Fall of the Roman republic.* Translated by R. Warner. Harmondsworth: Penguin.

Plutarch (1965) *The makers of Rome: nine lives by Plutarch.* Translated by I. Scott-Kilvert. London: Penguin.

Readings

Reading 1.1 Augustus on Cleopatra

Source: Cassius Dio (1987) *The Roman history: the age of Augustus*. **Translated by I. Scott-Kilvert. London: Penguin, pp. 52–5. Cassius Dio was writing in the early third century CE.**

We Romans are the rulers of the greatest and best parts of the world, and yet we find ourselves spurned and trampled upon by a woman of Egypt.

[…]

Would we not utterly dishonour ourselves if, after surpassing all other nations in valour, we then meekly endured the insults of this rabble, the natives of Alexandria and of Egypt, for what more ignoble or more exact name could one give them? They worship reptiles and beasts as gods, they embalm their bodies to make them appear immortal, they are most forward in effrontery, but most backward in courage. Worst of all, they are not ruled by a man, but are the slaves of a woman […]

Who would not tear his hair at the sight of Roman soldiers serving as bodyguards of this queen? Who would not groan at hearing that Roman knights and senators grovel before her like eunuchs? Who would not weep when he sees and hears what Antony has become? […] [He] has abandoned his whole ancestral way of life, has embraced alien and barbaric customs, has ceased to honour us, his fellow-countrymen, or our laws, or his fathers' gods.

[…]

He is either blind to reason or mad, for I have heard and can believe that he is bewitched by that accursed woman, and therefore disregards all our efforts to show him goodwill and humanity. And so, being enslaved by her, he plunges into war with all its attendant dangers which he has accepted for her sake, against ourselves and against his country. What choice, then, remains to us, save our duty to oppose him together with Cleopatra and fight him off?

[…]

And even if at one time he showed some valour when he served with our army, you can rest assured that he has now lost it beyond recall through the change in his manner of life. It is impossible for anyone who indulges in a life of royal luxury and pampers himself as a woman to conceive a manly thought or do a manly deed, since it cannot but follow that a man's whole being is moulded by the habits of his daily life.

[…]

To sum up, if it were a matter of being called upon to cavort in some ridiculous dance or cut some erotic caper, Antony would have no rival – for these are the specialities in which he has trained himself. But when it comes to weapons and fighting what has anyone to fear from him?

Reading 1.2 John, Bishop of Nikiu, on Cleopatra

Source: John, Bishop of Nikiu (1916) *The chronicle of John, Bishop of Nikiu*. Translated by R.H. Charles. London and Oxford: Williams & Northgate, p. 50. John, Bishop of Nikiu, was writing towards the end of the seventh century CE.

And she was great in herself and in her achievements (in) courage and strength. There was none of the kings who preceded her who wrought such achievements as she. 3. And she built in the confines of Alexandria a great (and) magnificent palace, and all that saw it admired it; for there was not the like in all the world. 4. And she built it on an island in the quarter of the north to the west of the city of Alexandria, outside the city and at a distance of four stadia. 5. And she raised a dike against the waters of the sea with stones and earth, and made the place of the waters over which they voyaged formerly in ships into dry land, and she made it passable on foot. 6. [...] [A] stupendous and difficult achievement [...] 7. And next she constructed a canal to the sea, and she brought water from the river Gihon and conducted it into the city. And by this means she brought it about that ships could approach and enter the city and by this means there was great abundance. 8. Now the city was formerly without access to water, but she brought all the water it required (lit. made it full of water) so that ships could sail thereon, and by this means fish became abundant in the city. 9. And she executed all these works in vigilant care for the well-being of the city. And before she died she executed many noble works and (created) important institutions. [...] the most illustrious and wise among women [...]

Chapter 2
Mary, the mother of Jesus

Stefanie Sinclair

Contents

1 Introduction

In 2005, a woman driving home from work noticed that a strange marking had appeared on a concrete wall in an underpass in Chicago, USA. In it, she saw the shape of the Virgin Mary. Following her discovery, hundreds of people also came to visit and pay homage to what they believed to be a miraculous manifestation of Jesus' mother – lighting candles, laying flowers, praying, singing songs and gently touching the wall (Figure 1).

Figure 1 'Our Lady of the Underpass' – Pilgrims pay homage to a marking in the shape of the Virgin Mary that appeared in a Chicago Expressway underpass in 2005. Photo: © Jeff Haynes/AFP/Getty Images.

Although the Illinois Department of Transportation explained the discolouring on the wall to be caused by a salt run-off, the underpass quickly became a shrine and pilgrimage site. Given that the appearance of this mark coincided with the week when the leadership of the Roman Catholic Church selected a new pope (Benedict XVI), some devotees also regarded it as a sign of the Virgin's approval of this decision. The strong public reaction to 'Our Lady of the Underpass' featured not just in local but also in international news, including the *Chicago Tribune*, *Fox News* and *BBC News*. It even inspired a critically acclaimed theatre play (*Our Lady of the Underpass*, 2010). Over the following years, the Chicago underpass continued to attract many visitors, and in that time the mark was defaced by graffiti, restored and has now faded away.

1.1 Who is Mary?

Jesus' mother Mary (also known as the Virgin Mary) is believed to have been born around 2000 years ago in ancient Palestine. She is not just an important figure in Christianity but also in other religious traditions, including Islam. Mary has been described as 'more of an inspiration to more people than any other woman who ever lived' (Pelikan, 1996, p. 2), inspiring worship, pilgrimage and a vast range of art and music across the world. As historian Miri Rubin (2010) points out:

> Women and men are named after her; so are places, towns, villages and churches. The figure of Mary is imprinted on the medieval fabric of modern Europe: in the images built into houses and walls of Italian towns, on cathedral façades in northern France, on roadside crosses in Austria and Bavaria, or in the **icons** of Greek churches.
>
> [...]
>
> For believers Mary is powerfully present [...and...] the culture of Mary is as diverse as that of the continents that bear her imprint [...]
>
> (Rubin, 2010, p. xxi)

This chapter will highlight the diversity of Mary's reputations – both past and present – within and between different religious traditions, as well as the fact that devotion to her is shared by many different traditions. It will also show that, although there have been many attempts by religious leaders to control different aspects of her reputation, Mary has had an almost uncontrollable popular appeal and people have found many different ways of relating to this powerful figure and of making her 'their own'.

> ## The name Mary
>
> 'Mary' is the English form of the name 'Mariam' (in Aramaic, a language widely spoken in ancient Palestine), 'Maria' (in Greek and Latin) and 'Miriam' (in Hebrew).

In studying the different reputations of Mary you will be introduced to the discipline of Religious Studies. This discipline draws on a range of different methods and approaches from the arts, languages and social sciences to explore the complex and multifaceted phenomenon of 'religion' – its history, art, ideas, practices, distinctive social institutions and the states of mind to which it can give rise.

Religious Studies is concerned with claims about truth, but also with the nature and power of the stories, myths and practices that shape cultures, both historically and in the present day. Therefore, the point of Religious Studies is not to promote a particular religion or religious commitment, but to gain a deeper understanding of how people make sense of the world – in this case, we will focus on how people have been making sense of Mary, the mother of Jesus.

Once you have finished the chapter, you will be invited back to the module website to take a closer look at the contemporary practices associated with Mary in both Christianity and Islam.

2 Textual sources about Mary

Though the figure of Mary has been very influential, she has been interpreted in many different and contrasting ways. In order to gain a deeper understanding of how Jesus' mother has been understood, let us start by considering representations of Mary in various early textual sources and how these might have influenced her reputation.

2.1 Mary in the New Testament

One of the earliest sources that mentions Jesus' mother Mary is what Christians call the New Testament, which contains accounts of the life, death and resurrection of Jesus, including teachings and acts of his early followers. Together with the Old Testament, this forms part of the central collection of texts included in the **Christian Bible**. The Old Testament, which was originally written in Hebrew, includes works that are also contained in Jewish scriptures, while the New Testament consists of specifically Christian texts, originally written in Ancient Greek. Following a series of extensive debates and councils that took place between the second and fourth centuries CE, members of the Christian church leadership decided which texts should be regarded as an authoritative part of the New Testament. At this time, the growing Christian communities felt a great need to agree on essential beliefs, texts and principles at the heart of Christianity. This included the identification of texts that were considered to be the most reliable, authentic and important out of the many that were in circulation in early Christian communities.

Jesus' mother Mary is mentioned in all of the four gospels (the Gospels of Matthew, Mark, Luke and John), as well as The Acts of the Apostles, which form part of the canon of the New Testament. While the four **canonical gospels** purport to tell the story of Jesus' life, The Acts of the Apostles (or 'Book of Acts') talks about events following Jesus' resurrection and his ascension into heaven; it also describes the missionary journeys of various significant characters in the new religious movement as well as the rise of the early Christian communities. These texts were originally based on oral (i.e. spoken) traditions, and were written down in the second half of the first century CE, several decades after Jesus is alleged to have ascended into heaven. Most biblical scholars agree that the Gospel of Mark is likely to be the oldest of the four canonical gospels and was probably written around 66–70 CE, followed by Matthew and Luke at around 85–90 CE and John in 90–110 CE. Most scholars also agree that the Book of Acts was written around the same time as the Gospel of Luke, and possibly by the same author.

Books of the New Testament

- Gospels: Matthew, Mark, Luke, John

- The Acts of the Apostles

- Epistles: Romans, I Corinthians, II Corinthians, Galatians, Ephesians, Philippians, Colossians, I Thessalonians, II Thessalonians, I Timothy, II Timothy, Titus, Philemon, Hebrews, James, I Peter, II Peter, I John, II John, III John, Jude

- The Revelation of St John the Divine.

Passages from the Bible are usually referred to by book name (or an abbreviation of it), chapter number and verse number. For example, 'Matt 1: 18' stands for 'Gospel of Matthew, Chapter 1, Verse 18'.

Although Mary is mentioned in these texts, relatively little information is given about her. For millions of Christians around the world, the divine conception of Jesus and the miraculous virgin birth form the centrepiece of Mary's story, which is why Christians often refer to her as the 'Virgin Mary'. Yet her status as a virgin is only mentioned in two of the four gospels: Matthew and Luke. So, let us take a closer look at the accounts of Jesus' conception and birth in the Gospels of Matthew and Luke.

Activity

(Allow around 60 minutes to complete this activity.)

Readings 2.1 and 2.2 contain descriptions of Jesus' conception and birth as told in the Gospels of Matthew (Matt 1: 18 – 2: 12) and Luke (Luke 1: 26–55 and Luke 2: 1–21). Note that in this chapter we have used the New Revised Standard Version of the Bible, which was translated into modern English by a committee of scholars representing different Christian traditions.

Read through the extracts now. As you do so, pay attention to the way that Mary has been described. Do you notice any similarities or differences between the accounts? You might find it helpful to highlight or underline relevant sections of the text.

Discussion

Similarities

Both accounts agree that Jesus' mother was a virgin when Jesus was conceived through the Holy Spirit. They both also mention Joseph, Mary's future husband, and identify Bethlehem as the place associated with Jesus' birth (though in Matthew it is not entirely clear how old Jesus is when the wise men visit him in Bethlehem – he is simply described as a child). Finally, they both mention an angel (or several angels according to Luke) taking on the role of messenger.

Differences

You may have noticed that the story in the Gospel of Luke is much more detailed and elaborate, with Mary having a much more central and active role than she has in the Gospel of Matthew. In fact, the extracts from the Gospel of Matthew tell us more about her 'righteous' future husband, Joseph (Matt 1: 19), than about Mary herself. Mary is described in relation to either her husband or her son: she is 'engaged to Joseph' and 'found to be with child from the Holy Spirit' (Matt 1: 18). The child is 'with Mary his mother' (Matt 2: 11) when 'wise men from the East' (Matt 2: 1) visit to pay homage to 'the child who has been born king of the Jews' (Matt 2: 2).

By contrast, in the Gospel of Luke, Mary is portrayed as a central figure in the story. Luke focuses on the moment when the angel Gabriel tells her that she is about to conceive a child by the Holy Spirit. According to this account, she is initially 'perplexed' by the encounter with the angel and 'ponders' on the meaning of the angel's greeting (Luke 1: 29). The account in the Gospel of Luke also gives Mary a voice. While no actual words are accredited to her in Matthew, in Luke's account Mary engages in a conversation with the angel Gabriel. She consciously accepts the responsibility of having this child. Later on, she enthusiastically gives praise to God in her meeting with her older relative Elizabeth, who is also miraculously expecting a baby.

The birth of Jesus is described much more elaborately in Luke than it is in Matthew. In Luke, Mary is depicted as thoughtful, 'treasuring' and 'pondering' (Luke 2: 19), the words of the shepherds paying homage to her baby. By contrast, Matthew emphasises Joseph's point of view. There are other significant differences in both stories. For example, Matthew does not mention Joseph's and Mary's journey to Bethlehem, or Jesus' birth away from home with his parents struggling to find a place to stay, or the story of the shepherds. On the other hand, Luke does not mention the visit of the wise men from the East at all.

Figure 2 Children performing a nativity play. Photo: Anyka/Alamy.

The story of Mary's pregnancy and Jesus' birth (the 'Nativity') is very well known in Christian popular culture. It has been, and continues to be, the subject of countless pieces of art and has been re-enacted around the world in many churches, community events and school performances at Christmas – the annual festival celebrating the birth of Jesus (Figure 2). Popular retellings of the story of the Nativity often deal with divergences between the different gospel accounts by weaving elements of both the Gospels of Matthew and Luke into one coherent narrative. The story typically goes like this:

- Mary is visited by the angel Gabriel who tells her that she is about to have a baby conceived through the Holy Spirit (the 'Annunciation') (Gospel of Luke).

- Joseph has a dream where he receives a message from an angel telling him to stay with Mary (Gospel of Matthew).

- Later, Joseph and the pregnant Mary travel to Bethlehem where Jesus is born in a stable (Gospel of Luke).

- Shepherds are told by angels of Jesus' birth and then find Mary, Joseph and the baby Jesus in the stable (Gospel of Luke).

- Wise men (often portrayed as three kings) visit to honour and bring gifts for the baby Jesus (Gospel of Matthew).

As the extracts from the Gospels of Matthew and Luke in Readings 2.1 and 2.2 show, the different gospels all pick up on different aspects of Mary's story, with some parallels and overlaps. While Mary features most prominently in Luke's account of her pregnancy and Jesus' birth, she also briefly appears in the context of other sections in the gospels relating to different stages of Jesus' life, where she is portrayed as a witness, parent and companion. Mary's story following Jesus' birth (according to the different gospels and The Acts of the Apostles) can be pieced together as follows (see also Maunder, 2007b, p. 13):

- Mary and Joseph take baby Jesus to the Temple in Jerusalem (Gospel of Luke).

- They flee to Egypt to escape King Herod and then return to Nazareth (Gospel of Matthew).

- Mary is concerned when twelve-year-old Jesus stays behind in the Temple in Jerusalem in conversation with teachers (Gospel of Luke).

- She is present at a wedding at Cana where the adult Jesus turns water into wine (Gospel of John).

- She is identified as Jesus' mother in front of crowds in Nazareth (Gospels of Mark, Matthew and Luke).

- Mary is present at her son's crucifixion at Golgotha (a site just outside the walls of Jerusalem) and Jesus asks 'the disciple whom he loved' to look after her (Gospel of John).

- Mary joins the early Christian community in Jerusalem in prayer after Jesus' ascension into heaven (The Acts of the Apostles).

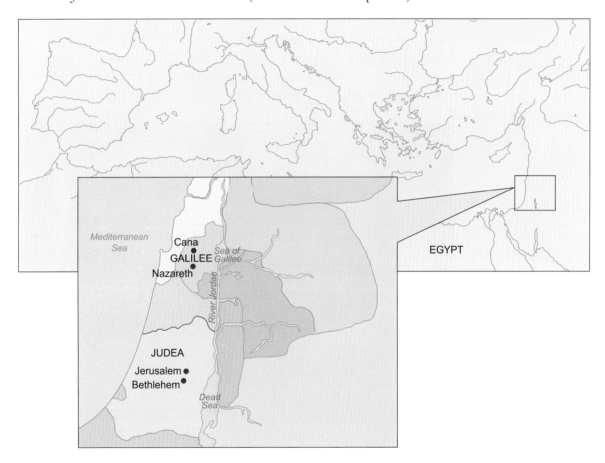

Figure 3 Map of ancient Palestine showing the locations of Nazareth, Bethlehem, Jerusalem and Cana in relation to Egypt.

What is particularly striking is that in the Gospel of Mark there are few references to Mary, including a very brief and indirect reference, where Jesus is referred to as 'the son of Mary' (Mark 6: 3) as well as a reference to 'his mother and his brothers […] standing outside' and calling him as Jesus addresses crowds (Mark 3: 31).

Apart from the four gospels and The Acts of the Apostles, the New Testament also includes letters (known as 'epistles') sent by leading early Christian missionaries (apostles) to members of early Christian communities. Most of these letters have been ascribed to the apostle Paul, though some biblical scholars argue that there was a wider range of early Christian authors. Mary is not mentioned in these epistles, apart from a reference to Jesus as 'born of a woman' in the letter to the Galatians (Galatians 4: 4). There is also a passage in the Book of Revelation describing apocalyptic visions of 'a woman clothed with the sun, with the moon under her feet, and on her head a crown of twelve stars' (Revelation 12: 10) being confronted by a dragon with seven heads as she gives birth to a son (Figure 4). Though this text does not explicitly mention Mary, it has been associated with her and has influenced portrayals of Mary in art and Christian culture.

Figure 4 Giusto di Giovanni de' Menabuoi, *The Woman Clothed with the Sun and the Seven-Headed Dragon*, 1360–70, fresco. Padua Baptistery, Padua. Photo: © Alinari/Bridgeman Images.

As historian Jaroslav Pelikan notes, 'the account of Mary in the New Testament is tantalizingly brief, and anyone who comes to consider biblical references to Mary […] must be surprised or even shocked how sparse they are' (1996, p. 8), especially in light of the prominence of Mary in Christian traditions.

2.2 Critical biblical scholarship

Divergences between the different gospel accounts and the fact that
these texts pick up on different elements of Mary's story are not
unique to her; they apply to many other aspects of the stories and
figures that feature in the New Testament. Critical biblical scholarship
has tried to explain these differences between accounts in the gospels
using a combination of analytical approaches and methods. An
approach combining historical and literary methods could explain
deviations between the gospel accounts by arguing that their authors
had access to different oral traditions or written sources. For example,
it could be argued that the Gospel of Luke talks more extensively
about Mary than the other gospels because Luke had access to sources
that were not available to the other authors. Mary's greater role in his
gospel could also be explained as a reflection of a greater interest in
Mary in Christian communities when this gospel was written, which
had not yet manifested itself at the time when the earlier Gospel of
Mark was written.

Some biblical scholars have argued that the gospels were not intended
to represent history in any literal sense. Instead, these texts are more
appropriately understood as faith documents or literary works that exist
in the context of contemporary oral or written sources, literary
traditions, and against the backdrop of the social and political history
of ancient Palestine in the first century CE. Differences in the gospel
narratives could be explained as the result of narrative techniques or
literary devices used by the authors of the gospels to characterise
figures like Mary in a particular way and to highlight specific
interpretations of the role and status of Jesus.

This means that accounts of the miraculous nature of Jesus'
conception and birth might reflect particular theological understandings
of Jesus' status as the Son of God, Christ or **Messiah**. From this point
of view, references to Mary's virginity could be understood as a literary
device used by the Gospels of Matthew and Luke to symbolise the
purity and innocence of Jesus' mother – reflecting Jesus' own purity,
virtuousness and divine origins (Maunder, 2007b). Others have
highlighted parallels between Jesus' birth and other virgin births in
classical mythology. As the historian and novelist Marina Warner
argues, 'the historical fact remains that in pre-Christian Roman empire

virgin birth was a shorthand symbol, commonly used to designate a man's divinity [and] that the virgin birth of heroes and sages was a widespread formula in the hellenistic world' (Warner, 2013, p. 35–6).

Therefore, it is very hard to deduce from the New Testament texts what Mary was really like, or whether she actually existed as a historical figure. As Warner points out, 'the amount of historical information about the Virgin is negligible. Her birth, her death, her age, her appearance are never mentioned' (Warner, 2013, p. 14). It could be argued that it is even more difficult to establish the 'historical Mary' than it is with other historical figures such as Cleopatra, given that Mary (and the New Testament as a source) continues to be central to highly emotionally charged religious beliefs, steeped in passion and intense devotion. These beliefs continue to be very popular and highly influential. As we saw in the example of 'Our Lady of the Underpass' introduced at the beginning of this chapter, Mary also continues to be very present to many people in powerful religious experiences.

It is also important to note that the New Testament is not the only early textual source that has influenced the reputations Mary has acquired. Let us briefly consider what other early sources there are.

2.3 Jewish scriptures

There are a number of prophecies in the **Hebrew Bible** that Christians have related to Mary, though she is not directly named in these texts. Most notably, this includes the prophecy of Isaiah, which is also quoted in the story of the Annunciation of Mary's pregnancy with Jesus in the Gospel of Matthew ('Look, the virgin shall conceive and bear a son' – see Reading 2.1). These links to prophecies in Jewish scriptures were particularly meaningful to followers of Jesus with a Jewish background (Rubin, 2010, p. 9).

2.4 Apocrypha

While the canonical gospels focus on Jesus' life and do not provide much information about Mary's origins or early life, there are other early Christian sources that offer more detailed accounts of her. However, these are regarded as **apocrypha**, as the Church leadership decided not to officially include them in the New Testament due to doubts around their authorship and authenticity.

This includes the Book of James (also known as the 'Protogospel' of James). Scholars estimate that this text was written in Syria or Egypt around 150 CE. The Book of James portrays Mary's own conception as miraculous and provides her 'with an early life fitting for the mother of God' (Rubin, 2010, p. 10), raised by doting, virtuous parents, Anne and Joachim, in a comfortable, wealthy home. It also suggests that Mary took a vow of virginity at a young age and argues that she remained a virgin throughout her life – including before and after giving birth to Jesus – and that she miraculously did not suffer any pain while giving birth (Warner, 2013, pp. 26–44).

Similarly, in the Book of Mary's Repose (a source that scholars have dated back to the third century CE and possibly earlier) Mary is presented as a revered figure who holds superior knowledge of the Christian faith and of cosmic mysteries, and possesses special powers to intercede with her son on behalf of sinners (Shoemaker, 2016).

Even though these texts were not included in the New Testament, narratives from the Book of James and other apocrypha, such as the Book of Mary's Repose, have had a strong and lasting influence on perceptions of Mary in Christian popular culture, including oral traditions, songs, mystery plays and art. The existence of these apocryphal sources in itself can also be seen as historical evidence of an emerging reverence for Mary in early Christian communities in the late second and third centuries CE (Shoemaker, 2016, p. 54).

2.5 Polemic

Early claims of Jesus' miraculous conception and virgin birth also became the source of strong written attacks and contemptuous ridicule, referred to as **polemic**. For example, there is evidence of accusations in relatively early anti-Christian polemic claiming that Jesus was illegitimate – born to parents who were not married to each other. This was a serious accusation in a society where genealogy and family lineage were regarded as very important, and where women who became pregnant outside of marriage were often rejected by their families and could be sold into slavery or even stoned to death.

These accusations were made by authors who were keen to discredit the growing early Christian cult. This included members of Jewish communities and some Greek and Roman authors, such as the pagan philosopher Celsus, who wrote a polemic against Christianity called

'The True Doctrine' in the late second century CE. The influence of Celsus' polemic is indicated by the fact that the early Christian theologian Origen of Alexandria (183–253 CE) felt compelled to write *Contra Celsus* to challenge Celsus' arguments (Ross and Potter, 2015; Rubin, 2010, pp. 12–16).

2.6 Mary in the Qur'an

Jesus' mother Mary is not only a figure of central importance within many forms of Christianity, but also holds a distinguished position within Islam. In fact, she is mentioned more often in the Islamic **Qur'an** than she is in the Christian Bible (34 times in the Qur'an in comparison to 19 times in the New Testament). Muslims believe that the Qur'an contains messages that God revealed to the Prophet Muhammad via the angel Gabriel (the same angel who is also believed to have visited Mary). As Muslims see it, these revelations to Muhammad confirm the same **monotheistic** message (based on the belief that there is only one God) that had been revealed to earlier prophets, including Adam, Abraham, Moses (who are also mentioned in the Jewish Hebrew Bible and the Old Testament of the Christian Bible) and Jesus. Muhammad is regarded as the last in this line of prophets. In Islam, Jesus is understood as a prophet and messenger of God who performed miracles, but not as the Son of God. In fact, the Qur'an refers to him as 'Isa son of Maryam'. The Qur'an was written in Arabic between 610 and 632 CE at a time when Mary was already becoming a prominent figure in Christian traditions.

Mary's story 'is by far the most complex and nuanced female portrait in the Qur'an' (McAuliffe, 1981, p. 19). The Qur'an dedicates one of its longer chapters (Sura 19) to Mary (referred to as Maryam). This includes an extended account of the Annunciation and Nativity, supporting the Gospels of Matthew and Luke's claims that Mary was a virgin when she conceived Jesus. However, the fact that Jesus is understood in Islam to be a prophet and not the Son of God also affects Muslim perceptions of Mary's status. The Qur'an portrays her 'as a woman of considerable integrity, sanctity, and autonomy in her own right; in fact, the Muslim Mary is not primarily celebrated as mother of Christ, but as a distinctive archetype of prayerfulness and patience in adversity' (Winter, 2007, p. 479).

Activity

(Allow around 30 minutes to complete this activity.)

Reading 2.3 reproduces part of the entry for 'Mary' by H. Chad Hillier in *The Qur'an: An Encyclopedia*. This extract provides an overview of the story of Jesus' conception and birth as told in the Qur'an, drawing on a range of sources.

Read through the extract now. How does Mary's story in the Qur'an differ from the narratives you have previously encountered in this unit?

Discussion

In contrast with the canonical gospels, but similar to the apocryphal Book of James, the Qur'an makes references to Mary's comfortable, respectable early life (her mother's name, Hanna, is likely to be a version or translation of the name Anne or Anna used in the Book of James). The story of the Annunciation is similar to the version told in the Gospel of Luke. However, Mary's husband Joseph is not mentioned in the Qur'an, and the baby Jesus is given a more active role.

Unlike the accounts in the Gospel of Luke, Mary gives birth alone under a palm tree. The Qur'an also describes Mary's painful labour, hunger, thirst and distress during childbirth, which is different to how she is portrayed in the Gospels of Matthew or Luke. However, in the Qur'an, she is comforted by a voice (possibly baby Jesus' voice) and God provides her with water and food. When she returns to her community with her son, she is confronted with scepticism and questions about her morality. According to the Qur'an, the baby miraculously speaks and 'asserts his prophetic mission in defence of his mother's chastity' (Hillier, 2006, p. 394).

You will be able to continue to explore Mary's reputation in Islam when you return to the module website at the end of the chapter.

3 Mary as a central figure in Christianity

In order to consider how Mary became such a central figure in Christianity, we will first look at how she was represented in art, and then at some of the popular beliefs and devotional practices that developed around her.

3.1 Imagining Mary

There are relatively few images of Mary in Islamic art due to the proscription in some forms of Islam against the creation of images of sentient beings, and of religious figures in particular. This is related to concerns that these images might become worshipped in themselves or distract from the worship of God. While the significance of images has also been contested in some Christian traditions, most notably in **Protestant** traditions that are particularly disapproving of the veneration of images, there is a remarkable wealth of representations of Mary in art within Christianity, especially in **Roman Catholic** and **Orthodox** Christian traditions.

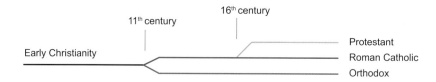

Figure 5 The three main branches of Christianity.

For many centuries, only a very small proportion of people could read, let alone translate, the biblical texts, and books like the Bible were unaffordable and inaccessible to most. So visual art – such as paintings, stained-glass church windows (Figures 6 and 7) and sculptures – was a very important way of sharing biblical (and apocryphal) stories and of bringing them alive.

This stained-glass window from a sixteenth-century French priory (Figure 7) illustrates the continuing powerful influence of apocryphal stories: it portrays Mary's interaction with her mother Anne, which forms part of The Book of James but is not mentioned in the New Testament.

Figure 6 (left) The Nativity depicted in a window, fifteenth century. Seville Cathedral. Photo: © akg-images/De Agostini Picture Lib./W. Buss.
Figure 7 (right) Window depicting St Anne teaching the Virgin to read, 1500–10. Ancient Priory of Saint-Lô, Bourg-Achard, France. Photo: © Bridgeman Images.

As Christianity spread and became more established, representations of the Virgin Mary interacted with different local cultures. Christian traditions adapted and incorporated images, shrines, rituals and customs from other religious traditions as Christianity established itself as a global faith (for example, old holy wells and pagan shrines were turned into Christian shrines). Some scholars have argued that some aspects of popular devotion to Mary were influenced by the worship of pagan goddesses, such as the Egyptian goddess Isis, the Roman goddess Diana or the Norse goddess Freya.

Activity

(Allow around 10 minutes to complete this activity.)

Look at Figures 8 and 9. Figure 8 shows a statue representing the Egyptian goddess Isis with her son Horus. Figure 9 shows a statue of the Virgin Mary with her son Jesus. What kind of similarities do you notice?

Discussion

There are striking similarities between both statues. For example, both portray the women seated in very similar positions on a chair or throne with a young child on their laps, breastfeeding them. Also, both figures wear crowns (although Isis' headgear is much more elaborate than Mary's) and are dressed as imperial, royal figures.

Some scholars have suggested that the parallels between Figures 8 and 9 might have been deliberately emphasised by early Christian missionaries to win over new converts and establish points of contact resonating with ancient local 'pagan' traditions (McGuckin, 2008, p. 11). It is also important to bear in mind that parallels with pre-Christian traditions were not limited to representations and devotional practices associated with the Virgin Mary, but have played a role in many other Christian practices and festivals, such as some rituals associated with Christmas.

Figure 8 (left) Gilded wood statuette from the tomb of Tutankhamun (d. *c.*1323 BCE), showing Egyptian goddess Isis with Horus, Egyptian civilisation XVIII Dynasty. Egyptian Museum, Cairo. Photo: © akg-images/De Agostini/ W. Bus. **Figure 9 (right)** *Shrine of the Virgin*; the Virgin nursing the Christ Child, *c.*1300, oak, linen covering, polychromy, gilding, gesso, 13 × 35 × 13 cm. Metropolitan Museum of Art, New York, Gift of J. Pierpont Morgan, 1917. Acc.n.: 17.190.185. Image copyright The Metropolitan Museum of Art/Art Resource/Scala, Florence.

Scholars have also highlighted the importance of understanding the growing popularity of devotion to the Virgin Mary 'as something that developed organically from within the early Christian tradition itself' (Shoemaker, 2016, p. 29) in the broader context of the emerging Christian veneration of martyrs and other figures of exceptional faith and sanctity, who were regarded as saints.

The fact that there is no physical description of Jesus' mother in the Bible has allowed artistic portrayals of Mary to be influenced by ideals of beauty as defined by particular historical, local and cultural contexts.

Different interpretations of her across different parts of the world are reflected in Figures 10, 11 and 12. These illustrate artistic interpretations of Mary to reflect a range of cultural contexts, portraying her and baby Jesus as members of a range of different ethnic groups. This adaptability has made her very relatable and attractive to people from a wide range of different backgrounds across the world in different historical and local contexts.

Figure 10 (left) Korean school, *Virgin and Child*, twentieth century, oil on canvas. Photo: © Boltin Picture Library/Bridgeman Images. **Figure 11 (centre)** *The Madonna and Child of Soweto*; 'The Black Madonna'. Regina Mundi Church, Soweto, Johannesburg. Photo: Blaine Harrington III/Alamy.
Figure 12 (right) Studio of Sandro Botticelli, *The Madonna and Child*, 1444/5–1510, oil on panel, 99 × 57 cm. Private collection. Photo: © Christie's Images/Bridgeman Images.

It is fair to say that representations of Mary in art have both reflected and shaped different aspects of her reputation. They have also reflected attempts to control or promote particular aspects of her reputation by political or religious leaders. Mary was adopted as the patroness of the Byzantine Empire and its capital Constantinople (modern-day Istanbul) from the fifth century CE. Her official portrayals in art subsequently became dominated by her representation as an imperial, queenly, poised, majestic figure, 'finely dressed, frontal, central and sometimes surrounded by angels and saints as attendants' (Rubin, 2010, p. 63).

Figure 13 *Mother of God*; Mural of Virgin Mary holding the baby infant Jesus in the domed interior, sitting on a jewelled throne, wearing a sumptuous blue robe against a golden background, *c.*843–67 CE. Hagia Sophia, Constantinople (modern-day Istanbul). Photo: © akg-images/Erich Lessing.

The convention of portraying Mary wearing a sumptuous blue cloak (Figure 13) can be traced back to the Byzantine Empire, *c.*500 CE, where blue was regarded as the colour of an empress and a symbol of the imperial cult. An explanation for the continuation of this representation of Mary in Europe throughout the medieval and Renaissance periods was that blue pigment was particularly valuable as it was derived from the rock lapis lazuli, which was imported from Afghanistan and was more precious than gold. The use of such a precious pigment in artistic portrayals of Mary originates in symbolic expressions of devotion and glorification, rather than realistic portrayals of her as a historical figure, as it is extremely unlikely that a Jewish woman in ancient Palestine would have worn a sumptuous blue cloak.

3.2 Controversies surrounding different aspects of Mary's reputation in Christianity

Representations of Mary in art also reflect the many different ways in which she has been understood in Christianity. Christians have venerated her as a saint, Queen of Heaven (Figure 14), Blessed Virgin, Second Eve, Bride of God, Bearer of God or Mother of God (though not as a deity in her own right) and Mother of the Church.

In light of the great diversity of popular beliefs and devotional practices associated with Mary, there have been fierce controversies amongst and within different branches of Christianity around the question of which beliefs associated with her should be regarded as compulsory **doctrines** (officially acknowledged as essential teachings by the church leadership). This includes disagreements around the question of whether Mary really was a virgin when she miraculously conceived Jesus through the Holy Spirit; whether she maintained a perpetual virginal status even after Jesus' birth; and whether she herself was conceived by a virgin. The virgin birth of Jesus was identified and acknowledged as an essential Christian belief by the First Council of Nicea held in 325 CE, where church leaders met in an effort to achieve an agreement on a range of issues among different branches of Christianity.

Figure 14 Master of the Legend of St Lucy, *Mary, Queen of Heaven*, fifteenth century, oil on panel, 199 × 162 cm. National Gallery of Art, Washington DC. Photo: © National Gallery of Art/Bridgeman Images.

Questions around Mary's virginity became particularly important in the context of the teachings of the early Christian theologian and philosopher Augustine of Hippo (354–430 CE), whose writings on the notion of 'original sin' became very influential, particularly in the Roman Catholic Church. Augustine argued that 'original sin' was passed on through sexual intercourse. Therefore, in order for Jesus to be holy and without sin, his conception and birth could not be the result of sex. Extended to his mother, this way of thinking strengthened the belief that Mary herself was conceived by a virgin and must have remained celibate all her life (as claimed by the apocryphal Book of James). For Augustine, original sin had begun with the first humans, Adam and Eve, whose story is told in the Book of Genesis in the Old Testament. As the idea became increasingly influential, Mary came to be seen as an inspirational model for asceticism and celibacy, influencing monastic practices.

It is worth noting that the **dogma** of Mary's Immaculate Conception was declared to be an essential aspect of the Roman Catholic faith as late as 1854 by Pope Pius IX. This stated the Roman Catholic Church leadership's conviction that Mary herself was miraculously conceived free from original sin, without sexual intercourse:

> We declare, pronounce, and define that the doctrine which holds that the most Blessed Virgin Mary, in the first instance of her conception, by a singular grace and privilege granted by Almighty God, in view of the merits of Jesus Christ, the Savior of the human race, was preserved free from all stain of original sin, is a doctrine revealed by God and therefore to be believed firmly and constantly by all the faithful.
>
> (Pope Bl. Pius IX, 2017 [1854])

However, the Council of Ephesus in 431 CE, where church leaders declared Mary to be 'Theotokos' (mother or 'bearer' of God), is widely regarded as the most important development – or watershed moment – as it signalled church leaders' official approval and promotion of devotion to the Virgin Mary, which is likely to have existed at the grass-roots level for some time before then. Coupled with the adoption of the Virgin Mary as the patroness of the Roman or Byzantine Empire and its capital Constantinople, this led to an 'explosion of Marian piety within the Christian empire and its church' from the fifth century CE onwards (Shoemaker, 2016, p. 29), giving 'rise to new feast days, churches, shrines, hymns, **relics**, and icons' (George-Tvrtković, 2018, p. 22).

Other debates about Mary's status have included disagreements around the question whether her body and soul were elevated and assumed into heaven before or after the end of her earthly life. While most

Protestant branches of Christianity neither teach nor believe in the Assumption of Mary into heaven, it became defined as a doctrine by the Roman Catholic Church as late as 1950, under the leadership of Pope Pius XII. This shows that these debates still continue even 2000 later, and illustrates the church leadership's ongoing attempts to define and control Mary's image.

The levels of importance assigned to the veneration of Mary, and the type of beliefs, experiences and devotional practices associated with her (and other Christian saints) have varied greatly amongst different Christian traditions. Whereas devotion to Mary has a central role within the Roman Catholic and Orthodox churches, many Protestant Reformers have criticised the extent of the veneration of Mary (and of all other saints) and devotional practices associated with her as being too excessive and a distraction from what they regard as the essentials of Christian biblical teachings.

You will explore some of the differences between different branches of Christianity in further detail in Book 2, Chapter 7.

3.3 Symbol of oppression or champion of the oppressed?

Some critics have argued that Mary's reputations have been deliberately manipulated by political and church leaders to support and legitimise particular agendas. We have already seen that the political leadership of the Byzantine Empire adopted her as a patroness of the Empire and of the capital Constantinople. This could be explained as a sign and symbol of the emperors' genuine devotion to Mary, but it could also be argued that her representation as a queenly, imperial figure also helped to legitimise and support the position and wealth of emperors and their families.

Figure 15 Edward Coley Burne-Jones, *The Annunciation*, 1863, watercolour and bodycolour on paper, 60 × 53 cm. Private collection. Photo: © Christie's Images/Bridgeman Images.

Some feminist theologians have argued that a predominantly male church leadership promoted representations of the Virgin Mary as a model of female compliance and quiet submissiveness and, ultimately, as a tool for the oppression of women. In particular, critics have claimed that the importance that male church leaders have assigned to Mary's virginity is linked to a repression and fear of female sexuality. From this point of view, the idealisation of her as an example of perfect, serene motherhood and spotless virginity has contributed to the association of the image of a 'good' woman with a submissive, demure and obedient role (Figures 15 and 16). Her paradoxical identity as both virgin and mother confronts women with rather unrealistic expectations, far removed from most women's experiences and everyday lives:

> [T]he ideal she presents of perfect mother as well as of spotless virgin has always had its negative aspects for women as well. It is an impossible ideal for a human mother to live up to. Feminists argue that that is partly why celibate male priests have encouraged it for so long: women can never attain the ideal of redeemed womanhood as presented by the virgin mother and feel confident in their femininity. The ideal is unattainable.
>
> (Drury, 1994, p. 52)

Feminist theologians have argued that ideas about gender and the role of women, including Mary, in Christian communities have been shaped by male church leaders. They claim that these ideas have been used to assign women to 'a secondary position within the Church' (Drury, 1994, p. 31), deny 'women an active and independent role in [the church's] ministry' (Warner, 2013, p. 194), and exclude them from priestly ordination, as they are in Roman Catholicism.

Figure 16 Giovan Battista Salvi, *Virgin Praying with Eyes Lowered*, 1647–52, oil on canvas. Castello Sforzesco, Museum of Ancient Art, Milan. Photo: © akg-images/Mondadori Portfolio/1992/Electa.

However, some also claim that parts of the New Testament's teaching about women is actually quite radical 'when understood against its contemporary background' (Drury, 1994, p. 30; see also Ruether, 1983; Schüssler Fiorenza, 1993). They believe that there is the possibility of a reform of the Christian tradition through the rediscovery of what they consider to be the original meaning of the biblical texts and Jesus' teachings, before their interpretation was 'hijacked' by male, wealthy authorities with a patriarchal agenda (which promotes a society controlled by men). The virgin birth could, for example, be understood as empowering to women in the sense that it did not even require the involvement of a man.

Activity

(Allow around 30 minutes to complete this activity.)

Reading 2.4 is an extract from a joint **ecumenical** statement prepared by a group of Asian Christian women at a conference held in Singapore in 1987, which brought together women from 16 countries in the Asia and Pacific regions.

Read through the extract and then answer the following questions: How is Mary portrayed in this text? How does this contrast with other portrayals of Mary?

Discussion

In this text, Mary is presented as 'the mother of suffering' and the mother 'of those who suffer'. She is described as 'a woman of the poor', bringing together Christians 'to liberate the poor and all victims of injustice', and her womb is portrayed as a 'place of struggle and suffering which brings new life' (Singapore Conference, 1994 [1987]).

This view of Mary stands in stark contrast with her representation as a model of submissiveness and passive receptiveness – instead, she is seen as an agent in her own right, who actively and freely accepts God's invitation. From this point of view, the virgin birth is seen as a symbol of the beginning of a new order and of a new humanity, where oppressive, divisive relationships as well as patterns of domination and subordination are overcome.

Mary's liberation from economic, cultural and political domination and subordination is understood as not only applying to women, but to all of humanity. From this point of view, Mary is regarded as a figure of hope and protector of the poor, oppressed and vulnerable – a portrayal standing in stark contrast to that of a 'jewelled and elaborately dressed' imperial figure or Queen of Heaven (1994 [1987], p. 274).

The statement in Reading 2.4 makes reference to the particular significance of Mary's 'Magnificat', which is also known as her 'Song of Praise' or Mary's Song. Its words are included in the Gospel of Luke (Luke 1: 46–55, which forms part of Reading 2.2). From this point of view, the following words from Mary's 'Song of Praise' have been interpreted as revolutionary, challenging the social order and established hierarchies:

> He has brought down the powerful from their thrones, and lifted up the lowly; he has filled the hungry with good things, and sent the rich away empty.
>
> (Luke 1: 52–3)

In line with the perception of her as a champion of the suffering and vulnerable, many bereaved parents have also regarded Mary as a powerful source of comfort, as a 'link with the dead, and an effective consoler of the living' (Rubin, 2010, p. 417). In particular, artistic representations of Mary cradling her dead son – also known as a *pietà* (Figures 17 and 18) – became very important symbols, particularly during the First World War, which many bereaved relatives of soldiers, especially their grieving mothers, could relate to. As Rubin notes, 'practically every parish in France has its own war memorial, so often the carved image of the Pietà: Mary holds her dead son, sometimes a soldier in uniform' (Rubin, 2010, p. 417).

Figure 17 (left) *Pietà*, German School, fifteenth century, State Hermitage Museum, Saint Petersburg. Photo: © Tarker/Bridgeman Images. **Figure 18 (right)** War memorial to the French dead of the Second World War at the Somme battlefield in Hamel. Photo: © BRIAN HARRIS/Alamy.

4 Interacting with Mary

To this day, Mary continues to be an incredibly popular figure, enormously revered across 'gender lines, with men as fervent as women if not more so' (Hall, 2004, p. 1). Particularly in Roman Catholic and Orthodox Christian traditions, there are a wide range of popular practices associated with Marian devotion. These can take on many forms including singing songs dedicated to Mary; carrying images, statues or relics of her (Figure 19) or displaying them in churches, homes or community spaces (Figure 20); building shrines for her; visiting existing Marian shrines; lighting candles or making offerings, such as flowers, to statues of Mary; touching, decorating or dressing Marian statues; or taking part in elaborate, colourful processions celebrating Marian festivals (Figure 21). In this section, we will be exploring a number of ways in which people interact with Mary, such as popular Marian festivals, prayers and rituals associated with her, and Marian apparitions.

Figure 19 (left) A Christian Lebanese woman holds a statue of Virgin Mary during a procession in a Beirut Christian dominated neighbourhood, 2016. Photo: © PATRICK BAZ/AFP/Getty Images.
Figure 20 (right) Men playing pool in Omo Valley, Ethiopia, 2011. Note that alongside the poster of Mary there are team photos of Liverpool and Manchester United football clubs and two of Didier Drogba, a devout Roman Catholic and twice African Footballer of the Year. Photo: ERIC LAFFORGUE/ Alamy.

Figure 21 Lebanese Christians walk behind a statue of the Virgin Mary mounted on a sport utility vehicle (SUV) during a procession marking the end of the month of the Virgin Mary, 2016. Photo: © PATRICK BAZ/AFP/ Getty Images.

4.1 Marian festivals

While the core of annual Christian festivals relate to events in Jesus' life (most notably Easter, commemorating his crucifixion and resurrection, and Christmas, celebrating his birth), many festivals specifically associated with Mary have also established themselves in the Christian church calendar, though the extent and manner in which they are celebrated varies between the different branches of Christianity.

The following table highlights the most widely celebrated Marian festivals, which are celebrated through vibrant rituals, such as elaborate processions. To this day, they often involve displays of very intense popular devotion to the Virgin Mary.

Major Marian festivals

Date	Festival
2 February	**Presentation/ Purification/ Candlemas** Celebrating Mary's ritual purification after childbirth through the presentation of her firstborn son, Jesus, to the Temple in Jerusalem. Given that a procession with candles became part of this festival, it has also come to be known as 'Candlemas'.
25 March	**Annunciation** Celebrating the angel Gabriel's visit to Mary to announce her pregnancy with Jesus.
31 May	**Visitation** Celebrating Mary's visit to Elizabeth.
15 August	**Assumption/ Dormition of Mary** Celebrating the taking up of Mary's body and soul into heaven at the end of her earthly life (celebrated as the 'Assumption' by the Roman Catholic Church and as the 'Dormition' – 'falling asleep' – of the Virgin Mary in the Orthodox Church).
8 September	**Nativity of Mary** Celebrating Mary's birth.

You will be able to watch a film about a Marian festival when you return to the module website at the end of the chapter.

4.2 Mary as intercessor and protector

Figure 22 Jean Mirailhet, *Virgin of Mercy*, (central panel), *c.*1429, tempera on panel. Musée d'Art et d'Histoire, Palais Masséna, Nice. Photo: © Bridgeman Images.

Devotees visiting Marian shrines or approaching Mary in prayer sometimes ask for protection, healing, fertility or other favours. While most Christian prayer is directly addressed to God or to Jesus, some branches of Christianity, particularly Roman Catholic and Orthodox traditions, regard Mary as an 'intercessor', mediator or bridge between God and human beings who devotees can approach through prayer to appeal to Jesus, intervene on their behalf and offer them protection. As the son of God's human mother, she is seen as an important link between humans and God and between the realms of heaven and earth. As Marina Warner explains:

> [T]he powers [...] attributed to her throughout Christianity are considered sovereign: the son can refuse his mother nothing. So a prayer to Mary, made in the spirit of repentance and resolve, is wonder-working. [...] The Virgin's intercession with her son can bring healing and fertility and consolation to the living; but by far the greatest function in the Catholic scheme of salvation is to reprieve the sufferings of sinners after death. She is 'the mother of mercy', the 'life, sweetness, and hope' of the fallen, the advocate who pleads humanity's cause before the judgement seat of God.
>
> (Warner, 2013, pp. 291, 322–3)

One especially well-known prayer addressed to Mary is referred to as the 'Hail Mary'. The words used for this particular prayer have been inspired by Elizabeth's words cited in Luke 1: 28 (see Reading 2.2):

> Hail Mary, full of grace, the Lord is with you. Blessed are you among women, and blessed is the fruit of your womb, Jesus. Holy Mary, mother of God, pray for us sinners now and at the hour of our death. Amen.
>
> ('Hail Mary' quoted in Molloy, 2017, p. 253)

This prayer forms part of practices associated with the rosary (Figure 23), which is a string of beads used for the recital of a particular sequence of prayers; this includes the 'Hail Mary' among others. (Prayer beads to help keep count of sequences of prayers are also used in other religious traditions, including Buddhism.) The rosary is held in the hand during prayer. While the beads are slowly gliding through the fingers, a prayer is said in relation to each bead. There are many variations of practices associated with the rosary, including visualising and meditating on the 'Mysteries of the Rosary'. This involves recalling and meditating on joyful, sorrowful, glorious and luminous experiences and events in Mary's and Jesus' lives described in the Christian Bible.

Figure 23 Prayer using a rosary.
Photo: Barry Mason/Alamy.

Praying the rosary can be both a solitary and communal practice – for example, today you can find websites that enable people from all over the world to pray the rosary together. Some Christians believe that those who are devoted to praying the rosary are granted special protection by the Virgin Mary, or are looking for salvation and deliverance from sin.

Mary's reputation as a protector is also linked to her adoption as a patron for cities like Constantinople. From this point of view, she has not just been represented but also experienced as giving strength in military conflicts. In her book *Christians, Muslims and Mary* (2018),

Rita George-Tvrtković highlights the diverse and changing nature of how devotees have related to Mary and experienced her presence in battles:

> early Byzantine texts depict her as directly involved in battles, while later writings ascribe her power to relics and icons rather than her person. For example, eyewitness accounts of the Avar siege of 626 describe Mary walking on the city walls and fighting the enemy herself. Her help is due to her physical presence. But eventually, Mary's power was transferred from her person to her robe, such that later accounts (of Avar, Arab, and Russian sieges) describe Christians processing with Mary's robe along the city walls. Still later accounts transfer Mary's power from her robe to her icon, and describe elaborate processions centred on specific Marian icons known for their power. An account of war with the Muslims of Aleppo in 1030 claims that by this time it was tradition for Byzantine emperors to carry Marian icons with them into battle.
>
> (George-Tvrtković, 2018, p. 25)

Notions of Mary's involvement as a protector range from her alleged physical participation in person (in the case of the Avar siege, more than 600 years after she is alleged to have been born), to the power associated with images or items of clothing associated with her. George-Tvrtković also points out that there were distinct differences between Byzantine Christian leaders, who tended to present Mary as a barrier and protector against all 'infidels' (including Muslims), and Arabic or Syriac-speaking Christians living in Muslim-controlled areas, who often displayed a more nuanced understanding of parallels between Islam and Christianity, and of the fact that Mary plays an important role in both traditions (George-Tvrtković, 2018, p. 27).

4.3 Marian apparitions

When studying the Virgin Mary, it is important to bear in mind that for many devotees, Mary is not just an abstract figure. Some see her as a figure that can physically appear, speak and interact with them in miraculous ways. Mary is reported to have miraculously appeared to thousands of people in many different cultural contexts and different periods of history. Marian apparitions and miraculous manifestations are reported up to the present day – as we noted at the beginning of this unit in relation to the relatively recent story of 'Our Lady of the Underpass' in Chicago. There are numerous shrines all over the world marking apparitions and miracles associated with Mary, which continue to be centres of intense popular devotion. Supernatural apparitions of Mary are believed to be ongoing, with new apparitions in many shapes and forms continuing to be reported.

Figure 24 Pilgrims praying at the Grotto of Massabielle in Lourdes at night. Photo: Agencja Fotograficzna Caro/Alamy.

Apparitions of Mary are often named after the place or town where they were reported (for example, 'Lady of Lourdes', 'Lady of Fátima', 'Our Lady of Walsingham', etc.). Places where Mary is believed to have appeared to devotees, such as in Guadalupe in Mexico, Lourdes in France or Fátima in Portugal, often become pilgrimage sites associated with miracles in popular culture. For example, the water from the spring in Lourdes at the grotto where Mary reportedly appeared in 1858 is believed to possess miraculous healing powers and has attracted people with illnesses hoping to be cured through Mary's intercession (Figure 24). This popular belief has inspired many people to travel to Lourdes to drink the water from this spring and bathe in it, or to collect water from the spring to share it with family or friends unable to visit. This has given rise to the emergence of many commercial organisations arranging trips to Lourdes or selling bottles with water from the spring at the grotto.

Some Marian apparitions – including that of the 'Lady of Lourdes' – have received official approval by the Vatican (the headquarters of the leadership of the Roman Catholic Church), headed by the Pope. Furthermore, the leadership of the Roman Catholic Church has established complex procedures and strict criteria to determine which cures linked to Lourdes are officially regarded as 'miraculous'. As part of these procedures, a local Medical Bureau refers claims of miraculous cures linked to Lourdes to an international committee, where medical experts from a range of different countries assess the medical evidence. Cases where no medical explanation can be found are referred to the patient's local bishop, who can then decide whether to take further steps for the cure to be officially declared miraculous by the Roman Catholic Church (Dowling, 1984). Regardless of whether these experiences are or should be seen as 'miraculous', some medical experts have highlighted the positive boost or changes in mental attitude devotees can experiences on pilgrimages, which can have a beneficial impact on how they experience various medical conditions (*Beyond Belief: Apparitions of Mary*, 2016).

Apparitions of Mary that have been reported in Medjugorje in Bosnia-Herzegovina since 1981 are still under investigation by the Vatican at the time of writing, and there are many more that have influenced popular culture but have not been officially recognised by the church leadership. Photography, film and social media have opened up new opportunities for devotees to share experiences of apparitions. In these instances, Mary allegedly appears physically (sometimes speaking to devotees), or appears in public manifestations (such as 'Our Lady of the Underpass'). Instances can also 'involve the miraculous appearance of an image on a window or a mirror, inside a cloak, hidden down a mineshaft, buried under a mosque' (Hall, 2004, p. 3) or on a piece of toast. Indeed, in 2004, a decade-old piece of toast that was believed to miraculously bear the image of the Virgin Mary and allegedly never went mouldy (Figure 25), reportedly sold on eBay for $28,000 (BBC News, 2004).

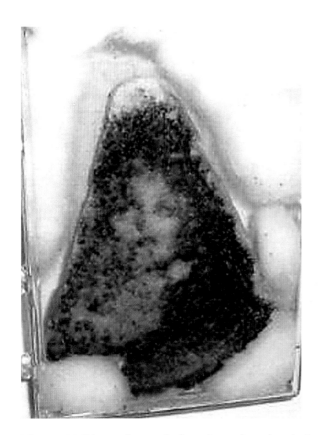

Figure 25 Piece of toast believed to miraculously bear the image of the Virgin Mary, which sold on eBay for $28,000 in 2004. Photo: © AFP/Getty Images.

It is also important to note that Marian apparitions have occurred in places of worship that are used by both Christians and Muslims (Keriakos, 2012) and that Marian shrines are not only visited by Christian devotees. For example, the Shrine of Our Lady of Lebanon 'has drawn Muslim visitors since it opened in 1908 […] They come as tourists, but also to pray and participate in Christian ceremonies at the site' (Blumberg, 2016). Interestingly, there has also reportedly been a 'rise in Hindus venerating the Virgin Mary alongside their own goddesses, like Pavarti and Durga [which highlights] her growing appeal across religious borders', including 'a rising number of Hindus visiting Lourdes' (Chamley, 2014; see also Fernandes, 2017; Ghosh, 2013).

Activity

(Allow around 30 minutes to complete this activity.)

Now that you have encountered a number of different approaches to the study of Mary, the mother of Jesus, take some time to look back at the example you were introduced to right at the beginning of this chapter: 'Our Lady of the Underpass', found in Chicago in 2005. How would you approach this case study now? What sort of questions would you be interested in asking? What kind of questions could be asked from a Religious Studies point of view?

Discussion

There are a wide range of questions you could be asking here. From a personal point of view, you might well be asking, 'Is this really a manifestation of the Virgin Mary?' However, having worked through this chapter, you might find yourself with other kinds of questions. Remember that we are not trying to question a religious commitment but to understand how people make sense of the world.

You might have ended up asking questions such as:

- Where, when, how and by whom was 'Our Lady of the Underpass' discovered?

- What do we know about the historical, local and cultural context of this event? How might this context influence practices or beliefs associated with 'Our Lady of the Underpass'?

- Who visits this site?

- What do people do when they visit?

- Why are people visiting? What do they see in 'Our Lady of the Underpass'?

- How have religious authorities or institutions been involved? Is this purely a popular or unofficial movement?

When studying apparitions or manifestations of the Virgin Mary in Religious Studies, the concern is not so much with making a judgement on whether or not Mary really appeared. Instead, the focus is on exploring the experiences of the people witnessing these apparitions or on gaining a deeper understanding of how pilgrims interact with places where apparitions reportedly occurred, taking local, social and historical contexts into account. As Chris Maunder (2007a), scholar of Religious Studies and Theology, argues:

> studies which recognize the rich and diverse layers of understanding and inspiration that apparitions engender; [...] which understand the fact that symbolic images are polyvalent [combine different meanings] and can never be limited to single and simple interpretations – these studies give the greatest insight into the human phenomena that are Marian apparitions.
>
> (2007a, p. 455)

5 Summary

The study of Mary, the mother of Jesus, illustrates that the use of symbols and stories – no matter whether they are 'true' or 'false' in a historical or scientific sense – can nonetheless be extremely powerful. Mary continues to be a very influential figure, even though we cannot know for sure whether she actually ever lived as a historical figure. The Virgin Mary has played an important role in official teachings of religious traditions and institutions, and there have been many attempts by religious and political institutions and their leaders to control her image. However, popular devotion to her has often gone much beyond the official framework of religious traditions as defined by their leadership. As Rubin concludes, 'As Christianity established itself as a global faith Mary emerged as a powerful and almost uncontrollable symbol, endlessly remade and reimagined by waves of devotees' (Rubin, 2010). The 'powerful, almost uncontrollable' symbolism associated with Mary has been a very fertile source of inspiration for culture and art, but it has equally been shaped and influenced by local, popular practices and traditions.

The figure of the Virgin Mary has also served as an important focal point for debates around different understandings of gender roles and of leadership and power in religious communities (and society as a whole). In this chapter, you have encountered a wide range of different, and sometimes conflicting, views of Mary: that of a model of serenity, purity, submissiveness and passiveness; of an intercessor, protector or warrior; of a queenly figure associated with symbols of wealth and high social status; of an active, powerful champion of the suffering and oppressed; and of a healing, comforting motherly figure full of unconditional love, peace and forgiveness. While different views of Mary have been the source of much controversy and division within and between different religious traditions and denominations, there are also many remarkable links and parallels between her role in different religious traditions, including not only different branches of Christianity but also Islam and Hinduism. As Dionigi Albera concludes, 'among the saints who act as bridges between religions, Mary has perhaps the dominant role' (Albera, 2008, p. 46).

You should now return to the module website to continue your study of this unit.

References

Albera, D. (2008) '"Why are you mixing what cannot be mixed?" Shared devotions in the monotheisms', *History and Anthropology*, 19(1), pp. 37–59.

BBC News (2004) '"Virgin Mary" toast fetches $28,000', 23 November. Available at: http://news.bbc.co.uk/1/hi/4034787.stm (Accessed: 5 June 2018).

Beyond belief: apparitions of Mary (2016) BBC Radio 4, 28 March. Available at: https://www.bbc.co.uk/programmes/b074x71z (Accessed: 6 May 2018).

Blumberg, A. (2016) 'Why Catholics and Muslims alike come to pray at this shrine to Mary', *Huffington Post*, 25 May. Available at: https://www.huffingtonpost.co.uk/entry/lebanon-mary-shrine-catholic-muslims_us_5745edfde4b0dacf7ad3bc85 (Accessed: 15 March 2019).

Chamley, S. (2014) 'Is Hindu worship of Marian shrines a sign of growing religious tolerance?', *Lapidomedia: Centre for Religious Literacy in Journalism*, 22 October. Available at: http://religiousliteracyinstitute.org/hindus-worshiping-virgin-mary (Accessed: 3 April 2018).

Dowling, S.J. (1984) 'Lourdes cures and their medical assessment', *Journal of the Royal Society of Medicine*, 77, pp. 634–8.

Drury, C. (1994) 'Christianity', in Holm, J. and Bowker, J. (eds) *Women in religion*. London: Printer Publishers, pp. 30–58.

Fernandes, D. (2017) 'How the Virgin Mary brings together different faiths in Pakistan and India', *The Conversation*, 3 February. Available at: https://theconversation.com/how-the-virgin-mary-brings-together-different-faiths-in-pakistan-and-india-71030 (Accessed: 22 January 2019).

George-Tvrtković, R. (2018) *Christians, Muslims and Mary: a history*. New York: Paulist Press.

Ghosh, P. (2013) 'Mary Matha: why Hindus in India venerate mother Mary, the blessed Virgin of Roman Catholicism', *International Business Times*, 11 July. Available at: http://www.ibtimes.com/mary-matha-why-hindus-india-venerate-mother-mary-blessed-virgin-roman-catholicism-1458716 (Accessed: 3 April 2018).

Hall, L.B. (2004) *Mary, mother and warrior: the Virgin in Spain and the Americas*. Austin, Tex.: University of Texas Press.

Hillier, H.C. (2006) 'Mary', in Leaman, O. (ed.) *The Qur'an: an encyclopedia*. London and New York: Routledge, pp. 393–4.

Keriakos, S. (2012) 'Apparitions of the Virgin in Egypt: improving relations between Copts and Muslims?', in Albera, D. and Couroucli, M. (eds) *Sharing sacred spaces in the Mediterranean: Christians, Muslims and Jews at shrines and sanctuaries*. Bloomington, Ind.: Indiana University Press, pp. 174–201.

Luke 1: 26–55 and Luke 2: 1–21, Holy Bible. New Revised Standard Version, Anglicised edition.

Matthew 1: 18 – 2: 12, Holy Bible. New Revised Standard Version, Anglicised edition.

Maunder, C. (2007a) 'Apparitions of Mary', in Boss, S.J. (ed.) *Mary: the complete resource*. London and New York: Continuum, pp 424–57.

Maunder, C. (2007b) 'Mary in the New Testament and apocrypha', in Boss, S. J. (ed.) *Mary: the complete resource*. London and New York: Continuum, pp. 11–46.

McAuliffe, J.D. (1981) 'Chosen of all women: Mary and Fatima in Qur'anic exegesis', *Islamochristiana*, 7, pp. 19–28.

McGuckin, J. (2008) 'The early cult of Mary and inter-religious contexts in the fifth-century church', in Maunder, C. (ed.) *The origins of the cult of the Virgin Mary*. London/New York: Burns and Oats/Continuum, pp. 1–22.

Molloy, M. (2017) *The Christian experience: an introduction to Christianity*. New York: Bloomsbury.

Pope Bl. Pius IX (2017 [1854]) 'Ineffabilis deus: the immaculate conception', *Papal Encyclicals Online*. Available at: http://www.papalencyclicals.net/pius09/p9ineff.htm (Accessed: 22 January 2019).

Pelikan, J. (1996) *Mary through the centuries: her place in the history of culture*. New Haven and London: Yale University Press.

Revelation 12: 10, Holy Bible. New Revised Standard Version, Anglicised edition.

Ross, W.D. and Potter, D. (2015) 'Celsus, Roman author of the true doctrine, late 2nd cent. CE', in *Oxford Classical Dictionary*. doi: 10.1093/acrefore/9780199381135.013.1456.

Rubin, M. (2010) *Mother of God: a history of the Virgin Mary*. London: Penguin Books.

Ruether, R.R. (1983) *Sexism and God-talk: toward a feminist theology*. London: SCM.

Schüssler Fiorenza, E. (1993) *Discipleship of equals: a critical feminist ekklēsialogy of liberation*. London: SCM.

Shoemaker, S.J. (2016) *Mary in early Christian faith and devotion*. New Haven and London: Yale University Press.

Singapore Conference (1994 [1987]) 'Summary statement on feminist mariology' in King, U. (ed.) *Feminist theology from the third world: a reader*. London: SPCK/Orbis Press.

Warner, M. (2013) *Alone of all her sex: the Virgin myth & cult of the Virgin Mary*. 2nd edn. Oxford: Oxford University Press.

Winter, T. (2007) 'Mary in Islam', in Boss, S.J. (ed.) *Mary: the complete resource*. London and New York: Continuum, pp. 479–502.

Our lady of the underpass by Tanya Saracho (2010) Directed by Aandra Marquez [16th Street Theater and Teatro Vista, Berwyn, Chicago. April].

Readings

Reading 2.1 Matthew 1: 18 – 2: 12

Source: Matthew 1: 18 – 2: 12, Holy Bible. New Revised Standard Version, Anglicised edition.

1 The Birth of Jesus the Messiah

^{18} Now the birth of Jesus the Messiah took place in this way. When his mother Mary had been engaged to Joseph, but before they lived together, she was found to be with child from the Holy Spirit. ^{19} Her husband Joseph, being a righteous man and unwilling to expose her to public disgrace, planned to dismiss her quietly. ^{20} But just when he had resolved to do this, an angel of the Lord appeared to him in a dream and said, 'Joseph, son of David, do not be afraid to take Mary as your wife, for the child conceived in her is from the Holy Spirit. ^{21} She will bear a son, and you are to name him Jesus, for he will save his people from their sins.' ^{22} All this took place to fulfil what had been spoken by the Lord through the prophet:

^{23} 'Look, the virgin shall conceive and bear a son, and they shall name him Emmanuel', which means, 'God is with us.' ^{24} When Joseph awoke from sleep, he did as the angel of the Lord commanded him; he took her as his wife, ^{25} but had no marital relations with her until she had borne a son; and he named him Jesus.

2 The Visit of the Wise Men

^{1} In the time of King Herod, after Jesus was born in Bethlehem of Judea, wise men from the East came to Jerusalem, ^{2} asking, 'Where is the child who has been born king of the Jews? For we observed his star at its rising, and have come to pay him homage.' [3] When King Herod heard this, he was frightened, and all Jerusalem with him; [4] and calling together all the chief priests and scribes of the people, he inquired of them where the Messiah was to be born. [5] They told him, 'In Bethlehem of Judea; for so it has been written by the prophet:

[6] "And you, Bethlehem, in the land of Judah, are by no means least among the rulers of Judah; for from you shall come a ruler who is to shepherd my people Israel."

[7] Then Herod secretly called for the wise men and learned from them the exact time when the star had appeared. [8] Then he sent them to Bethlehem, saying, 'Go and search diligently for the child; and when you have found him, bring me word so that I may also go and pay him homage.' [9] When they had heard the king, they set out; and there, ahead of them, went the star that they had seen at its rising, until it stopped over the place where the child was. [10] When they saw that the star had stopped, they were overwhelmed with joy. [11] On entering the house, they saw the child with Mary his mother; and they knelt down and paid him homage. Then, opening their treasure-chests, they offered him gifts of gold, frankincense and myrrh. [12] And having been warned in a dream not to return to Herod, they left for their own country by another road.

Reading 2.2 Luke 1: 26–55 and Luke 2: 1–21

Source: Luke 1: 26–55 and Luke 2: 1–21, Holy Bible. New Revised Standard Version, Anglicised edition.

1 The Birth of Jesus Foretold

[26] … the angel Gabriel was sent by God to a town in Galilee called Nazareth, [27] to a virgin engaged to a man whose name was Joseph, of the house of David. The virgin's name was Mary. [28] And he came to her and said, 'Greetings, favoured one! The Lord is with you.' [29] But she was much perplexed by his words and pondered what sort of greeting this might be. [30] The angel said to her, 'Do not be afraid, Mary, for you have found favour with God. [31] And now you will conceive in your womb and bear a son, and you will name him Jesus. [32] He will be great, and will be called the Son of the Most High, and the Lord God will give to him the throne of his ancestor David. [33] He will reign over the house of Jacob for ever, and of his kingdom there will be no end.' [34] Mary said to the angel, 'How can this be, since I am a virgin?' [35] The angel said to her, 'The Holy Spirit will come upon you, and the power of the Most High will overshadow you; therefore the child to be born will be holy; he will be called Son of God. [36] And now, your relative Elizabeth in her old age has also conceived a son; and this is the sixth month for her who was said to be barren. [37] For nothing will be impossible with God.' [38] Then Mary said, 'Here am I, the servant of the Lord; let it be with me according to your word.' Then the angel departed from her.

Mary Visits Elizabeth

[39] In those days Mary set out and went with haste to a Judean town in the hill country, [40] where she entered the house of Zechariah and greeted Elizabeth. [41] When Elizabeth heard Mary's greeting, the child leapt in her womb. And Elizabeth was filled with the Holy Spirit [42] and exclaimed with a loud

cry, 'Blessed are you among women, and blessed is the fruit of your womb. [43] And why has this happened to me, that the mother of my Lord comes to me? [44] For as soon as I heard the sound of your greeting, the child in my womb leapt for joy. [45] And blessed is she who believed that there would be a fulfilment of what was spoken to her by the Lord.'

Mary's Song of Praise

[46] And Mary said,
'My soul magnifies the Lord,
[47] and my spirit rejoices in God
        my Saviour,
[48] for he has looked with favour on the
        lowliness of his servant.
    Surely, from now on all generations
        will call me blessed;
[49] for the Mighty One has done great things
        for me,
    and holy is his name.
[50] His mercy is for those who fear him
    from generation to generation.
[51] He has shown strength with his arm;
    he has scattered the proud in the
        thoughts of their hearts.
[52] He has brought down the powerful from
        their thrones,
    and lifted up the lowly;
[53] he has filled the hungry with
        good things,
    and sent the rich away empty.
[54] He has helped his servant Israel,
    in remembrance of his mercy,
[55] according to the promise he made to our
        ancestors,
    to Abraham and to his descendants for
        ever.

[...]

2 The Birth of Jesus

In those days a decree went out from Emperor Augustus that all the world should be registered. [2] This was the first registration and was taken while Quirinius was governor of Syria. [3] All went to their own towns to be registered. [4] Joseph also went from the town of Nazareth in Galilee to Judea, to the city of David called Bethlehem, because he was descended from the house and family of David. [5] He went to be registered with Mary, to whom he was engaged and who was expecting a child. [6] While they were there, the time came for her to deliver her child. [7] And she gave birth to her firstborn son and wrapped him in bands of cloth, and laid him in a manger, because there was no place for them in the inn.

The Shepherds and the Angels

[8] In that region there were shepherds living in the fields, keeping watch over their flock by night. [9] Then an angel of the Lord stood before them, and the glory of the Lord shone around them, and they were terrified. [10] But the angel said to them. 'Do not be afraid; for see – I am bringing you good news of great joy for all the people: [11] to you is born this day in the city of David a Saviour, who is the Messiah, the Lord. [12] This will be a sign for you: you will find a child wrapped in bands of cloth and lying in a manger.' [13] And suddenly there was with the angel a multitude of the heavenly host, praising God and saying,

[14] 'Glory to God in the highest heaven, and on earth peace among those whom he favours!'

[15] When the angels had left them and gone into heaven, the shepherds said to one another, 'Let us go now to Bethlehem and see this thing that has taken place, which the Lord has made known to us.' [16] So they went with haste and found Mary and Joseph, and the child lying in the manger. [17] When

they saw this, they made known what had been told them about this child; [18] and all who heard it were amazed at what the shepherds told them. [19] But Mary treasured all these words and pondered them in her heart. [20] The shepherds returned, glorifying and praising God for all they had heard and seen, as it had been told them.

Jesus Is Named

[21] After eight days had passed, it was time to circumcise the child, and he was called Jesus, the name given by the angel before he was conceived in the womb.

Reading 2.3 Mary in the Qur'an

Source: Hillier, H.C. (2006) 'Mary', in Leaman, O. (ed.) *The Qur'an: an encyclopaedia*. London and New York: Routledge, pp. 393–4.

Mary (Maryam, meaning 'pious') is the most prominent woman in the Qur'an. Highly regarded because of her virtue and devotion to God (66.12), she is considered the best woman of her day (3.42) and a 'sign to the nations' (21.91). The only woman mentioned by her proper name, Mary is found over thirty times within the scripture. Traditional sayings of the Prophet Muhammad state that she is one of the four most praise-worthy women of history and is the only woman to be protected from the touch of Satan at birth, a protection shared by her son Jesus ('Isa).

As in the New Testament, the Qur'anic story of Mary is intimately linked with that of her son. This is made evident, aside from the number of times the name 'Jesus, son of Mary' appears, from the placement of Mary's life story within the larger nativity narrative of Jesus. The story of Mary begins with the prayer of her mother, the 'wife of Imran', who, being childless, desired to become pregnant. Mary's mother, not named in the Qur'an but known as Hanna by Muslim historians and commentators, dedicated her future child to God's service (3.35). In discovering that she had given birth to a girl, perhaps previously assuming that it would be a boy, Hanna invoked divine protection on Mary and her offspring (3.36). As such, the Lord accepted Mary, raised her in 'purity and beauty', and assigned her to the guardianship of Zachariah, the father of John the Baptist. Residing in a chamber of the Jerusalem Temple, Zachariah is repeatedly surprised to find her divinely provided for, whereby Mary reminds him that God provides for whomever he wills without limit (3.37).

Some time later, Mary withdraws to a 'place in the east' (19.16), possibly referring to an eastern chamber within the Temple, a cave or an eastern city such as Bethlehem. There she receives an announcement from an angelic messenger: 'O Mary! God gives you glad tidings through a word from him; his name will be Christ Jesus, the son of Mary' (3.45). Mary, astonished at the message, asks how this can be so, since she is chaste. The reply, rejecting pagan concepts of divine–human sexual relations, is that God does what he wills and he merely needs to say the word and it will occur. (3.47; 19.20–21)

Muslim commentators and historians have elaborated these narratives. For instance, there are different accounts of Mary's encounter with Gabriel. Commonly, historians such as al-Tabari recount that, when Mary and Joseph lived in the Temple, she, for one reason or another, made a temporary sojourn out of the Temple. While away, perhaps travelling eastward, Mary encounters Gabriel, who, appearing as a man, announces that he is sent by God to give her a son. Fearful of the man, Mary cries out to God for protection, upon which Gabriel assures her that it was God giving her the child, not he, then blowing the divine breath into her chest through her sleeve she becomes pregnant. Upon her return, her husband Joseph, who is not mentioned in the Qur'an, is the first to notice and, eventually, acknowledge the miraculous event.

On the occasion of her labour, the Qur'an portrays Mary, wishing she were dead, driven to a palm tree in anguish. At that point, a voice from beneath her, perhaps Jesus, comforts her by saying that God has provided a small brook for drinking and ripe dates from the tree to eat, but she must refrain from talking to any person (19.24–26). Subsequently, the Qur'an moves forward to a later time, when Mary returns to her people with her infant son. There they ask why she has brought this 'strange thing' to them, since her mother and father were neither immoral nor unchaste people. In response, Mary points to the infant in her arms, expecting some response from the child. Her critics snort: 'How should we speak to one who is a child in the cradle?' (19.29). At which point, the infant Jesus speaks and asserts his prophetic mission in defence of his mother's chastity.

Reading 2.4 Mary as a woman of the poor

Source: King, U. (1994) 'Feminist theology from the third world', *Singapore conference*. Singapore, 20–29 November. London: SPCK/Orbis Press, pp. 273–4.

Mary as one of the bases of feminist theology

Each of us, within our own culture, has found different strengths in the process of reclaiming and redefining Mary. We can look at Mary the mother and see her womb as the place of the action of the Holy Spirit – a place of struggle and suffering which brings new life. The struggle of mothers in the Asia/Pacific context, who struggle with and for their children, to give birth to a new and just reality. Mary is the mother of suffering, of those who suffer.

If we recognize that Mary is a woman of the poor, we must also challenge the lie that depicts her as jewelled and elaborately dressed. Because the good news of the Magnificat is bad news for the rich, we reject Mary's hijacking by a wealthy Church – for the consolation of the rich. This simply reinforces the oppression of the poor. If we understand the virgin birth as the beginning of a new order, in which patriarchy can no longer be the basis of human life, we must hear the angel's greeting, "Hail, full of grace," as addressed to all of us. We too must participate in changing oppressive relationships and cultural symbols – overcoming patterns of domination and subordination between north and south, rich and poor, male and female, black and white.

The Magnificat is the rallying point for ecumenism, as Christians join together working to liberate the poor and all victims of injustice. It is the liberation song of women, who are, with their children, the poorest of the poor. However, in the context of the indigenous struggles of Aotearoa and Australia, it is necessary for women of the dominant group to remember that while we are oppressed by patriarchy, we also benefit from institutionalized racism, so our sisterhood is not one of equality. So while we too sing the Magnificat in our countries, we must learn the response of relinquishing power as indigenous women take control of their own lives.

We acknowledge that in Asia and the Pacific the need for economic
and political liberation is often used to trivialize women's struggle.
However, the struggle of indigenous women is a fight for a people's
survival. If feminist theology is concerned only with sexism, and not
with the liberation of the whole human race, it too is oppressive. We
see feminist Mariology as a liberation theology that gives hope of
humanization to all the world.

Chapter 3
Elizabeth I

Gemma Allen and Neil Younger

Contents

1 Introduction

In this chapter, we will examine the reputation of Elizabeth I, queen of England and Ireland, from a variety of perspectives so that we can consider what History is and what historians do.

The first part of this chapter looks at Elizabeth's reputation during her own lifetime, and how different people sought to mould it. In the process, you will be introduced to the use of various types of written and visual evidence created at the time.

In the second part of the chapter, we will look at historians' views of Elizabeth's reputation, and how and why they have differed over time. For example, do historians view Elizabeth as a successful monarch? How have they judged her actions in important matters, such as the attempted attack of the Spanish Armada in 1588 and her refusal to marry?

2 Elizabeth as queen

Figure 1 Unknown artist, *Family of Henry VIII, c.*1545, oil on canvas, 141 × 355 cm. Photo: © Getty Images/SuperStock/Peter Barritt.
Left to right (main figures): Princess Mary, Prince Edward, Henry VIII, Jane Seymour and Princess Elizabeth.

Born in 1533, Elizabeth (Figure 1) was the second child of King Henry VIII. Her mother Anne Boleyn was executed after facing charges of adultery, incest and treason when Elizabeth was only two years old. When Henry VIII died in 1547, he was succeeded on the throne firstly by his son, Edward VI (reigned 1547–53), and then by his elder daughter, Mary I (reigned 1553–58). As heir to the throne, Elizabeth led a troubled existence during the reign of her half-sister Mary, being briefly imprisoned in the Tower of London in 1554 when she was 20. It was only after Mary's death that Elizabeth became queen of England in November 1558. (You can find a chart showing the relationship of these monarchs in Figure 11, later in the chapter.)

Elizabeth faced many challenges as monarch. In the years preceding her reign, England had experienced religious turmoil, with her father Henry VIII ending the authority of the Roman Catholic pope over the English church in the early 1530s and beginning to introduce Protestant worship. Under Edward VI's rule, a much more thorough reform of worship was implemented, creating a genuinely Protestant church in England, but under Mary I, England returned to Catholicism. Elizabeth always appeared to have been a firm Protestant, and when she became queen she restored Protestantism. Despite this, there were ongoing religious tensions in England. As queen, Elizabeth faced Catholic plots to assassinate her, and in 1570 the Pope issued a papal bull declaring that her subjects need not obey her.

You were introduced to some of the differences between Roman Catholic and Protestant forms of Christianity in the previous chapter on Mary, the mother of Jesus.

As a female ruler, another major challenge for Elizabeth was her gender. Sixteenth-century England was a patriarchal society, where it was expected that fathers and husbands should rule within their own households and a male ruler would rule the country. Many people who lived during that time believed that women were incapable of ruling effectively. In 1558, the year Elizabeth came to the throne, the Scottish Protestant clergyman John Knox published *The First Blast of the Trumpet Against the Monstruous Regiment of Women*. In it, he argued that female rule was against biblical principles and therefore a 'monstrous' thing: 'God, by his sentence, has dejected [deprived] all woman from empire and dominion above man' (Knox, 1588, p. 13). Books and sermons of the time also insisted that women should be silent and obedient to their husbands and fathers. However, it was not only Elizabeth's suitableness as a woman to rule that was challenged. As you will learn later in this chapter, her gender also created other problems for her as ruler: her potential marriage, and the related issue of who would succeed her as monarch, caused repeated political upheaval throughout her reign.

2.1 Creating the royal image

As a result of these challenges to her rule, Elizabeth and her advisers were confronted with an image problem. How should she present herself to her people as a monarch, and more pressingly, as a female monarch? How should she seek to construct her reputation? The need to create a royal image was not something that originated with Elizabeth I: male monarchs before her had also sought to ensure a positive royal image. The historian Kevin Sharpe has argued that the need to craft the royal reputation became particularly important under Elizabeth's father, Henry VIII. As he unleashed religious change upon

Figure 2 Hans Holbein the Younger, *Henry VIII with Henry VII*, *c*.1536–37, ink and watercolour, 258 × 137 cm. National Portrait Gallery, London, NPG 4027. © National Portrait Gallery, London.

the country, Henry VIII sought to develop a royal image that would ensure his subjects' obedience. He used portraits, pageants and authorised texts to gain his people's adoration (Sharpe, 2009). For example, consider Figure 2, a famous portrait of Henry by Hans Holbein.

The most notable aspects of the image are Henry's masculine strength and particularly his codpiece, highlighting his virility. With this image, Henry sought to represent his authority and power over his people, albeit to the limited audience that would have seen the picture. Elizabeth, however, could not imitate this presentation strategy: she could not present herself as physically strong, especially as this was a time when female sexuality was feared as uncontrollable and potentially dangerous.

Elizabeth's half-sister, Mary, had struggled with presenting herself as a female monarch. For Mary's coronation, there was indecision over how the queen should be dressed: kings had traditionally dressed for their coronations in purple velvet trimmed with ermine, but Mary I was instead presented in the traditional manner for a queen consort (the wife of the male monarch), all in white with her hair loose (Richards, 1997, pp. 901–2); her status as a ruler was downplayed, even for her own coronation.

Creating a royal image for Elizabeth as an unmarried female monarch was therefore still difficult. Elizabeth herself admitted the importance she placed on ensuring her own reputation in 1586 when she remarked, 'we princes, I tell you, are set on stages in the sight and view of all the world duly observed. The eyes of many behold our actions; a spot is soon spied in our garments; a blemish quickly noted in our doings' (Marcus et al., 2000, p. 194).

2.2 The primary sources

If we want to find out about how Elizabeth's reputation was created or constructed, we should turn to the contemporary evidence; this is at the heart of what historians do – to find out about the past, they look for evidence, the traces of the past that have been left behind. To do this, they use **primary sources**, by which we mean evidence produced in the period being studied. So, to think about the formation of Elizabeth's contemporary reputation, there are all sorts of primary sources from her own time that we could use, including portraits, speeches, letters and literature.

You were introduced to a range of primary sources in your study of Cleopatra and Mary, the mother of Jesus.

One of the most important elements of studying History is learning how to read or interpret these primary sources. This involves understanding them in their own terms, thinking about why they were produced, for whom, and the context in which they were created. Therefore, a key skill you will develop as a History student is the ability to read, interpret and contextualise historical evidence.

Here are some of the questions that a historian might keep in mind when confronted with a new primary source:

1   What kind of document is it?

2   What is its historical context?

3   How does it help us to study a particular period of history?

Of course, these questions are just a starting point and, when you are examining a single document, you won't necessarily be able to answer all of them. In the following section, we will look at two types of primary sources to help us understand Elizabeth's contemporary reputation: her speeches and her portraits.

2.3 The speeches

Let's start by looking at Elizabeth's speeches. First, we might ask what her speeches can tell us about the creation of her reputation. One answer is that she was a skilled orator (public speaker), who controlled the content of her own speeches and was highly educated for a woman by the standards of her time, meaning she could deliver rousing speeches 'off the cuff'. In 1597, without a moment's preparation, she gave a devastating speech in Latin to a Polish ambassador, who had foolishly dared to chastise her for supposedly disrupting Polish shipping trade with Spain (Green, 2000). Therefore, we can use Elizabeth's speeches to think about how she wanted to create her own reputation: in other words, her self-representation.

However, speeches are also problematic as primary sources for historians, as they were often only copied down from memory by those who had heard them. In the case of Elizabeth's speeches to her Parliaments, these transcripts were often checked by the queen herself and by her ministers prior to publication, but many other records of her speeches had no such 'quality-control' procedures (Marcus et al., 2000, p. xxi).

You may recognise at least a few lines from one of Elizabeth's most famous speeches. It was given to the troops assembled at Tilbury in Essex to defend the country against the attack by the Spanish Armada, the fleet of Spanish ships sent to attack England in 1588 (you will look at this event in more detail later in the chapter). The Tilbury speech was a piece of 'spin' (a public relations exercise), rather than a necessary act to inspire the troops to fight: by the time Elizabeth gave her speech, the Spanish fleet was already known to be damaged and at least temporarily in retreat (Trim, 2016, p. 85). Yet the speech still offers an opportunity to consider how Elizabeth presented herself both to her people and to foreign observers.

Activity

(Allow around 45 minutes to complete this activity.)

Reading 3.1 provides the text of Elizabeth's speech at Tilbury. Two versions have been provided: the original text and a version that has been rendered into modern English.

Read the contemporary version of the speech first, as historians should always try to work with original primary sources. You might want to use the modern English version to help your understanding.

As you read the speech, think about these questions:

1   What kind of document is it? There are lots of things you could think about when considering this issue, but here you should focus on whether the words of this document were written down by Elizabeth herself or not. This will help us think about whether this document is an official text. The italics at the beginning of the reading refer to the way the speech was recorded, so pay close attention to them.

2   How does this document help us study this period of history? Again, there are lots of things you could think about here, but in this instance you should focus on how the speech presents Elizabeth as a monarch. Does she:

(a) present herself as feminine or masculine, as a queen or as a king?

(b) refer to God in her speech?

Discussion

1   The opening lines of the document suggest that the speech was noted down by somebody 'that heard it'. So, the recorded words of the speech were not necessarily exactly those delivered by Elizabeth. The opening lines do state that the speech was then supposedly sent to Elizabeth herself, but we have no confirmation of whether that actually happened, or whether she approved the text as accurate. Therefore, this is not an official document.

2

   (a) In this speech, Elizabeth acknowledges that she has the body of a woman, but suggests that her courage and pragmatism are that of a male king. You might also have noticed that she plays down women in general in the speech as 'weak and feeble' (Marcus et al., 2000, p. 326).

   (b) Elizabeth refers to God quite a lot in the speech, highlighting God's favour to her as a monarch.

Why is it important for us to recognise that the text reproduced in Reading 3.1 is not an official document? This version of the speech was from a letter written by Dr Leonel Sharpe, who served Robert Dudley, the earl of Leicester, at Tilbury and supposedly repeated the speech the day after Elizabeth had given it. Therefore, Sharpe was a witness of Elizabeth's speech. He suggests that he was instructed to send a copy of his transcript to Elizabeth herself ('commanded [...] to send it gathered to the queen herself' (Marcus et al., 2000, p. 325)). However, the only written copy of the speech that we know about was included in a letter he wrote around 1623, which was 35 years later. The delay between the speech and the creation of this document is concerning for a historian: we can all forget a lot in 35 years! The good news is that there are other records of this speech. A version is displayed beneath a painting of Elizabeth at Tilbury in St Faith's Church in Gaywood, Norfolk; this may have been created just after the defeat of the Armada in 1588, but there is evidence to suggest that in actuality it may not have been commissioned until 1605, as the painting was hung next to one of the Gunpowder Plot of that year. Additionally, another version of the speech was printed in a sermon in 1612 (Frye, 1992, pp. 101–2). All the versions of the speech share a lot of Elizabeth's comments about her gender, so we can be reasonably confident that Elizabeth made some of those references, although the version used in Reading 3.1 is the most detailed on that theme.

This speech also reveals much about how Elizabeth thought of herself as a kind of male monarch. When she refers to 'the heart and stomach of a king' (Marcus et al., 2000, p. 326), it is because at the time the heart was thought to be the source of courage, and the stomach the source of pragmatism and the ability to commit violence when necessary. Although Elizabeth, as a woman, could not lead her troops into battle (she notes that her 'lieutenant general shall be in my stead'), she portrays herself as a warrior prince, prepared to die with her troops. Indeed, we can see that she refers to herself as a 'prince' rather than a 'princess', implying that she saw herself as above other 'weak and feeble' women (Marcus et al., 2000, p. 326). Elizabeth, like many powerful women throughout history, did not seek to improve the lot of women as a whole, only to safeguard her own (in many ways vulnerable) position.

The speech also gives us evidence that Elizabeth thought herself to be favoured by God. Presenting herself as an instrument of God was a favourite tactic of hers throughout her reign. In a period in which it was believed that God continually intervened in earthly events, this was a good defence against anyone who questioned her rule as a female monarch.

Analysing this speech tells us a lot about how Elizabeth sought to present herself, but there are also problems about the nature of the source that we, as historians, need to consider. How might we try and further establish the legitimacy of the self-representation in this document? One way would be to look at other speeches of Elizabeth I, particularly those that were recorded more accurately, such as her parliamentary speeches, and see if there are many similarities or differences between them.

Figure 3 Unknown artist, 'Queen Elizabeth in Parliament', frontispiece to Simonds D'Ewes, *Journals of All the Parliaments during the Reign of Queen Elizabeth*, 1682. British Museum, London, Y,8.20. Photo: © Trustees of the British Museum.
This image can be seen in more detail in the online gallery on the module website.

Activity

(Allow around 30 minutes to complete this activity.)

Readings 3.2 and 3.3 are extracts from two speeches that Elizabeth gave to her (all male) Parliament (see Figure 3). The first is from 1566 and the second is from 1593, meaning one speech was given relatively early in Elizabeth's reign and one much later, thus helping us to consider her self-representation across her reign.

As before, the Readings provide the contemporary primary source of the speech as well as a modernised version. As you read the two speeches, think again about how these sources can help us study this period of history.

As with the previous activity, focus on how the speeches present Elizabeth as a monarch. Does she:

(a) present herself as a female or a male ruler?

(b) refer to God in her speech?

Remember that the references to Elizabeth's father are to Henry VIII; her claim to the throne comes from her descent from her father.

Discussion

(a) As in the Tilbury speech, Elizabeth emphasises in both her parliamentary speeches that she is an exceptional woman, imbued with special qualities. In the 1593 speech, she goes further, again characterising her rule as that of a prince (rather than a princess), and as one of the greatest ever monarchs of England. You might also have noticed that she emphasises her royal status comes from a king: her father, Henry VIII.

(b) Elizabeth does not mention God in the 1593 speech. However, in the 1566 speech, she highlights that she is an 'anointed queen' (Marcus et al., 2000, p. 97) (meaning a queen blessed by God) and thanks God for the qualities of her character.

The similarities between these speeches and the Tilbury speech suggest Elizabeth repeatedly tried to present herself as an exceptional woman, sent by God, taking on the persona of the male ruler. The male monarch she most closely connects herself to is her father, Henry VIII. These references are important, as Elizabeth regularly sought to define her rule in terms of legitimate descent from her father. The historian Christopher Haigh has suggested that in acknowledging her womanhood whilst emphasising her masculine traits, Elizabeth wanted to create a reputation for herself as a 'political hermaphrodite' (Haigh, 1988, p. 30): someone who was politically both male and female.

2.4 The portraits

In the previous section, we looked at written primary sources; however, historians also use visual primary sources as evidence. In doing so, historians often borrow techniques from a related subject area, Art History. Historians draw on a range of methods and approaches to help us understand our sources.

You will discover more about the approaches of Art History later in this book.

We can ask the same questions of visual sources as we do of written primary sources:

- What kind of image is it?

- What is its historical context?

- How does the image help us to study a particular period of history?

The culture of Elizabethan England was very visual, and educated people of the time had the skills to 'decode' quite complex stories and symbolism in images. Therefore, portraits of Elizabeth provide rich evidence of how her reputation was formed in her lifetime. We have to be careful though, as these portraits were only owned or seen by a small number of people from the highest levels of society. However, they help us see how these people understood Elizabeth's reputation, especially as they were often very influential figures.

Whilst you might be able to call to mind some images of Elizabeth during her later years, you might not be familiar with pictures of her during the early part of her reign. The first example we will consider in detail is now known as the 'Hampden Portrait' and dates from around 1563, a few years into Elizabeth's reign, when she was aged around 30. This is the earliest full-length image of the queen, an imposing image about two metres high. This portrait is significant, as it was one of the first attempts to create and control Elizabeth's visual image, which is important to remember if we want to think about the context in which the portrait was produced. In the same year it was painted, 1563, a royal proclamation had been drafted complaining that painters were making poor quality images of the queen and that 'none hath sufficiently expressed the natural representation of her majesty's

Figure 4 Unknown artist, the 'Clopton Portrait', *c*.1558, oil on panel. Private collection. Photo: © Philip Mould Ltd, London/Bridgeman Images.

person, favor, or grace' (Hughes and Larkin, 1969, p. 240). The type of portraits that were being criticised showed Elizabeth dressed quite modestly in black, which, although a symbol of piety, did little to advance the prestige of the new queen (for example, the 'Clopton Portrait', as shown in Figure 4).

The 'Hampden Portrait' (Figure 5) was therefore the first of a new type of portrait of Elizabeth I, painted during negotiations for a possible marriage match between Elizabeth and the Roman Catholic Archduke Charles of Austria. The queen had nearly died of smallpox that year, causing anxiety over who would succeed her as monarch when she died, and fuelling the desire for her to marry and produce an heir.

The 'Hampden Portrait' presents Elizabeth as a marriageable young queen, in the hope of attracting a good royal match. The symbols and signs in the portrait back up this interpretation, with a lot of the symbols aiming to convey her royal status. The Tudor rose on her shoulder highlights her descent from the Tudor royal line, and she is standing in front of a throne and a golden cloth of state bearing the royal coat of arms. Other symbols stress her readiness to marry. She is holding a gillyflower, or pink carnation, in her right hand, which symbolises betrothal or impending marriage. There are lush fruits to the right of the painting, including peas about to burst forth from their pods, suggesting Elizabeth's fertility. Her dress is a striking red, which was understood as the colour of sexuality and was sometimes the colour of sixteenth-century wedding dresses (Walker, 1998, p. 274). If you look closely, you can see there are pearls on the girdle chain around her waist and down the front of the dress; pearls were a symbol of virginity at the time. Placed alongside the signs of her sexuality, they are intended to suggest that Elizabeth, though a virgin, is ripe for marriage and childbearing.

Although Elizabeth is clearly shown as royal and extremely wealthy, there is no particular attempt to bolster or create her royal image with this portrait; instead, it highlights her potential as a suitable marriage match. We don't know precisely who commissioned the 'Hampden Portrait' (though it must have been a courtier close to the marriage negotiations), but considering it was a new type of image of the queen, it is likely she approved of how it portrayed her.

Figure 5 Steven van der Meulen/Steven van Herwijck (attributed), the 'Hampden Portrait', *c*.1563, oil on panel transferred onto canvas, 196 × 140 cm. Private collection. Photo: © Philip Mould Ltd, London/ Bridgeman Images.

Figure 6 George Gower (attributed), the 'Armada Portrait', *c*.1588, oil on panel, 134 × 106 cm. Woburn Abbey, Bedfordshire. Photo: © Bridgeman Images.

Activity

(Allow around 15 minutes to complete this activity.)

Let's look at another image of Elizabeth I. In doing so, we're going to analyse this visual source to see what it can tell us about the period we're studying, as we did with the written sources.

This portrait, known as the 'Armada Portrait' (Figure 6), dates from 1588 and is a commemorative image painted after the defeat of the Spanish Armada: the queen was about 55 years old at the time. Several versions of this portrait exist, all dating from the same year.

As you look at the image, try to answer the following questions:

1   Given that this image was produced following the defeat of the Spanish attack, what might be the significance of the two scenes between the columns behind Elizabeth? Remember, you can look more closely at this painting in the online gallery on the module website.

2 How is Elizabeth presented as a monarch in this image? You may choose to focus on the following:

   (a) How Elizabeth is presented compared to the 'Hampden Portrait' in Figure 5 (i.e. is she shown as lifelike or not? Are symbols of virginity shown prominently)?

   (b) Can you identify any symbols of Elizabeth's royal status in the 'Armada Portrait'?

Discussion

1 You will probably have identified that the scene on the left shows ships at sea, and you may have noticed that the ships towards the back of the scene are on fire. This is an image of the English fireships that were sent to scatter the Spanish Armada: a defensive manoeuvre against the Spanish attack. The scene on the right of Elizabeth is of ships in a storm, with ships hitting the rocks. This is the shipwreck of the same Spanish ships in Scotland or Ireland. The two scenes tell a story of Elizabeth's victory over the Spanish: the first scene being the dispersal of the Spanish fleet with fireships, and the second being the impact of the weather on the attacking ships.

2

   (a) You might have noticed that in the 'Armada Portrait' the queen looks less lifelike than in earlier pictures: her dress is huge and conceals most of her body; and her face and hands are so pale they are almost white. She appears ageless and almost superhuman, and the many pearls in the portrait clearly symbolise her virginity. In the 'Hampden Portrait' there are a few discreet pearls signifying her ripeness for marriage, but here there are pearls all over her dress, headdress and crown.

   (b) You might have noticed the crown on the left, which symbolises Elizabeth's royal status. You might have also noticed that in the 'Armada Portrait' she stands in front of a richly decorated chair; this is a chair of state, a sort of throne, similar to the one in the 'Hampden Portrait'.

In the 'Armada Portrait', Elizabeth is transformed into a queen in full majesty. Her womanly body is concealed and she becomes a symbol of other-worldly royalty. Her hand rests on a globe and that's another important message: her hand rests on America, acknowledging English hopes of expansion and trade with the New World. The crown, shown above the globe, is an 'imperial' crown (a closed crown with arches), meaning that Elizabeth is portrayed as an empress, acknowledging no superior (Strong, 1987, p. 132). You have already noted the many pearls in this portrait, representing her virginity, but they are not the only symbol of virginity in the picture: you may have seen the mermaid carved into the arm of the chair of state, for example. Mermaids, the temptresses of sailors, were symbols of 'uncontrolled female sexuality' (Belsey and Belsey, 1990, p. 14). In this image, Elizabeth turns her back on dangerous female sexuality and is presented as the Virgin Queen of England.

In understanding this image and Elizabeth's representation as a virgin queen, we need to again think about its historical context. It was painted around 1588, when she was about 55 years old. Later in her life, portraits of Elizabeth started to make explicit and unmistakable reference to her virginity. In Figure 7, you can see one of a series of portraits painted between 1579 and 1583 that featured Elizabeth with a sieve: the 'Sieve Portrait' by Quentin Metsys the Younger. In Elizabethan times, the sieve was a symbol of virginity, alluding to Tuccia, a Roman priestess who proved her virginity by filling a sieve with water from the River Tiber; Tuccia's sieve did not shed a drop of water, proving her virginity. There are other symbols of virginity in the 'Sieve Portrait' too. The pillar to the left is covered with pictures showing the classical story of Dido and Aeneas. The tale is a symbol of chastity because Aeneas did not give in to Dido's advances before founding the Roman Empire. You may have also noticed that, once again, there are lots of pearls in this image: the portrait emphasises Elizabeth's virginity at every turn.

Figure 7 Quentin Metsys the Younger, *Portrait of Elizabeth of England* (the 'Sieve Portrait'), *c.*1583, oil on canvas, 124 × 92 cm. Pinacoteca Nazionale, Siena. Photo: Scala, Florence – courtesy of the Ministero Beni e Att. Culturali e del Turismo.

So, why did portraits start to represent Elizabeth as a virgin in the late 1570s and 1580s, when earlier portraits, such as the 'Hampden Portrait' (Figure 5), did not focus on this? We can find a clue in the 'Sieve Portrait'. This painting was almost certainly commissioned by Christopher Hatton, a leading courtier of Elizabeth's, in 1583. The third figure to the right behind Elizabeth may be Hatton himself – his badge of a golden hind is just visible on the figure's cloak. In the late 1570s and early 1580s, another potential husband for Elizabeth was proposed: the French prince Francis, duke of Anjou. Many courtiers, including Hatton, opposed the match, wanting Elizabeth to continue to reject marriage, thus remaining a virgin queen. Hatton's commissioning of the portrait is a commemoration of the triumph of his opposition to the match.

Consequently, the historian Patrick Collinson has commented that it was only in the late 1570s and early 1580s that 'the persona of the Virgin Queen was invented, or at least perfected' (Collinson, 2007, p. 40). This started with courtiers opposed to Elizabeth's proposed marriage to Anjou, but gathered pace thereafter as it was increasingly accepted that the queen would die unmarried and childless. From the 1580s, Elizabeth came to be depicted as the Virgin Queen, a goddess, the untouchable and other-worldly queen of the 'Armada Portrait'.

As you started work on this unit, you might have held the view that Elizabeth was the Virgin Queen. But did Elizabeth herself encourage this reputation? You might want to look back at the speeches you studied earlier to see if you can find any evidence of this. It turns out that Elizabeth made few references to her virginity in her speeches. When Parliament demanded she marry in 1559, at the very start of her reign, she did tell them that 'in the end this shall be for me sufficient: that a marble stone shall declare that a queen, having reigned such a time, lived and died a virgin' (Marcus et al., 2000, p. 58). Yet Elizabeth said this in the context of resisting pressure to marry, so a reference to virginity might be expected. Beyond that, Elizabeth rarely portrayed herself as a virgin queen. The idea only seems to have become common at the time of the Anjou marriage proposal, in the years around 1580, when it was expressed in portraits (as you have seen) as well as in other forms, such as poetry. Elizabeth did not commission these portraits and poems, but they were designed to please and win favour with the queen, so she must have approved of being represented in this way. Moreover, she did commission miniatures (small images of herself), which showed her as the classical virgin goddesses Diana and Cynthia (Figure 8).

Figure 8 Nicholas Hilliard, *Miniature of Elizabeth I*, 1586–87, watercolour on vellum stuck onto plain card, 5 × 4 cm. Victoria and Albert Museum, London, museum no. P23-1975. © Victoria and Albert Museum, London.
The crescent shaped piece of jewellery in Elizabeth's hair refers to Cynthia or Diana, the virgin moon goddesses.

As we come to the end of this section of the chapter, what can we say about Elizabeth's reputation in her own lifetime? You have seen the very different representations of Elizabeth that can be drawn from different primary sources: her speeches highlight different ideas about her queenship than her portraits do. The historian Susan Doran has argued that 'multiple images' of Elizabeth circulated during her lifetime, more so than earlier English rulers: at different times she was the female ruler sent by God, the warrior prince, and, later on, the Virgin Queen (Doran, 2011, p. 54). These multiple reputations were undoubtedly the result of Elizabeth's gender and her unmarried status, and texts and images reflected the times in which they were created. Doran also highlights the importance of a culture that embraced religious and classical symbolism (Doran, 2011, p. 55). The success of the creation of Elizabeth's multiple personas in the late sixteenth century can be seen in the fact that over 400 years later, we can still think of Elizabeth as both the warrior prince of Tilbury and the Virgin Queen. Her personal motto may have been '*Semper eadem*' ('Always the same'), but the power of her reputation stemmed from its variability – she was one woman with multiple reputations.

3 Elizabeth I's historical reputation

For the remainder of this chapter, we will move on from looking at the reputation Elizabeth had during her own life and how this was constructed, to how she has been regarded by later historians – what we might call her historical reputation.

Elizabeth I is often regarded as having been a very successful monarch. Yet, in some ways, it is hard to pinpoint why that should be. She had a long reign, it is true, and was fortunate enough to reign in the time of William Shakespeare, but she achieved few of the successes that are usually regarded as the marks of a 'great' ruler: she did not make major conquests of territory; she made no major legal reforms; and living standards for the people were, in fact, declining during her reign. The most decisive steps in the religious Reformation (the Protestant split from the Roman Catholic Church) were instigated by her father Henry VIII, not Elizabeth herself. She did not found a new dynasty; she did not even continue her own dynasty, but left the succession to the throne unsettled for the whole of her reign. Yet Elizabeth retains a reputation of having presided over a 'golden age'. It's possible that you thought of her this way when you began to study the unit.

Activity

(Allow around 30 minutes to complete this activity.)

Turn to Reading 3.4, which is an extract from a biography about Elizabeth I written by a leading scholar, Patrick Collinson, at the beginning of the twenty-first century, in which he describes the views of both historians and non-historians concerning Elizabeth's reputation. Make a note of the key points he makes about her reputation: does he view this as something that has changed or remained stable?

Discussion

Collinson notes that the public's fascination with Elizabeth remains very strong, yet also points out that it is potentially difficult to see why this is. He goes on to point out that despite this popular interest, professional historians tend to be more critical of her reputation, particularly with regard to her cautious tendency to avoid making decisions. His wording stresses that this reputation has shifted over the years, and might even go in 'phases' (Collinson, 2004).

As Collinson makes clear in this passage, the judgements historians pass on historical figures do not remain constant; they vary over time and they vary between historians. In this section of the chapter we will look at how and why this happens.

3.1 Historians and the interpretation of the past

So far we have seen that historians need to be very careful and critical about how they use primary sources relating to historical figures. The same is true with the other main type of sources used by historians, **secondary sources**. These are sources written after the event, usually by historians themselves, and published as books or scholarly articles, or more recently as television or radio programmes, blogs, and so on. All of these secondary sources present a picture or an account of some element of the past, some part of history. Yet just like primary sources, secondary sources must be regarded critically, which is to say that we should not believe that they are definitive. In history, as in every field of knowledge, we should never assume that what is currently believed is the fixed truth.

As we first saw with the figure of Cleopatra, Elizabeth has become an iconic historical figure not only because of her own actions but also because of the way her story has been told by historians. She is one of the most closely studied women in world history, the subject of countless books and articles. Naturally, not all of those who have closely studied her life have come to precisely the same conclusions about her. We should not find this surprising. After all, you would not necessarily be surprised if you had a very different opinion to a friend or relative about the merits of a particular politician, artist or athlete. It's also quite possible that two people describing the same event, or two witnesses in a trial, may give differing versions of the same story. In a similar way, two historians will give somewhat different accounts of the same historical event or person.

There can be many reasons for these differences. It is seldom because of deliberate efforts to mislead, or to suppress certain facts. Assessing events in the past is complex (just as determining the guilt or innocence of the accused in a trial can be very difficult), for a whole host of different reasons: the evidence may be incomplete or contradictory; the cause of particular events can be very difficult to identify; or the consequences of actions may be difficult to assess, and may look very different in the short term than they do in the long term. Historians may have different assessments of historical figures depending on moral questions. For example, as we will see, Elizabeth ordered the execution of her cousin Mary, Queen of Scots. Was this an act of cruel murder or pragmatic statesmanship? Historians may also make different judgements about what is important, or ask different questions about historical figures. One might ask, 'Did Elizabeth make England a great military power?', while another might just as reasonably ask the sort of question by which we might judge a modern prime minister or president, such as, 'Did Elizabeth provide a high standard of living for her people?' As well as this, historians particularly concerned with one aspect of her legacy might draw conclusions based on that particular aspect: historians of Ireland, for example, may be much more critical of Elizabeth than English historians, since Elizabeth's record as ruler of Ireland was marked by a great deal of instability and violence.

Thus, historians reach different conclusions about people in the past for a wide range of legitimate reasons. We refer to these as historical interpretations. Human beings, after all, are complex, and it is difficult to provide an assessment of their lives which is at once short enough to be digestible and detailed enough to do justice to the subject. It is especially difficult to judge the 'success' or 'failure' of a ruler like Elizabeth, since she inherited problems from her predecessors, and the outcomes of her actions were not of her making alone, but were dependent on the actions of the many other people she dealt with at home and abroad. Furthermore, historians do not work in isolation. Their work is influenced by that of other historians both past and current, and their research responds to, builds on, supports or challenges that of others. In this way, historians seek over time to improve our knowledge of the past.

In this next section, we will look at some of these issues by considering different ways in which Elizabeth's actions have been assessed by historians and why historians have come to different conclusions about them. We will do this by looking further at two important aspects of her legacy: her role in the defeat of the Spanish Armada, and her decisions about marriage and her succession.

3.2 Elizabeth and the Spanish Armada

First, we will look at an event that we have already touched on in this chapter, an event which, perhaps more than anything else, Elizabeth's popular reputation rests on – the defeat of the Spanish Armada. In later centuries, this became an event of talismanic significance in English history. Not only was this a defeat of a great Roman Catholic enemy by Protestant England but it was also an early sign of the naval power that later became the backbone of the British Empire.

Elizabeth disliked war and she sought to avoid it for most of her reign. She maintained peace despite ongoing tension between England and Spain (the most powerful nation in Western Europe of the time), tension which largely arose from religious differences between Protestant England and Catholic Spain. Elizabeth finally decided to go to war in 1585, sending troops to support the Dutch who were rebelling against Spanish rule. She did this in an attempt to limit Spanish power in northern Europe, because she feared that if Spain regained control of the Netherlands, they would use it as a base to attack England. Therefore, despite the popular image of a fearsomely powerful Spain attacking a relatively weak England, Elizabeth had made the first aggressive move. By doing so, she arguably made the attack she feared all the more likely, and so it proved: in 1586, Philip II of Spain ordered the preparation of a great fleet, an Armada, to attack England. This fleet intended to sail from Lisbon in Portugal (then part of the Spanish empire) to the English Channel, rendezvous with the Army of Flanders (the Spanish forces already in the Netherlands to fight the Dutch), and then escort them across to England and descend on London (see Figure 9).

This strategy assumed that the English fleet would not be able to disrupt the plan. Initially, this assumption proved accurate: the two fleets made contact off the coast of Cornwall on 21 July 1588, and

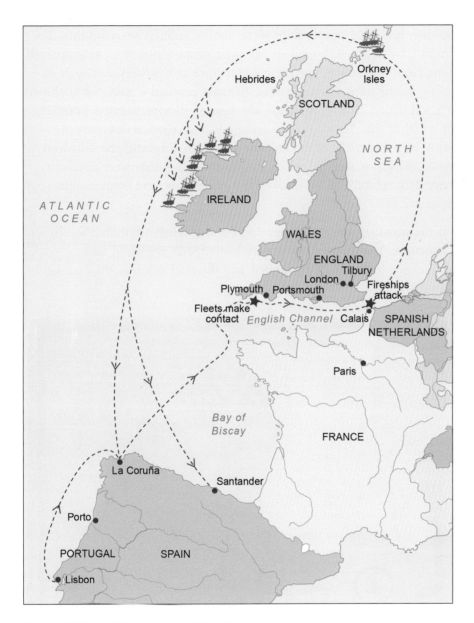

Figure 9 Map of the voyage of the Armada.
After the fireships attack and the battles in the English Channel, the Armada became dispersed, and its ships sought to make their way back to Spain. Many were wrecked on the Scottish and Irish coasts.

engaged in intermittent fighting for the next several days as they sailed eastwards along the south coast of England. However, neither side was able to inflict much damage on the other. The Spanish hoped to destroy English ships by making contact and engaging in hand-to-hand fighting, but the English ships were nimble enough to avoid this. The English, by contrast, hoped to use their cannon power to sink Spanish ships from a distance, but the cannon were not powerful enough to have a major impact; the Spanish Armada reached Calais and anchored in good order. At that moment, the fate of Europe seemed to hinge on whether the Armada could accomplish its rendezvous with the Army of Flanders. If it did and then invaded England, the kingdom would quite possibly fall, since England's land forces were relatively weak. If England fell, so would the Netherlands, and Spain would reign supreme.

On the night of the 28–29 July 1588, the English attempted a different manoeuvre. Eight small ships were loaded with firewood and gunpowder, and were then ignited and directed towards the Spanish fleet (Figure 10).

Figure 10 Chart showing the fireships attack. Robert Adams, engraved by Augustine Ryther, 'Expeditionis Hispanorum in Angliam vera descriptio. Anno Do: M D LXXXVIII', 1590. Intended to accompany: Petruccio Ubaldini, *A discourse concerninge the Spanishe fleete invadinge Englande in the yeare 1588*. London, 1590. Library of Congress, Geography and Map Division, call number G1816.S45 1588 .A3.

This caused panic in the anchored fleet; the Spanish shipmasters cut their anchors and, in disarray, were pushed by the tides north-eastward, up the coast of the Netherlands. The next morning, the English fleet (by then reinforced) attacked the disorganised Armada again, while the winds helped to drive the Armada into the North Sea. The Armada's commander decided that his best option was to head for home by sailing around the north and west coasts of the British Isles. There, the unseasonably bad weather and the unfamiliar coasts doomed many ships to destruction.

England was saved and a legend was born. The Armada was defeated, but had Elizabeth defeated it? Clearly Elizabeth personally did not fight it off; as you've seen, female monarchs were unable to lead their troops into battle. However, can we claim that her own actions made the difference between success and failure? Let's think now whether it is true to say that 'Elizabeth defeated the Armada'.

Activity

(Allow around 15 minutes to complete this activity.)

Look back over the preceding account of events and note down what the main factors in the failure of the Armada appear to have been.

Discussion

There appear to have been multiple factors that contributed to the failure of the Armada. These include:

1   The Armada's problematic strategy for attacking England, which did not account for resistance from the English fleet.
2   The design of the ships on each side, in particular the effectiveness and speed of the English ships.
3   The two sides' tactics, which allowed neither side to inflict serious damage on the other.
4   The fireships attack, which disrupted the Spanish formation.
5   The weather.

Let us consider the factors that contributed to the defeat of the Armada further. Two of them were clearly beyond Elizabeth's control: the weather (5) and Spain's strategy (1). Others were much more in her control: the strength of the English navy (2), the tactics they adopted (3), and in particular the fireships attack (4), were her responsibility as ruler. So, can we credit her with success in these regards?

With regard to point (2), had Elizabeth made a decision to invest heavily in her naval defences? The answer to this appears to be mostly yes. Nicholas Rodger, a leading expert on naval history, writes:

> the queen herself, and a large proportion of those to whom she looked for support, had strong reasons to keep up naval strength. The reasons were almost exclusively political and defensive. [...] Survival was her priority, over many years when the odds seemed to be heavily against it, and the queen's ships were designed and maintained almost exclusively for this purpose. Hers was a navy intended, not to found the British Empire, but to defend the country by dominating the Channel and the North Sea.
>
> (Rodger, 2004, pp. 196–7)

Rodger argues that a conscious decision was made to create a navy not for conquest (as both earlier and later monarchs would do), but in order to defend England and its seemingly rather weak ruler. This view is supported by Geoffrey Parker, a historian who has compared England and Spain in this period:

> From the 1570s onward, her naval experts deliberately sought to link her simple yet realistic defence strategy with the appropriate tactics and thus [...] with an equally appropriate ship design. [...] Philip and his advisers, by contrast, devoted little thought to such matters.
>
> (Parker, 1998, p. 268)

Parker perhaps lays more stress on Elizabeth's 'naval experts' rather than Elizabeth herself. As with all political decisions, it is hard to say precisely how much was down to the queen and how much was down to her advisers and experts, but it was the policy of her government (approved by Elizabeth), hence, we can chalk it up as her success.

What about the role of tactics in the defeat of the Spanish Armada? Again, it is hard to pin down Elizabeth's personal role. We know that the instructions for her commander, Admiral Lord Howard of Effingham, were issued in her name and that she signed them. She must have approved them, as she did not put her name to documents lightly, but did she herself conceive these instructions? It surely seems likely that she relied heavily on the advice of her ministers and (perhaps most importantly) on her naval commanders themselves, who had experience in naval tactics. We cannot say that she did not play an important role in approving the documents, but nor can we say she planned the defence in any meaningful way.

Historians offer somewhat different interpretations of whether Elizabeth's orders provided an effective plan for defeating the Armada. Parker writes that 'when in late December 1587 Queen Elizabeth ordered her fleet to put to sea, her Instructions to Admiral Howard revealed almost total confusion about Philip's intentions' (1998, p. 225), a judgement which suggests poor planning (or poor information) on Elizabeth's part. On the other hand, Rodger places a much more positive interpretation on her orders: 'the Queen has sometimes been accused of interfering with her admirals, but few commanders-in-chief in so critical a situation have ever been trusted with such complete discretion as Howard of Effingham was' (2004, p. 263). In this interpretation, Elizabeth left decisions in the hands of those with greater expertise, which can be regarded as very good leadership.

With regard to the fireships attack, we have no record of whose plan this was, but Rodger refers to it as an 'obvious enough' plan and a 'well-known form of attack', which the Spanish were expecting (2004, p. 269). If so, then we return again to attributing the failure of the Armada to the weaknesses in the original conception of their plan.

On close examination, it is hard to pinpoint specific points at which Elizabeth's personal involvement was critical in the outcome. The Spanish plan was badly conceived from the beginning and one could argue that Elizabeth merely took the obvious steps to ensure its defeat. Can we give her any credit at all, then? One can argue that Elizabeth appointed the ministers and commanders, and therefore their successes were her successes, but this is not an argument everyone would accept. One could even make the argument that the English soldiers and sailors fought as bravely as they did because of the loyalty Elizabeth inspired in them – but again, this smacks of wishful thinking. Some historians, such as James McDermott, have tended to argue that Elizabeth was simply lucky:

> If Englishmen could count it as a victory, it was one bestowed largely by unseasonably foul weather and Spanish [ship]masters' inadequate understanding of the treacherous waters through which their battered ships were obliged to struggle home.

> (McDermott, 2005, p. 307)

This debate shows us that historians can reach a variety of legitimate conclusions about how to explain these complex events, with some reflecting well on Elizabeth and others much less so.

3.3 Elizabeth, marriage, Mary and the succession

A second key dispute concerning Elizabeth's actions relates to the question of the succession to the throne, a constant worry throughout her reign. Elizabeth was the last surviving child of Henry VIII and came to the throne without an obvious successor: no children, siblings, nephews or nieces. Owing to legal and genealogical complexities, it was distinctly unclear who the next legal heir to the throne was. One strong candidate was Mary Stuart, Queen of Scots, a descendent of Henry VIII's elder sister, who was both foreign and a Roman Catholic (see Figure 11).

Other possible successors included the Grey sisters, descended from Henry's younger sister Mary, who were Protestant and English. None of these seemed entirely suitable; needless to say, most English people would have preferred a male heir. In light of this, the obvious solution would have been for Elizabeth to marry and hopefully bear children, but famously she did not. As you have seen, she told the members of the House of Commons early in her reign that she was happy to be remembered as having 'lived and died a virgin' (Marcus et al., 2000, p. 58).

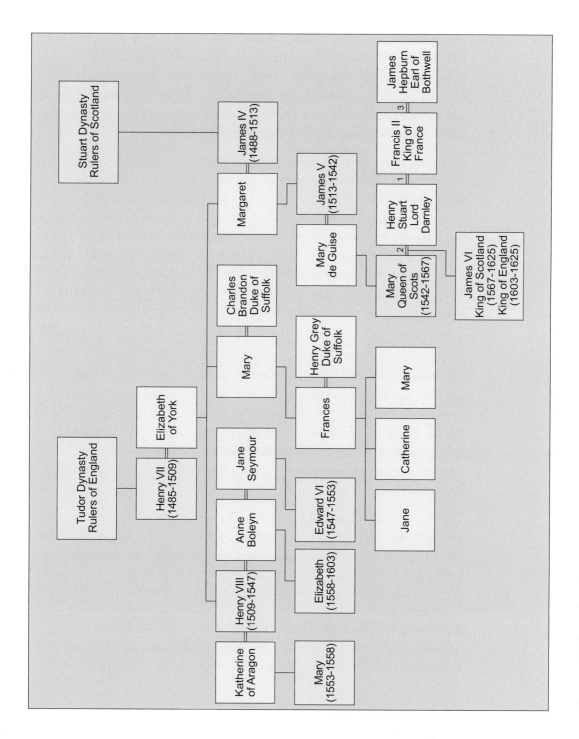

Figure 11 Chart showing the relationship of the House of Tudor (English monarchs) and House of Stuart (Scottish monarchs). The dates show regnal years.

This did not stop people seeking to arrange a marriage, and Elizabeth had many suitors. Early in her reign, foreign princes and kings from Sweden to Spain made overtures of marriage. Elizabeth and her ministers held serious and sustained talks about arranging a marriage with a prince of the royal families of Austria in the 1560s, and France in the 1570s and early 1580s. These efforts failed, however, over the reluctance of the princes in question to conform to Elizabeth's Protestant church. There were also several serious prospects among the English nobility. Elizabeth seems to have seriously considered marrying her court favourite, Robert Dudley, earl of Leicester, but again this was problematic because of his chequered private life.

It is clear that, in spite of her public statement, Elizabeth did not wholly close off the possibility of marriage. Should we therefore conclude that she was not opposed to marrying in principle? It certainly appeared so when in 1581 she gave a ring to a French suitor, the duke of Anjou, and said that she would marry him (Doran, 1996, p. 187). What stopped her marrying was simply that she could never bring her personal wishes into line with the political and religious constraints that bound her at any given moment. Clearly, this casts Elizabeth's image as the 'Virgin Queen' in some doubt, but as we have seen, this was an image of her that became prevalent quite late in her life.

However, none of this resolved the issue of the succession, and every day that the realm was left without an heir was dangerous. Elizabeth could have resolved this by naming an heir, and perhaps by passing an Act of Parliament to ease the transition. She chose not to, believing that naming a successor would weaken her own position by encouraging her subjects to focus on ingratiating themselves with the future ruler.

Matters were complicated further by the behaviour of the person who was probably regarded as the most likely successor to the throne, Mary, Queen of Scots (Figure 12). Having fled to England in 1568 to escape a rebellion in Scotland, Mary was imprisoned by Elizabeth for nearly 20 years. She was a Catholic, and as such was viewed by Elizabeth's Protestant ministers and subjects as an entirely unsuitable successor; they urged Elizabeth to put her to death, but she refused. Mary, naturally frustrated by her captivity, eventually took to plotting against Elizabeth. In 1586, Mary signalled her support for a plot to murder

Figure 12 François Clouet, *Mary, Queen of Scots*, *c.*1558, watercolour and body colour on vellum rebacked with card, 8 × 6 cm. Royal Collection Trust © Her Majesty Queen Elizabeth II, 2018/Bridgeman Images.

Elizabeth, the Babington Plot. Presented with this proof of treachery, Elizabeth agreed to have Mary tried, convicted and sentenced to death. Even then, Elizabeth's ministers had to despatch the death warrant in secret to prevent her from changing her mind at the last minute. Although Elizabeth executed Mary, it seems she did so very reluctantly.

It is also notable that Mary was sentenced to death only after her son and successor James VI of Scotland had grown to adulthood and was capable of succeeding Elizabeth himself. Yet, as late as 1601, English writer Thomas Wilson was able to name at least 12 people whom he thought might plausibly succeed Elizabeth (Wilson, 1936 [1601], pp. 2–5). Nevertheless, the succession issue was resolved smoothly and peacefully. When Elizabeth died in 1603, James VI of Scotland was invited to succeed her as king. Elizabeth had engaged in a very lengthy and potentially dangerous gamble, but ultimately the worst had been averted.

Activity

(Allow around 35 minutes to complete this activity.)

We can now consider how different historians have judged Elizabeth's decisions relating to the issue of succession.

Reading 3.5 and Reading 3.6 present extracts from the work of two modern historians: Patrick Collinson and John Guy. Read them through now and answer the questions below:

1   What are Collinson's and Guy's assessments of Elizabeth's decisions in the matter of the succession?

2   How do their assessments differ?

Discussion

Both historians note the dangers of Elizabeth's decisions: for Collinson (2004), she 'gambled with the succession on the stake of her own life'; for Guy 'her attitude was deeply irresponsible' (2016, p. 401). Both, too, suggest that the decision was in many ways a matter of balancing Elizabeth's personal interests and those of her people. Guy seems to give her the benefit of the doubt, primarily on the grounds that things turned out well in the end. Collinson, however, is a little more critical, pointing out that Elizabeth's decision served her own interests, but 'was not seen to be in the interest of her people'.

It is worth considering whether you find Collinson's and Guy's arguments convincing. Certainly, a more critical judgement could easily be made. One might argue that Elizabeth owed it to the country to preserve her own position, and this justified not naming a successor early in her reign. Yet, after the death of Mary, Queen of Scots, when Elizabeth seems to have intended that James VI should succeed her, there seems no reason not to name him as such and avoid the risk of disruption after her death. Ultimately, Elizabeth never grasped the nettle, something that casts doubt on her effectiveness as a leader.

4 Summary

As you have seen in this chapter, the reputations of individuals from the past are very often complex and varied, both in their own time and after their deaths.

We might think of Elizabeth I today as the Virgin Queen; however, as we have seen, it is questionable how far this was an image that she herself wished to emphasise. Instead, Elizabeth preferred to present herself as a powerful monarch who ruled her people justly. Her reputation as the Virgin Queen seems to have come about later in her life, and was stressed by those around her in view of her decision not to marry.

Elizabeth's historical reputation, examined in the second half of this chapter, is also more complex than we might think: though she is often seen as one of the most successful of English monarchs, when we look closely at the decisions she made as queen, a more complex and mixed picture emerges. Inevitably, she was by no means wholly responsible for many of the glories of her reign, and some of her decisions (most notably over the succession) might very well have proved to be less successful than they turned out to be.

You should now return to the module website to continue your study of this unit.

References

Belsey, A. and Belsey, C. (1990) 'Icons of divinity: portraits of Elizabeth I', in Gent, L. and Llewellyn, N. (eds) *Renaissance bodies: the human figure in English culture, c.1540–1660*. London: Reaktion Books, pp. 11–35.

Collinson, P. (2004) 'Elizabeth I (1533–1603)', in *Oxford dictionary of national biography*. Oxford: Oxford University Press.

Collinson, P. (2007) *Elizabeth I*. Oxford: Oxford University Press.

Doran, S. (1996) *Monarchy and matrimony: the courtships of Elizabeth I*. London: Routledge.

Doran, S. (2011) 'The queen', in Doran, S. and Jones, N. (eds) *The Elizabethan world*. Abingdon: Routledge, pp. 35–58.

Frye, S. (1992) 'The myth of Elizabeth at Tilbury', *The Sixteenth Century Journal*, 23(1), pp. 95–114.

Green, J.M. (2000) 'Queen Elizabeth I's Latin reply to the Polish ambassador', *The Sixteenth Century Journal*, 31(4), pp. 987–1008.

Guy, J. (ed.) (2016) *Elizabeth: the forgotten years*. London: Viking, pp. 400–1.

Haigh, C. (1988) *Elizabeth I*, Harlow and London: Longman.

Hughes, P. and Larkin, J. (eds) (1969) *Tudor royal proclamations: volume II: the later Tudors, 1553–1587*. New Haven and London: Yale University Press.

Knox, J. (1558) *The first blast of the trumpet against the monstrous regiment of women*. Geneva: J. Poullain and A. Rebul.

Marcus, L.S., Mueller, J. and Rose, M.B. (2000) *Elizabeth I: collected works*. Chicago: University of Chicago Press.

McDermott, J. (2005) *England and the Spanish Armada: the necessary quarrel*. New Haven: Yale University Press.

Parker, G. (1998) *The grand strategy of Philip II*. New Haven: Yale University Press.

Richards, J.M. (1997) 'Mary Tudor as "sole queen"?: Gendering Tudor monarchy', *Historical Journal*, 40(4), pp. 895–924.

Rodger, N.A.M. (2004) *The safeguard of the sea: a naval history of Britain 660–1649*. London: Penguin.

Sharpe, K. (2009) *Selling the Tudor monarchy: authority and image in sixteenth-century England*. London and New Haven: Yale University Press.

Strong, R. (1987) *Gloriana: the portraits of Queen Elizabeth I*. London: Thames and Hudson.

Trim, D. (2016) 'War, soldiers, and high politics under Elizabeth I', in Smuts, R.M. (ed.) *The Oxford handbook of the age of Shakespeare*. Oxford: Oxford University Press, pp. 82–102.

Walker, J.M. (1998) 'Bones of contention: posthumous images of Elizabeth and Stuart politics', in Walker, J.M. (ed.) *Dissing Elizabeth: negative representations of Gloriana*. Durham and London: Duke University Press, p. 252–76.

Wilson, T. (1936 [1601]) 'The state of England anno dom. 1600', in Fisher, F. J. (ed.) *Camden miscellany 16*. London: Royal Historical Society, pp. 1–47.

Readings

Reading 3.1 Elizabeth's speech at Tilbury

Source: Marcus, L.S., Mueller, J. and Rose, M.B. (2000)
'Queen Elizabeth's Armada speech to the troops at Tilbury,
August 9, 1588', in *Elizabeth I: collected works*. Chicago:
Chicago University Press, pp. 325–6.

*Gathered by one that heard it and was commanded to utter it to the whole
army the next day, to send it gathered to the queen herself.*

My loving people, I have been persuaded by some that are careful of
my safety to take heed how I committed myself to armed multitudes,
for fear of treachery. But I tell you that I would not desire to live to
distrust my faithful and loving people. Let tyrants fear: I have so
behaved myself that under God I have placed my chiefest strength and
safeguard in the loyal hearts and goodwill of my subjects. Wherefore I
am come among you at this time but for my recreation and pleasure,
being resolved in the midst and heat of the battle to live and die
amongst you all, to lay down for my God and for my kingdom and for
my people mine honour and my blood even in the dust.

I know I have the body but of a weak and feeble woman, but I have
the heart and stomach of a king and of a king of England too—and
take foul scorn that Parma [Alessandro Farnese, duke of Parma,
commander of the Spanish forces] or any prince of Europe should
dare to invade the borders of my realm. To the which rather than any
dishonour shall grow by me, I myself will venter my royal blood; I
myself will be your general, judge, and rewarder of your virtue in the
field. I know that already for your forwardness you have deserved
rewards and crowns, and I assure you in the word of a prince you shall
not fail of them. In the meantime, my lieutenant general [Robert
Dudley, earl of Leicester] shall be in my stead, than whom never prince
commanded a more noble or worthy subject. Not doubting but by
your concord in the camp and valor in the field and your obedience to
myself and my general, we shall shortly have a famous victory over
these enemies of my God and of my kingdom.

Modernised version (Gemma Allen)

Written down by someone that heard the speech and was ordered to give it again to the whole army the next day, and then to send it written down to the queen herself.

My loving people, I have been advised by those who worry about my safety to be careful about placing my trust in troops who could betray me. But I tell you that I would not want to live to distrust my faithful and loving people. Let overbearing or distrustful monarchs worry: I have so behaved myself that under God I have placed my greatest strength and guarantee of safety in the loyal hearts and goodwill of my subjects. This is why I stand among you at this time, not for my recreation and pleasure, but because I have resolved in the middle and heat of the battle to live and die among you all, to lay down for my God and for my kingdom and for my people my honour and my blood even to death.

I know I have the body but of a weak and feeble woman, but I have the heart and stomach of a king and of a king of England too – and pour scorn on how Parma [Alessandro Farnese, duke of Parma, commander of the Spanish forces] or any prince in Europe should dare to invade the borders of my country. To which end, rather than any dishonour shall be caused by my actions, I will offer up my royal blood; I will be your general, judge, and rewarder of your virtue in the field of battle. I know already that because of your eagerness to engage in battle you deserve rewards and crowns, and I assure you in the word of a prince you shall not be deprived of such rewards. In the meantime, my lieutenant general [Robert Dudley, earl of Leicester] shall lead the army in my place, and a prince has never commanded a more noble or worthy subject than him. Not doubting that by agreeableness in the army camp and bravery in the field of battle and your obedience to myself and my general, we shall shortly have a famous victory over these enemies of my God and of my kingdom.

Reading 3.2 Elizabeth's speech to the Lords and Commons, 1566

Source: Extract from Marcus, L.S., Mueller, J. and Rose, M. B. (2000) 'Queen Elizabeth's speech to a joint delegation of Lords and Commons, November 5, 1566', in *Elizabeth I: collected works*. Chicago: Chicago University Press, p. 97.

As for my own part, I care not for death, for all men are mortal; and though I be a woman, yet I have as good a courage answerable to my place as ever my father had. I am your anointed queen. I will never be by violence constrained to do anything. I thank God I am indeed endued with such qualities that if I were turned out of the realm in my petticoat, I were able to live in any place of Christendom.

Modernised version (Gemma Allen)

As for me, I don't worry about dying, for all men must die; and though I am a woman, yet I have as much bravery as fitting to my place in life as my father ever had. I am your sacred queen. I will not be made by violence to do anything. I thank God I am possessed of such characteristics that if I were banished from England in my petticoat [underwear], I would be able to live in any place in the Christian world.

Reading 3.3 Elizabeth's speech at the closing of Parliament, 1593

Source: Extract from Marcus, L.S., Mueller, J. and Rose, M. B. (2000) 'Queen Elizabeth's speech at the closing of Parliament, April 10, 1593', in *Elizabeth I: collected works*. Chicago: Chicago University Press, p. 329.

This kingdom hath had many noble and victorious princes. I will not compare with any of them in wisdom, fortitude, and other virtues; but (saving the duty of a child that is not to compare with her father) in love, care, sincerity and justice, I will compare with any prince that ever you had or ever shall have. It may be thought simplicity in me that all this time of my reign I have not sought to advance my territories and enlarged my dominions, for both opportunity have served me to do it, and my strength was able to have done it. I acknowledge my womanhood and weakness in that respect, but it hath not been fear to obtain or doubt how to keep the things so obtained that hath withholden me from these attempts; only, my mind was never to invade my neighbors, nor to usurp upon any, only contented to reign over my own and to rule as a just prince.

Modernised version (Gemma Allen)

England has had many noble and victorious princes. I cannot compare to any of them in wisdom, courage in the face of adversity, and other virtues; but (with the exception that the duty of a child should not be to compare herself with her father) in love, care, sincerity and justice, I can compare with any prince you ever had or ever will have. It might be thought a lack in my judgement that during my reign I have not tried to expand the territories and enlarge the land I rule over, for I have had the opportunity to do so, and the strength to have done it. I acknowledge my femininity and weakness in that respect, but it has not been due to fear about how to gain or how to keep these new lands that has stopped me making such attempts; it has only been that my intention was not to invade neighbouring countries, nor to unjustly claim any neighbouring countries as my own, as I am happy to rule only over my own country and to rule as a just prince.

Reading 3.4 Collinson on Elizabeth's reputation

Source: Collinson, P. (2004) 'Elizabeth I (1553–1603)', in *Oxford dictionary of national biography.* **Oxford: Oxford University Press.**

As the country braced itself to commemorate the fourth centenary of Elizabeth's death in 2003, her posthumous fame was never greater, Gloriana never so glorious. She was for ever on the television screens, thanks only in part to [David] Starkey's skills as publicist and communicator. Publishers were commissioning any plausible author in sight to contribute yet another biography to the heap which already exists, confident that they would not lose their investment. It is not all that easy to explain why this should have been so. Asked why Elizabeth was great, the viewers of those programmes and the readers of those books would probably refer to her charm and affability. People would also have in mind great things that happened in Elizabeth's reign, as always, the defeat of the Armada, as ever, Shakespeare.

At the same time, professional historians have in many cases ceased to be dazzled. Paradoxically, this is one of those phases in Elizabeth's posthumous reputation when her personal stock has fallen in value. This is not because her political skills are unappreciated. On the contrary, an enriched sense of the texture of Elizabethan politics enjoyed by this generation of Elizabethan historians has if anything enhanced admiration of those skills. It is true that her instinctive reluctance to take decisive and creative action has never been so emphasized. Not even [the historian James] Froude called Elizabeth a do-nothing queen, which his successors have dared to do, but some biographers have decided that often it was the wisest course to do nothing, or to put off until tomorrow what need not be done today. Elizabeth has been praised not as the great achiever but as the consummate survivor, although others would say that that was not something that she could ever guarantee, and that throughout her long reign she gambled with the lives and fortunes of her subjects, above all through failing to make arrangements for their future government.

Reading 3.5 Collinson on Elizabeth's approach to the succession

Source: Collinson, P. (2004) 'Elizabeth I (1553–1603)', in *Oxford dictionary of national biography.* **Oxford: Oxford University Press.**

Historians and biographers have praised Elizabeth for choosing celibacy but, leaving aside the question of how far that choice was simply hers, as long as she remained single and without heirs of her own body she gambled with the succession on the stake of her own life. As a speaker in the Commons put it in 1567: 'if God should take her Majestie, the succession being not established, I know not what shall become of my self, my wife, my children, landes, goodes, friendes or cuntrie' (Hartley, 1.138 [Hartley, T.E. (ed.) (1981) *Proceedings in the Parliaments of Elizabeth I, volume I 1558–1581*. Leicester: Leicester University Press, p. 138]). In 1572, when the point at issue was the execution of Mary, queen of Scots, another MP demanded: 'since the Queene in respect of her owne safety is not to bee induced hereunto, let us make petition shee will doe it in respect of our safety' (ibid., 376). This was also an exclusion crisis [a debate about whether to prevent an heir succeeding to the throne], since to limit the succession was to exclude Mary. The pitting of the interests of subject and monarch against one another was debilitating from the royal perspective and enabling for the wider political nation.

[…]

Elizabeth's refusal to name a successor, another of her *semper eadem*s, was in her own interest, since as the 'second person' [heir to the throne] in her sister's reign she more than anyone had experience of the double threat which that posed. It was not seen to be in the interest of her people.'

Reading 3.6 Guy on Elizabeth's approach to the succession

Source: Guy, J. (ed.) (2016) *Elizabeth: the forgotten years*. London: Viking, pp. 400–1.

[W]hen unable to extricate herself from difficult corners, [Elizabeth] preferred to wait and see what time might to do rescue her. [...] To assure the continuation of the dynasty, she would need an heir, and that meant marriage, with all the vexing problems of finding a suitable husband and risking having to submit herself, and her country, to his authority, as her half-sister had done. Opting to remain single, on the other hand, could lead to chaos or even to civil war. When still of childbearing age, she had been lobbied repeatedly to marry or name an heir. [...] The menopause had liberated her, as there was no point in urging marriage on a barren woman, but it also highlighted the succession issue all the more acutely. Unlike her privy councillors, Elizabeth believed she would end up weaker, not stronger, if she named an heir rather than leaving the question in limbo. While at one level her attitude was deeply irresponsible, it was firmly rooted in her searing experiences in her half-brother's and half-sister's reigns. Things might have been different as she approached her late sixties had she actually liked James but, judging by her tetchy letters to him, she found his waywardness and presumption exasperating. She preferred to promise nothing and leave all to time. Time worked in her favour in the end, though it took its toll on a personal level.

Chapter 4
Mozart

Helen Coffey

Contents

3 Mozart today

Remember: there are two ways to study this unit. You can either choose to work through the printed chapter or to study exactly the same material on the module website. If you study from the book, you will need to download a playlist of tracks and refer back to the website to watch the videos.

The section and figure numbers in this chapter correspond to the numbering of the online unit.

Although Mozart lived over 200 years ago, his life and music continue to fascinate people today. He regularly tops polls seeking to identify the greatest ever composers and his music continues to sell out concert halls all over the world. His extraordinary achievements have been the subject of plays, novels and films; his homes in Salzburg and Vienna are now museums; and his image continues to appear on all kinds of merchandise, from Christmas tree decorations to chocolates.

Figure 2 (left) Tom Hulce as Mozart in *Amadeus*, dir. Miloš Forman (Orion Pictures, 1984). Photo: SNAP/REX/Shutterstock. **Figure 3 (centre)** Mozart Christmas tree decoration. Photo: Helen Coffey. **Figure 4 (right)** Mozart chocolates, Salzburg. Photo: © Richard Nebesky/Robert Harding/age fotostock.

Activity

To begin with, I would like you to familiarise yourself with a number of Mozart's best-known works, which were written in the later years of his life and are still regularly heard today.

Before you listen to the following tracks, take some time to think about your preconceptions of Mozart and his music. What are your impressions of Mozart? What do you think his music is going to sound like? Where do your impressions of Mozart come from?

- **Unit 4: Track 1** Piano Sonata No. 11, III. Rondo alla turca (written Vienna?, 1783)

- **Unit 4: Track 2** Horn Concerto No. 4, III. Rondo (written Vienna, 1786)

- **Unit 4: Track 3** Symphony No. 40, I. Molto allegro (written Vienna, 1788)

- **Unit 4: Track 4** Aria from the opera *The Magic Flute* (written Vienna, 1791)

You can download these tracks from the module website.

Even if you do not know Mozart's music very well, you may still have heard of him and be aware of his fame as a great musician. In this chapter, you will explore what it is about Mozart's life and works that appears to have captured people's imaginations, possibly more than any other composer.

In examining Mozart's reputation, you will be introduced to the musical genres and instruments that he mastered during his lifetime. Therefore, you will not only gain insight into the different factors that contributed to his reputation as a musical genius but will also develop your skills in the study of Music.

3.1 Exploring Mozart's reputation

Figure 5 Mozart's funeral, engraving. Photo: © Granger/Bridgeman Images.

Mozart died in Vienna on 5 December 1791, just two months before his thirty-sixth birthday. Two days later, a Viennese newspaper reported on this great loss to the musical world:

> In the night of the 4th and 5th of this month there died here the Imperial & Royal court chamber composer Wolfgang Mozart. Known from his childhood as the possessor of the finest musical talent in all Europe, through the fortunate development of his exceptional natural gifts and through persistent application he climbed the pinnacle of the greatest Masters; his works, loved and admired by all, bear witness to this, and are the measure of the irreplaceable loss that the noble art of music has suffered by his death.
>
> (*Wiener Zeitung*, 7 December 1791; quoted in Deutsch, 1966, p. 418)

This obituary indicates that Mozart's reputation stood high at his death and that he was a composer who had achieved widespread fame during his short lifetime. The obituary also recounts how this reputation had been nurtured from childhood, and while there is no doubt here of Mozart's 'exceptional natural gifts', his success as a musician is also described as a result of 'persistent application' of these talents. In this chapter you will examine how both these factors – extraordinary musical talent and continuous hard work – contributed to the creation of Mozart's reputation as a musical genius. In addition to exploring the development of his skills, you will consider the decisions he and his father, Leopold, made to encourage success in his career, and how these decisions were informed by the circumstances in which they lived and worked. Following your study of Mozart's fame during his lifetime, you will finish the chapter by considering how his reputation has endured to the present day, and how the extraordinary achievements of this prolific composer have invited interest and intrigue since his death.

4 Leopold Mozart and the child prodigy

In Figure 6, 24-year-old Wolfgang Amadeus Mozart can be seen surrounded by members of his immediate family, all of whom played an important part in the development of his reputation as a gifted musician. Wolfgang had been born to Leopold Mozart, violinist at the court of the Archbishop of Salzburg, and his wife Anna Maria on 27 January 1756. Leopold is shown here on the right holding a violin, while his wife is presented in the portrait on the wall between Wolfgang and his father (Anna Maria had died two years before this picture was painted). Next to Wolfgang at the keyboard, we can see his sister Maria Anna (known as 'Nannerl'), who was five years older than her brother.

Figure 6 Johann Nepomuk della Croce, *The Mozart family*, 1780–81, oil on canvas. Mozart Museum, Salzburg. Photo: © Alinari/Bridgeman Images.

Both Wolfgang and Nannerl benefited from the experience and talents of their musician father, as well as the unceasing support of their mother. The children exhibited their musical gifts at an early age: Nannerl started to play the keyboard at 7 years old, and by his fourth birthday Wolfgang had learned a number of pieces written in a music book that had been given to his sister. Such precociousness demanded an individually tailored education, and as far as is known, Leopold educated his children not only in music but also in other subjects, such as mathematics, literature and languages. Besides composing, Wolfgang learned to play the keyboard, the violin and he also sang (Halliwell, 1998, pp. 30–2; Komlós, 2011, pp. 215, 219).

4.1 Mozart and the harpsichord

Figure 7 Harpsichord belonging to Franz Joseph Haydn, eighteenth century. Kunsthistorisches Museum, Vienna. Photo: © Bridgeman Images.

While Mozart made use of various keyboard instruments, during the early years of his life it was the harpsichord that he played most of all (Figure 7).

Activity

(Allow around 10 minutes to complete this activity.)

I would now like you to listen to a performance on the harpsichord of one of the pieces written in the music book given to Nannerl.

As you listen to the track, jot down how you would describe the sound of the instrument: is it mellow and sonorous (that is, a rich and full sound) or more brittle and clipped? Loud or soft? Does the musician play high notes or low?

- **Unit 4: Track 5**

  You can download this track from the module website.

Discussion

The instrument sounds quite brittle and clipped, rather than mellow and sonorous. At the beginning the music is quite loud but suddenly, at 00:19 of the recording, it goes very quiet before returning to the original volume at 00:23. This occurs again at 00:34, returning to the original volume at 00:38. The harpsichord sounds both very high (in the right hand of the keyboardist) and low (in the left hand).

When discussing music, the term **pitch** is used to describe how high or low an instrument sounds (in this example, you might describe the right hand of the keyboardist as playing at a high pitch, whereas the left hand plays notes of a lower pitch). The difference between the highest and lowest pitch of an instrument is its **range**. The unique sound quality of an instrument is its **timbre** (so the timbre of the harpsichord can be described as brittle and clipped, whereas the timbre of another instrument or voice would be described differently). The volume with which music is performed (loud or soft) is described as its **dynamics**. To learn more about the harpsichord, watch the video 'Introducing the harpsichord'.

You can find the video 'Introducing the harpsichord' in Section 4.1 of the unit on the module website.

Nannerl's music book

Figure 8 Page from Nannerl's music book, 1761. The Morgan Library and Museum, New York, Mary Flagler Cary Music Coll., call No. M9397.P581, fo. 2r. © 2018. Photo: The Morgan Library & Museum/ Art Resource, NY/Scala, Florence.

The piece you listened to earlier is claimed to have been written by the young Wolfgang just a month before his sixth birthday, when it was added to his sister's music book by their father. If you look closely at Figure 8, you might just be able to make out '**Allegro**' – a common term in music indicating that the piece should be 'cheerful' and 'lively' – and that underneath Leopold has written 'Sgr: Wolfgango Mozart. 11ten Decembris 1761' ('Signor Wolfgang Mozart. 11th December 1761'). Not all of the pieces in the book are by the young Mozart – other composers of the time, including his father Leopold, are also represented here. Leopold's input into the development of Wolfgang's musical skills and the reputation arising from these was considerable. Father and son worked closely together for many years, and Leopold continued to proofread and correct his son's musical compositions until the early 1770s. However, Leopold didn't just help Wolfgang's artistic development by being his teacher; as you will see in the next section, he also put in place professional opportunities that would enable the growth of his son's reputation as a musician (Eisen, 2001).

4.2 On the road with the Mozarts

Whereas today Wolfgang Mozart might be thought of primarily as a composer, during his lifetime he acquired fame early on in his life as both composer and performer. By the time Wolfgang was 6 and Nannerl was 10, Leopold regarded their musical talents to be sufficiently advanced to be exhibited outside of their hometown. Between 1762 and 1769, they visited cities across Austria and Germany as well as London, the Netherlands, Paris and Switzerland, returning to their home in Salzburg after each tour.

Figures 9 and 10 Wolfgang (left) and Nannerl (right) Mozart, 1763, Pietro Antonio Lorenzoni (1721–1782). Photo: © Bridgeman Images.

Both children performed in concerts that showcased their talents to European royalty and nobility. While both would perform on the harpsichord, Wolfgang also demonstrated his skill in singing and on the violin. Leopold not only made these opportunities possible for his children but also ensured that news of their musical successes reached the ears of influential people back in Salzburg through open letters to his acquaintances there. In a letter dated 8 June 1764, Leopold, then in London, informed his banker Lorenz Hagenauer:

> My little girl, although she is only twelve years old, is one of the most skilful players in Europe, and […] in a word, my boy knows in this his eighth year what one would expect only from a man of forty. Indeed only he who sees and hears him can believe it. You yourself and all our Salzburg friends have no idea of Wolfgang's progress; for he is quite different now.
>
> (Anderson, 1966, pp. 48–9)

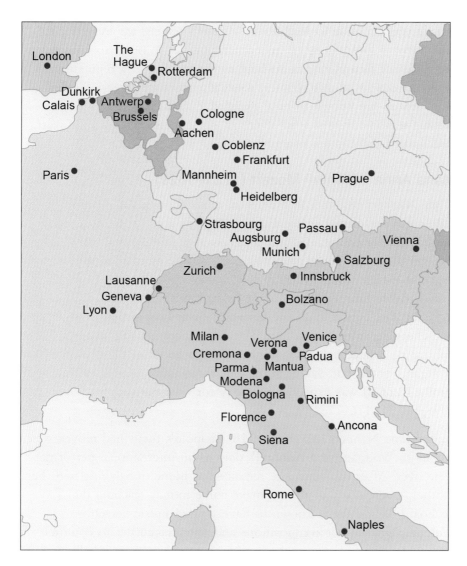

Figure 11 Map of Europe in Mozart's time showing the chief places he visited. Based on a map in Robbins Landon, H.C. (ed.), *The Mozart Compendium* (London, 1990).

From 1769 onwards, Nannerl was no longer permitted to tour Europe with her father and brother, as she was by that time of marriageable age. Wolfgang, however, went on to undertake several additional tours accompanied by his father or mother, continuing to build his international reputation as a performer and composer of the highest calibre. The chief places visited by Wolfgang are shown in Figure 11.

Before you continue to read about Mozart's travels, we are going to take a closer look at one of his contemporaries in order to consider the different factors that contribute to the making of a reputation. Over the course of this chapter, you will encounter three individuals, all of whom are known to have excelled as musicians, but who, for various reasons, have not achieved the same level of fame as Mozart. The first of these is his sister Nannerl.

Maria Anna 'Nannerl' Mozart (1751–1829)

While Nannerl received an exemplary musical education from her father and performed across Europe to great acclaim, from an early age her gender constrained her progress as a professional musician. As the two Mozart children grew older, the nature of their education began to differ; while Wolfgang was taught a variety of skills that would enable him to make a living as a musician, Nannerl, though still receiving instruction upon the keyboard from Leopold, learned housekeeping from her mother. The differences in the children's upbringing reflect eighteenth-century beliefs about gender: while Wolfgang would one day be financially responsible for his whole family, Nannerl was expected to marry for financial support (Halliwell, 1998, pp. 31, 116–17, 190).

By the time Nannerl had reached 18, Leopold's focus had moved wholly to Wolfgang and Nannerl's days as an international performer were over. After this time, she remained at home in Salzburg with her mother, where she was able to make some money teaching the keyboard. While she is known to have written music herself – Wolfgang praised her compositions and encouraged her to continue writing – none of these works survive. Unlike her more rebellious brother, Nannerl married at the age of 33 in accordance with her father's wishes, abiding by the contemporary ideas of femininity in her propriety and modesty (Rieger, 2001).

Figure 12 Unknown artist, *Portrait of Maria Anna Walburga Ignatia Mozart*, eighteenth century. Mozart's birthplace museum, Getreidegasse, Salzburg. Photo: © De Agostini Picture Library/A. Dagli Orti/Bridgeman Images.

4.3 Mozart in Mantua

Wolfgang left Salzburg for his first tour without Nannerl on 13 December 1769, which was also his first trip to Italy. One notable performance during this tour took place on 16 January 1770 in Mantua. This concert and subsequent performances elsewhere in Italy were huge successes. On 19 January 1770, a Mantuan newspaper described Wolfgang as 'a miracle in music', commenting on 'the amazing talent and extraordinary mastery which he already possesses in music at the age of 13' (Deutsch, 1966, pp. 107–8).

The programme of the Mantua concert was as follows:

1   Symphony composed by Sig. W. Amadeo Mozart, Parts 1 and 2.

2   Concerto for Harpsichord presented and performed by him at sight.

3   Aria contributed by the tenor of the Opera, Signor Uttini.

4   Sonata for Harpsichord performed at sight by the youth [...]

5   Concerto for a Violin [...] by a Professor.

6   Aria composed and sung at the same time by Signor Amadeo extempore, with the proper Accompaniments performed on the Harpsichord, to words made for the purpose, but not previously seen by him.

7   Another Harpsichord Sonata, both composed and performed by the same, on a musical theme proposed to him extempore by the first violin.

8   Aria contributed and sung by a Signorina Galliani.

9   Concerto for Oboe [...] by a Professor.

10 Musical Fugue, composed and performed by Signor Amadeo on the Harpsichord [...]

11 Symphony by the same, performed with all the parts on the Harpsichord from a single Violin part, openly submitted to him extempore.

12 Duet of Professors.

13 Trio in which Signor Amadeo will play an improvised Violin part.

14 Final Symphony by the same Sig. Mozzard.

(quoted in Deutsch, 1966, p. 106)

This programme sums up the musical achievements of 13-year-old Mozart (named here as 'Signor W. Amadeo Mozart', 'Signor Amadeo' and 'Sig. Mozzard'), which had been nurtured by his father, and for which Wolfgang was by then well known. He played harpsichord, violin and sang; he presented his own compositions, as well as a number of works by other composers; and he played at sight (i.e. from music presented to him on the day) and improvised (performed 'extempore').

While it is not possible to identify all the works performed on this occasion (especially as several were improvised and not written down), the different kinds of pieces listed in this programme – symphony, concerto, aria and sonata – were the musical genres typically heard and also expected in concerts during this period, which Mozart and his fellow composers therefore adopted in their work.

These different musical genres can be described as follows:

- **Symphony:** *(from the Greek 'syn' ('together') and 'phōnē' ('sounding'))* A large-scale piece for an orchestra (a large group of instrumentalists that does not depend on the virtuosity of soloists).

- **Concerto:** *(from the Latin 'concertare', meaning both 'to contend, dispute, debate' and also 'to work together with someone')* A work that provides contrast between an orchestra and solo instrumentalist(s).

- **Aria:** *(Italian for 'air')* A lyrical song for a solo voice with instrumental accompaniment, performed independently or in a larger work such as opera.

- **Sonata:** *(from the Italian word 'suonare' ('to sound'))* An instrumental piece for a soloist or small ensemble.

Identifying musical genres

Activity

(Allow around 10 minutes to complete this activity.)

Listen to the following four recordings and identify which of these is a symphony, a concerto, an aria and a sonata.

When trying to identify what kind of work each piece of music is, listen for whether you can hear a full orchestra (for the symphony), one or two instruments (for the sonata), a solo singer (for an aria), or a solo instrumentalist accompanied by orchestra (for the concerto). Bear in mind the definition of each genre, given previously.

- **Unit 4: Track 6**

- **Unit 4: Track 7**

- **Unit 4: Track 8**

- **Unit 4: Track 9**

You can download these tracks from the module website.

Discussion

Track 6: This is from a sonata. It is played by a very small group of musicians. I can hear only two instruments here: a harpsichord and a violin.

Track 7: This is an aria. Here, a singer can be heard accompanied by a group of instruments.

Track 8: This is from a symphony. A large and diverse group of instruments can be heard playing together in an orchestra. There is no soloist, either vocal or instrumental.

Track 9: This is from a concerto. The orchestra can be heard playing from the start. The solo instrumentalist (violinist) then becomes prominent from around 00:47.

The sonata you have just listened to (No. 3, for keyboard and violin) was written by Mozart in 1763–64 at the age of 7, during a visit to Paris. The aria is from Mozart's opera *La finta semplice*, written in 1768 when he was just 12. The symphony (No. 6) was composed in 1769 or early 1770 when Mozart was 18. He wrote the concerto (No. 1 for violin) in 1773 at the age of 22.

These examples not only demonstrate the kinds of pieces that would be performed at Mozart's concerts but also show the breadth of his work from an early age. He would continue to compose in these forms – sonata, symphony, concerto, aria – for the rest of his life. In fact, at the start of this chapter you listened to examples of these genres written in his final years. His work was not restricted to these genres, yet they remained central to his career as a composer and performer.

In the remainder of this chapter, you are going to explore how Mozart combined musical talent with professional astuteness in his music, and how the decisions he made about his compositions both met and challenged his audience's expectations, thereby contributing to the formation of his reputation as a fine musician. We will focus here on his works for keyboard: the versatility of keyboard instruments as part of an ensemble or as a solo instrument in both private and public music-making resulted in these becoming his primary medium as a musician, allowing him to showcase his talents as both performer and composer in a single concert. The two genres that embody the versatility of the keyboard and the development of Mozart's career and reputation are the sonata and concerto, which you will examine further in the following sections.

4.4 The sonata

The term 'sonata' had been used to describe various kinds of instrumental pieces before Mozart's time. By the second half of the eighteenth century, it referred to a particular kind of instrumental work for either solo keyboard or for single instrument (most frequently violin) and keyboard. The sonata was intended primarily for domestic use in the drawing room or private home, rather than the stage or public theatre.

Mozart's frequent performances of his sonatas during the tours of his youth were usually in private or semi-private settings, such as in royal or noble residences, or halls hired by a private music society (as in the Mantua concert you studied in the previous section). In addition to these private performances before the social elite, sonatas also had a pedagogic function, many being composed for teaching ladies of high social standing: musical ability was regarded as socially desirable (Irving, 2007, p. 469).

During Mozart's early years, the sonata was the ideal form for him to showcase his skills as both composer and performer to the European elite. His earliest known works in this form were for violin and keyboard. During a tour to Paris, London and the Low Countries (now the Netherlands, Belgium and Luxembourg) from 1763 to 1766, Wolfgang wrote 16 such works, which were published in each of the cities he visited. We will focus on one of the sonatas published in Paris in 1764, where Mozart was hailed in one French newspaper (*L'Avant-Coureur*, 5 March 1764) as 'a veritable prodigy' for his skills in composition, performance and improvisation (Deutsch, 1966, p. 30).

Besides the sonata being written for one or two instruments, one of its defining features, which Mozart was to adopt, was its structure: the work as a whole typically comprised three (sometimes four) movements, in the same way that a book might be divided into three or four chapters.

Figure 13 Michel Ollivier, Afternoon tea at the house of the Princesse de Conti, Palais du Temple, Paris with the Young Mozart at the keyboard, 1766, oil on canvas, 53 × 68 cm. Château de Versailles. Photo: © Bridgeman Images.

Activity

(Allow around 15 minutes to complete this activity.)

Listen to the excerpts from the three movements of Mozart's sonata for keyboard and violin, written in Paris in 1763–64. As you do, try to tap along to the **pulse** of the music – the pulse is the regular pattern of even-length stresses (referred to individually as beats) that run throughout a piece of music.

Is the pulse of the music at the same speed in each movement? How would you describe the mood of each excerpt?

- **Unit 4: Track 10** First movement

- **Unit 4: Track 11** Second movement

- **Unit 4: Track 12** Third movement

You can download these tracks from the module website.

Discussion

The first movement of the sonata is quite lively, with rapid, light notes, especially in the harpsichord. I would describe the mood of the movement as cheerful.

The second movement is slower and calmer than the first, and is more tender and sentimental.

The third movement is faster than the second, with a lighter and more playful mood.

Do not worry if you found it difficult to identify the pulse of each movement. The excerpts are presented again in the following tracks with clicks identifying the pulse in each case.

- **Unit 4: Track 13** First movement

- **Unit 4: Track 14** Second movement

- **Unit 4: Track 15** Third movement

The differences in mood between the three movements were typical of the sonatas written by Mozart and his contemporaries: a lively, fast movement was usually followed by a second slower, gentle movement, and then a final movement that ended the piece in a lighter mood. The speed of the pulse is called the **tempo**: composers like Mozart often wrote different sections of a work in contrasting tempos and moods to create interest.

Local musical styles

Figure 14 Unknown artist, *Portrait of Johann Schobert*. Photo: The Picture Art Collection/Alamy.

While Mozart adopted these widespread conventions in his composition of sonatas, he also absorbed local musical styles that he encountered in his journeys across Europe. This was all part of Leopold's plan for his son: in addition to showcasing Wolfgang's musical talents to the European elite, these tours also exposed the young Mozart to the best composers outside of Salzburg. The influence of these local musical styles on Wolfgang not only assisted his unique musical development but also endeared him to the different audiences that he encountered at each location, enhancing his reputation as a fine musician. Leopold instilled in his son early on the need to cater for his audiences' tastes. During a later visit of Wolfgang to Paris, Leopold wrote to his son from Salzburg that he should 'listen in advance to what is being composed and what people like best' (Schroeder, 2011).

In the sonatas written by Mozart during the tour of 1763 to 1766, it is possible to trace influences of local musical styles and of composers based in Paris, London and the Low Countries. It was in Paris at this time that the 'accompanied sonata' (i.e. keyboard accompanied by violin) was particularly popular, especially in the works of Johann Schobert (Figure 14), whom Leopold, Nannerl and Wolfgang met in the French capital.

Activity

(Allow around 10 minutes to complete this activity.)

Listen to the second movement of one of Schobert's sonatas for keyboard and violin.

Which of the two instruments playing here is prominent?

- **Unit 4: Track 16**

You can download this track from the module website.

Discussion

The harpsichord is more prominent here and the violin plays an accompanying role to the keyboard instrument.

Activity

(Allow around 10 minutes to complete this activity.)

Now listen again to the beginning of the second movement of Mozart's sonata for keyboard and violin that you heard earlier, written in Paris in 1763–64.

How would you describe the interaction of the violin and harpsichord here, and which is more prominent?

- **Unit 4: Track 17**

You can download this track from the module website.

Discussion

While the violin can be heard more clearly here, it is the harpsichord that is again the most prominent. The violin supports the keyboard instrument, emphasising certain notes played by the harpsichord and enriching its sound.

The prominence of the harpsichord and the accompanying role of the violin was made clear in the titles of both Mozart's and Schobert's publications of their sonatas: 'Sonatas for the harpsichord which can be played with violin accompaniment'. While this is only one element of Parisian musical practice that Mozart appears to have adopted, it demonstrates how he was able to absorb various national styles during his travels and thereby please every audience that he met.

Mozart's tours as a child prodigy were a huge success and this was in no small part due to his father's careful planning and influence. It was Leopold who provided an exemplary musical education, both at home in Salzburg and by introducing his son to the best musicians across Europe. It was Leopold who arranged for both of his children to perform to the European elite and who enabled the international communication of their musical success. It was also Leopold who made Wolfgang very aware of the need to please each audience he encountered. Therefore, it was thanks to Leopold that Wolfgang's reputation as a fine musician had an auspicious start that would ensure his success in the years to come.

Joseph Boulogne, Chevalier de Saint-Georges (1745–1799)

Figure 15 W. Ward after Mather Brown, *Joseph Boulogne Monsieur de St. George*, 1788, engraving, 38 × 28 cm. Photo: © Bridgeman Images.

Before you study Mozart's subsequent work, I would like you to consider the reputation of another musician who was working in Paris at the time of his visit – Joseph Boulogne (or Bologne), the son of a Guadeloupe planter and his African slave, who had been brought to France by his parents at a young age.

More than ten years older than Mozart, Boulogne was a gifted violinist and a prolific composer who wrote several operas, violin concertos, symphonies and smaller works to critical acclaim. Although it is not known whether Mozart ever met Boulogne, by the time Wolfgang returned to Paris in 1778, Boulogne's works were all the rage. In a letter from this period, Mozart mentions the Parisian orchestra of which Boulogne was director (Banat, 1990, p. 189).

Combining his musical activities with a successful military career, Boulogne was embraced by the French elite. Yet despite this popularity, Boulogne's career was not without its challenges: his proposal to become director of the Paris Opéra was blocked by a number of its leading ladies on grounds of his ethnicity, and he was also caught up in the tensions of the French Revolution that resulted in his brief imprisonment.

The relatively short time Boulogne was active as a composer has been suggested as one of the reasons for the neglect of his music since his death, as has the fact that, despite his success in Paris, the style of his compositions has always been overshadowed by that of Mozart and Haydn (Banat, 1990). You will take a brief look at the career of the composer Joseph Haydn later, in Section 5.

4.5 The concerto

By the time Leopold and his children returned to Salzburg from their tour of 1763 to 1766, Wolfgang had already achieved a significant reputation as both composer and performer. As a result of this, in October 1769, at the age of 13, he received his first permanent appointment as a musician, at the court of the Archbishop of Salzburg (Leopold had also instilled in his son the need for steady employment).

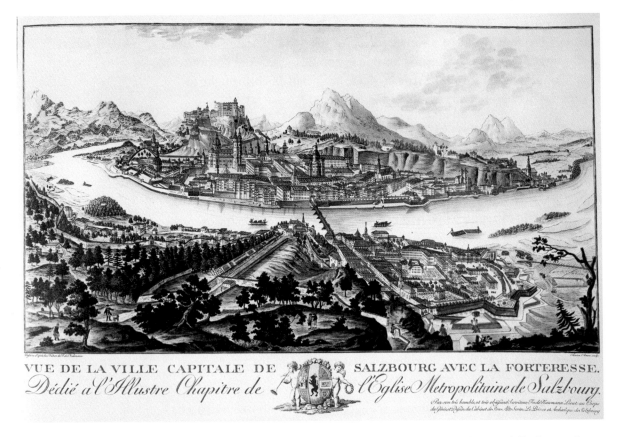

Figure 16 Anton Amon after Friedrich Gotthard Naumann, *View of the Capital City and Fortress of Salzburg*, dedicated to the Illustrious Chapter of the Metropolitan Church of Salzburg, 1791, engraving. Photo: © Bridgeman Images.

Archbishop Siegmund Christoph, Count Schrattenbach (ruled 1753–71; see Figure 17) was a staunch patron of music and of the Mozarts, often subsidising their travels abroad. During Schrattenbach's reign, orchestral music was greatly cultivated at the Salzburg court, Leopold being one of the main composers of this music. It was under these circumstances that Wolfgang started to explore yet another musical genre that would have implications for his reputation as a composer: the concerto.

Figure 17 Franz Xaver König, *Portrait of Archbishop Siegmund Christoph, Count Schrattenbach*, eighteenth century. Photo: © De Agostini Picture Library/A. Dagli Orti/Bridgeman Images.

Like the term 'sonata', 'concerto' has been used to describe different kinds of instrumental works over the years. By Mozart's time, it referred primarily to a piece for solo instrumentalist and orchestra. Wolfgang's first attempts at writing concertos demonstrate Leopold's ongoing influence. These attempts also demonstrate the impact of their travels and the fortuitous circumstances in Salzburg that encouraged the composition of orchestral music.

Mozart's second concerto for keyboard

Activity

(Allow around 15 minutes to complete this activity.)

Let's now look at one of Mozart's orchestral pieces to see how he made use of available instrumental resources and traditional musical forms in his work.

Listen to the following extracts from the three movements of Mozart's second concerto for keyboard, written in Salzburg in 1767.

How would you describe the tempo and mood of each movement? How does this overall structure compare to that of the sonata which you looked at earlier?

- **Unit 4: Track 18** First movement
- **Unit 4: Track 19** Second movement
- **Unit 4: Track 20** Third movement

> You can download these tracks from the module website.

Discussion

The first movement is at a moderate pace and cheerful; the second is slightly slower, perhaps more stately; the third is faster and brighter, with very rapid notes in the harpsichord. Like the sonata, the concerto has three movements: fast, slow, fast.

Activity

(Allow around 10 minutes to complete this activity.)

Now listen to this longer extract from the second movement of the concerto, paying close attention to the relationship between the solo harpsichordist and the orchestra.

- **Unit 4: Track 21** Second movement

> You can download this track from the module website.

Complete the following table by entering 'harpsichord' next to the sections when you think the keyboardist is more prominent, and 'full orchestra' where all instruments can be heard.

Audio timings	Harpsichord or full orchestra?
00:00–00:31	
00:31–01:36	
01:37–02:08	
02:08–03:11	

Discussion

Audio timings	Harpsichord or full orchestra?
00:00–00:31	Full orchestra
00:31–01:36	Harpsichord
01:37–02:08	Full orchestra
02:08–03:11	Harpsichord

When describing the contrast between soloist and orchestra, the term 'tutti' (Italian for 'all') is often used for the sections for full orchestra, and 'solo' (Italian for 'alone') for those for instrumental soloist. The table might therefore be presented as follows:

Audio timings	Solo or Tutti?
00:00–00:31	Tutti
00:31–01:36	Solo
01:37–02:08	Tutti
02:08–03:11	Solo

The two traits you looked at in the previous activities – (i) three movements with tempos fast, slow, fast; and (ii) contrasting sections within each movement for orchestra and soloist – were typical of the late eighteenth-century concerto. These musical traditions provided a framework upon which Mozart could develop his work – and therefore his reputation – as a performer and composer, while also meeting the expectations of his audiences in Salzburg and further afield. In addition to the musical genres (sonata, concerto) and instruments (harpsichord, orchestra) that he accommodated in his writing, other musical influences are also evident in his early keyboard concertos, as you shall discover in the next activity.

Musical influences

Activity

(Allow around 10 minutes to complete this activity.)

Now listen to this excerpt from 00:46 to 01:36 of Mozart's concerto, and compare this to the opening of the first movement of another sonata for keyboard and violin by Johann Schobert.

What do you notice about these two excerpts?

- **Unit 4: Track 22** Mozart keyboard concerto, second movement
- **Unit 4: Track 23** Schobert sonata for keyboard and violin

You can download these tracks from the module website.

Discussion

The music in both excerpts is almost identical, although the tempo of Schobert's movement is much faster than Mozart's. Don't worry if you found it difficult to hear the similarities between the two excerpts – the different tempos make this quite tricky. You might find it easier to focus on the last ten seconds of both excerpts to listen for their similarities: try starting Track 22 from 00:42 and then Track 23 from 00:31.

The reason for the similarities in the two works is that, while Mozart's later works would exhibit great originality, his earliest keyboard concertos, written in 1767, are in fact based on keyboard and violin sonatas by composers he had met on his tours of Europe – for this movement, he used the first movement of one of Schobert's sonatas for keyboard and violin. Mozart added 'tutti' sections to the transcribed sonata material that he retained for the solo keyboardist. It would seem that Leopold may have given the young Wolfgang these pieces as an educational exercise: his corrections can be seen on the original score of the piece.

4.6 The piano

Figure 18 Mozart's piano. Mozart's birthplace museum, Getreidegasse, Salzburg. Photo: © akg-images/Erich Lessing.

Mozart's travels outside Salzburg continued to influence his music into the 1770s. After Leopold and Wolfgang returned from their successful Italian tour of 1773 (which included the Mantua concert you examined earlier), Wolfgang's days as a travelling child prodigy were effectively over. For the next few years, his career was firmly focused on his home town, but further occasional tours would prove highly influential for the young musician. It was through these that he was able to experience a new instrument that was, as far as we know, not yet available in Salzburg: the piano (Figure 18).

The first reference to Wolfgang playing the piano was in the course of his travels in 1777–78 that took him to Munich, Augsburg, Mannheim and Paris. At the end of 1777, his mother reported to Leopold from Mannheim that '[e]veryone thinks the world of Wolfgang, but indeed he plays quite differently from what he used to in Salzburg – for there are pianofortes here, on which he plays so extraordinarily well that people say they have never heard the like' (quoted in Komlós, 2011, p. 219). The impact of this instrument on Mozart was immeasurable: he soon began to perform and teach on the piano, and it was during these tours that his first sonatas for piano were to appear.

Activity

(Allow around 10 minutes to complete this activity.)

Now listen to this excerpt from the first movement of Mozart's Piano Sonata, No. 7, written at Mannheim for Rosina Cannabich, the daughter of the local Kapellmeister (the musician in charge of a choir or orchestra).

How would you describe the timbre and dynamic range of the piano in comparison to the harpsichord you listened to earlier?

- **Unit 4: Track 24**

You can download this track from the module website.

Discussion

The timbre of the piano is not as brittle or clipped as the harpsichord. It has a softer, mellower timbre. The music is very expressive; the dynamics are more subtle than on the harpsichord and wider-ranging.

The greater expressivity of the piano, due to its ability to play louder or softer depending on the pressure applied to the keys, gave it a great advantage over the harpsichord. In order to find out more about this new instrument, watch the video 'Introducing Mozart's fortepiano'. As you do so, think about its capabilities and appeal to Mozart as a composer.

You can find the video 'Introducing Mozart's fortepiano' in Section 4.6 of the unit on the module website.

Activity

(Allow around 10 minutes to complete this activity.)

It was not only sonatas that Mozart began to perform on the piano. Listen to the following recording of another piece he is known to have performed during his 1777–78 tour.

What genre of work is this – symphony, sonata, concerto or aria? Why have you identified it as such?

- **Unit 4: Track 25**

You can download this track from the module website.

Discussion

This is a concerto. The exchange between orchestra and piano can be heard early on, and continues with impressive orchestral and solo piano passages.

Mozart had in fact written this piece of music back in Salzburg, where the harpsichord was still the norm (Irving, 2017, pp. 128–9). It was now outside Salzburg that Mozart wowed his audiences with brilliant performances of both his sonatas and concertos for the keyboard, on the piano. One such concert in Augsburg on 22 October 1777 was described in a local newspaper as follows:

> the rendering on the fortepiano so neat, so clean, so full of expression, and yet at the same time extraordinarily rapid, so that one hardly knew what to give attention to first, and all the hearers were enraptured. One found here mastery in the thought, mastery in the performance, mastery in the instruments, all at the same time.
>
> (*Augsburgische Staats- und Gelehrten Zeitung*, 28 October 1777, quoted in Deutsch, 1966, p. 168)

This review of one of Mozart's concerts hints at the increasing complexity in his compositions in the late 1770s, which challenged his listeners.

Mozart's ninth concerto for keyboard

Activity

(Allow around 20 minutes to complete this activity.)

Let us explore the challenging nature of these particular compositions by listening again to the first movement of Mozart's ninth concerto for keyboard.

As you listen, complete the following table, adding timings for where the soloist is more prominent ('solo'), and where the full orchestra ('tutti') can be heard. I have entered the first three timings as examples.

- **Unit 4: Track 25**

You can download this track from the module website.

Audio timings	Solo or Tutti?
00:00–00:02	Tutti
00:02–00:05	Solo
00:05–00:07	Tutti

Discussion

My attempt at completing the table is as follows:

Audio timings	Solo or Tutti?
00:00–00:02	Tutti
00:02–00:05	Solo
00:05–00:07	Tutti
00:07–00:10	Solo
00:10–01:42	Tutti
01:42–01:49	Solo
01:50–01:52	Tutti
01:52–01:55	Solo
01:55–01:57	Tutti

Audio timings	Solo or Tutti?
01:57–03:01	Solo
03:01–03:09	Tutti
03:09–03:57	Solo
03:57–04:06	Tutti
04:07–04:14	Solo
04:14–04:21	Tutti

You may have found this activity quite challenging for a number of reasons:

1   The exchange between soloist and tutti is very rapid: at the start of the movement, the orchestra only plays for two seconds before the soloist enters, and this quick dialogue continues until the longer 'tutti' section from 00:10–01:42, after which the opening rapid exchange between orchestra and pianist returns. If you compare this opening to the second movement of the second concerto for keyboard you examined in Section 4.5, you will see that the earlier work has a longer tutti section before the soloist enters at 00:31.

2   The solo and tutti sections are not always clearly defined in the ninth concerto, creating a subtle dialogue between the orchestra and pianist: at 01:37, for example, the piano enters with a long **trill** towards the end of the tutti section.

The relationship between soloist and orchestra is therefore more subtle and complex than in Mozart's earlier concertos: the early entry of the pianist here, after two seconds, would certainly have been a surprise to the audience. So, while Mozart retained the traditional use of solo and tutti, he also began to explore the capabilities of this dialogue, both astounding and challenging his audiences.

4.7 The break with Salzburg

While Mozart's new works were received with acclaim in Augsburg, such expressivity and complexity in orchestral music were not to everyone's taste. Back in conservative Salzburg, Mozart's ambitions as a composer and performer were frustrated. Following Leopold's lead and encouraged by the orchestral repertoire that had been cultivated there in previous years, Wolfgang had become the chief composer of orchestral music in the city. There, he wrote at least 17 symphonies and 11 concertos: five for violin and six for keyboard. Yet, these were not composed for the archbishop's court where Mozart was employed.

Count Colloredo (Figure 19), who had become archbishop in 1772, did not encourage the composition of orchestral music, so Mozart withdrew from court life, instead writing concertos and symphonies for the local nobility. The relationship between the conservative archbishop and the ambitious musician deteriorated to such an extent that a visit to Vienna opened Mozart's eyes to opportunities that would better suit his ambitions. He thus requested his discharge from the archbishop's service and on 8 June 1781, this was finally granted (Eisen and Sadie, 2001).

You have now traced the development of Mozart's reputation as a musician from his childhood, when he was heralded as a 'miracle in music', to his later visits to Augsburg where 'all the hearers were enraptured'. In this chapter so far, you have seen various aspects of Mozart's reputation as a musician begin to emerge: a gifted child prodigy, acclaimed throughout Europe, who in later years astounded audiences with the complexity and expressivity of his music for piano, taking the musical genres that his audiences were used to in new directions. However, it was not only Mozart's natural gifts that contributed to his fame: his father played a key role, educating young Wolfgang, organising tours that showcased his talents, and instilling in him the need to please his audience and to ultimately find steady employment as a musician. Now with his break from Salzburg – and the direct influence of his father – a new phase in Mozart's career began.

Figure 19 Johann Michael Greite, *Hieronymus Count Colloredo*, *c.*1775, oil on canvas. Museum Carolino Augusteum, Salzburg. Photo: © akg-images.

5 Mozart in Vienna

Figure 20 Johann Adam Delsenbach, *New Market, Vienna, c.*1750, copper engraving (later coloured). Photo: © akg-images.

With his move to Vienna, Wolfgang defied his father's wish that he should remain in Salzburg (Wolfgang's permanent position at the archbishop's court and its steady salary were, according to Leopold, not to be dismissed lightly). However, Wolfgang recognised the opportunities that Vienna had to offer to a freelance musician and, in letters to Leopold, tried to convince his sceptical father that leaving Salzburg was the right thing to do. On 4 April 1781, he wrote to Leopold: 'I can assure you that this here is a Magnificent place – and for my Métier [career] the best place in the world' (quoted in Link, 2011, p. 22).

As the capital of the Holy Roman Empire, Vienna was the location of the emperor's court, which offered several employment opportunities to an aspiring musician. Mozart's ultimate aim was to become a composer at the court, and in 1788 his wish was granted when he was finally made composer of the emperor's chamber music. This appointment provided him with the stable employment and steady salary that he had last enjoyed in Salzburg as well as advancement in his social standing.

Figure 21 Unknown artist, *Emperor Joseph II*, *c.*1790, oil on canvas, 96 × 73 cm. Deutsches Historisches Museum, Berlin. Photo: © Bridgeman Images.

How, then, in the meantime, did Mozart establish himself as a musician in the city and gain the emperor's favour? Like his father, he made careful decisions about his career and took advantage of every opportunity available to a musician. Mozart's hard work in Vienna resonates with the obituary that you read at the start of this chapter, which refers to the 'persistent application' of his musical talents. Through his teaching, performing, composing and in having his music published, Mozart was able to develop a reputation as one of the foremost musicians in the city.

The different professional opportunities in Vienna allowed Mozart to compose all kinds of music, including the musical genres that had been so important to him since his childhood. While sonatas were primarily written for his pupils and performed in private concerts, operas, symphonies and concertos were composed for public performances in a variety of venues, extending his reputation across the city.

Activity

(Allow around 15 minutes to complete this activity.)

Now listen to a number of the works composed by Mozart during his first years in Vienna.

As you listen, note the musical genre of each work, and explain why you have selected that genre based on the voices and/or instruments you can hear. In the following discussion, I have added further details of each work to demonstrate how these pieces contributed to Mozart's reputation in Vienna.

- **Unit 4: Track 26**
- **Unit 4: Track 27**
- **Unit 4: Track 28**

You can download these tracks from the module website.

Discussion

Track 26: This is a sonata. The only instrument I can hear is the piano.

This is in fact a sonata for two pianos (do not worry if you did not spot that two instruments were being played – this is difficult to hear). It was written by Mozart for his pupil Josepha von Auernhammer, whom he started to teach in the summer of 1781. Mozart performed the sonata with Josepha in a private concert at her family residence in November that year, which, he wrote to his father, was a great success.

Track 27: This is an aria from an opera. After an orchestral introduction, a singer can be heard from 00:14.

The opera is *Die Entführung aus dem Serail* ('The Abduction from the Seraglio'), which was first performed in Vienna in July 1782, catapulting Mozart to international fame. The German playwright Johann Wolfgang von Goethe wrote years later in 1787: 'All our endeavour [...] to confine ourselves to what is simple [...] was lost when Mozart appeared. *Die Entführung aus dem Serail* conquered all [...]' (quoted in Deutsch, 1966, p. 305).

Track 28: This is a symphony (No. 35). I can hear a full orchestra playing here, without soloists.

A Hamburg newspaper reported of its first performance on 22 March 1783: 'Our Monarch, who, against his habit, attended the whole of the concert, as well as the entire audience, accorded him [Mozart] such unanimous applause as has never been heard of here' (quoted in Deutsch, 1966, p. 215).

5.1 The piano concerto in Vienna

Mozart would go on to compose some of his best-known works while living in Vienna, including those pieces that you heard at the beginning of this chapter. The genre that allowed Mozart to showcase his talents as both performer and composer in a single concert was, however, the piano concerto.

In June 1781, Mozart wrote to his father that 'Vienna is certainly the land of the clavier [keyboard]!' (quoted in Komlós, 2011, p. 221) and over the next few months, he was to establish himself as the finest pianist in the city. In the coming years, Mozart was to give many performances that showcased his pianistic skills at private soirées in the residences of the nobility and in public spaces such as theatres. It was in these performances that he presented his newly composed piano concertos that would become the most important pieces of their kind. As ever, Mozart was aware of the need to please his audience with these works, expressing this view in a letter to his father of 28 December 1782, in which he refers to the three new piano concertos that he was composing at that time:

> These concertos [...] are very brilliant, pleasing to the ear, and natural, without being vapid. There are passages here and there from which the connoisseurs alone can derive satisfaction; but these passages are written in such a way that the less learned cannot fail to be pleased, though without knowing why.
>
> (quoted in Keefe, 2011, p. 78)

Figure 22 Joseph Lange, *Portrait of Wolfgang Amadeus Mozart at the Piano*, 1789, oil on canvas. Mozart Museum, Salzburg. Photo: © Alinari/ Bridgeman Images.

In addition to reassuring his father of the intended broad appeal of these works (to both connoisseurs and the 'less learned'), Mozart also indicates here his response to criticisms of the concerto genre at that time by music critics and theorists. While listeners expected these works to display the brilliance of the soloist (who was often required to perform very complex music), this was not to be empty virtuosity that distracted from the emotional depth of a work. Mozart's concertos therefore firmly asserted his own brilliance as a pianist and also ensured greater musical content through a more fluid dialogue between soloist and orchestra – you have already encountered an example of this in Mozart's ninth concerto for keyboard (in Section 4.6). The resulting greater expression of feeling through the dialogue was likened to the dramatic processes of a play on the stage, which were carefully crafted to engage the audience (Keefe, 2011, pp. 80–1).

Mozart's Piano Concerto No. 21

Activity

(Allow around 15 minutes to complete this activity.)

Explore Mozart's further development of the concerto by listening to an extract from the second movement of his Piano Concerto No. 21, written in Vienna in 1785.

Write a description of the dialogue between the orchestra and soloist in the extract, including track timings.

- **Unit 4: Track 29**

You can download this track from the module website.

Discussion

The passage begins with the full orchestra. The piano joins seamlessly at 01:19, repeating the musical material that has just been played by the orchestra. From 01:44 the accompaniment by the orchestra of the piano's solo becomes more prominent. The orchestra plays alone from 02:02, introducing the return of the piano solo at 02:08. From around 02:33, the exchange between soloist and orchestra becomes more subtle and frequent until they play the same music together at 02.53.

The division between soloist and orchestra in this extract is very subtle, with the relationship between the two becoming more equal as time goes on. This greater interplay and parity between soloist and orchestra were just some of the significant contributions Mozart made to the concerto genre.

This dramatic dialogue between instruments was not lost on Mozart's audience. In 1785, a Viennese newspaper reported on Mozart's performance of one of his piano concertos: 'the favourable reception of which we forbear to mention, since our praise is superfluous in view of the deserved fame of this master, as well known as he is universally valued.' (*Wiener Zeitung*, quoted in Deutsch, 1966, p. 259). Even Leopold, initially sceptical of his son's ability to succeed in Vienna, was astounded by the piano concertos that he heard his son perform at a concert the same year. From Vienna, he wrote to Nannerl: 'I had the great pleasure of hearing so clearly all the interplay of the instruments that for sheer delight tears came into my eyes. When your brother left the platform the Emperor waved his hat and called out "Bravo, Mozart!" ' (quoted in Komlós, 2011, p. 223).

In order to establish himself in Vienna and extend his reputation there as a great musician, Mozart had again combined his natural musical talents with professional astuteness, showcasing his talents as a performer while also composing works that met the tastes of the discerning Viennese audience. Mozart wrote a total of 17 piano concertos in Vienna, the last being composed months before his death in 1791. His concertos for keyboard span nearly his entire adult career, and therefore demonstrate both his growth as a composer and his important contribution to the development of the piano concerto genre.

Before you move on to the final section of this chapter, I would like you to take a brief look at the career of another Austrian musician who gained widespread fame during his lifetime: Joseph Haydn.

(Franz) Joseph Haydn (1732–1809)

Figure 23 Thomas Hardy, *Joseph Haydn*, 1791, oil on canvas, 77 × 64 cm. Royal College of Music, London, accession No.: PPHC000001. Photo: © akg-images.

Mozart and Haydn are thought to have first met at a private musical gathering in Vienna in 1783/84. In 1785, Haydn (Figure 23) wrote to Leopold Mozart that Wolfgang was 'the greatest composer known to me either in person or by name' (Wyn Jones, 2011, p. 50), and that same year, Wolfgang dedicated an edition of string quartets to Haydn. Yet, despite both composers enjoying widespread fame, their careers were very different.

Haydn was much older than Mozart and by the 1780s, had become the most celebrated musician of the time. While Haydn is unlikely to have heard Mozart's music before the latter moved to Vienna, Mozart would have known Haydn's music through his travels across Europe. Haydn worked at the Esterházy court and was only in Vienna for a few weeks every year, whereas Mozart was a freelance musician who responded to the circumstances of life in the Austrian capital (Wyn Jones, 2011, pp. 50–1).

Despite Haydn's huge popularity during his lifetime, his reputation suffered in the nineteenth century, with his music often being viewed as conservative and old-fashioned. While today, Haydn, along with Beethoven (1770–1827) and Mozart, is regarded as one of the greatest composers of the eighteenth century (he is known as the 'father of the symphony' due to his composition of at least 100 such works), it might be argued that his life and character (as the respectable 'Papa Haydn') has not captured the imagination as much as Mozart's, as we shall see in the next section.

6 The musical genius

Figure 24 Tom Hulce as Mozart in *Amadeus*, dir. Miloš Forman (Orion Pictures, 1984). Photo: SNAP/REX/Shutterstock.

It is not only Mozart's achievements as a musician that have continued to be of interest since his death in 1791. The character of a man destined from childhood to be one of the greatest musicians of all time has continued to fascinate music lovers worldwide. Over the last 200 years, the life – and death – of Mozart have inspired numerous biographical accounts in print, on stage and on screen, which attempt to portray aspects of his personality.

Yet, determining the nature of Mozart's character is a difficult task, and so these representations of the composer are often contradictory, shaped by different preconceptions of what a musical genius should be like. Despite the variances in Mozart biographies, they have all contributed to the composer's reputation since his death and how we might view him today.

Activity

(Allow around 20 minutes to complete this activity.)

You should now watch the video 'Exploring Mozart's genius', which presents several views of Mozart's character that have emerged since his death (indeed, your own views of Mozart may have been coloured by these accounts).

As you watch the video, make a note of the contrasting ways in which biographers have perceived Mozart's personality.

> You can find the video 'Exploring Mozart's genius' in Section 6 of the unit on the module website.

Discussion

The video outlines three accounts of Mozart's character, as shaped by different concepts of how a genius should behave. The first of these is the view of Mozart's genius as a gift from God, as was expressed by his own father in 1768. His effortless, spontaneous compositions were regarded as divinely inspired, while Mozart himself was deemed unworldly but lovable, and his music balanced and orderly.

The second view of his character is as a tragic genius inspired by dark other-worldly forces that drove him to his death. This was portrayed in Eduard Mörike's novel *Mozart's Journey to Prague* of 1855, in which the heroine expresses the fear that, like the title character in his opera *Don Giovanni*, Mozart would also be the cause of his own demise.

The third perception is of Mozart the eternal child, a vulgar, childish and disrespectful man who has no regard for social etiquette, as first expressed by Friedrich Schlichtegroll in his 1793 biography of the composer, who also claimed that Mozart's childish irresponsibility was the cause of his financial ruin.

We have now encountered three different views of Mozart's character – divinely inspired, demonic and childlike – all of which are shaped by notions of genius, which are removed from the social norm in some way.

So what was Mozart really like? Well, that is still difficult to say. Unlike the versions of his character portrayed in the video, we know that Mozart was not a genius detached from society, but was a gifted musician who engaged with his patrons and audience, taking great care in the works he prepared for them. We can now also establish that many of the events presented in *Amadeus* and other biographical narratives are inaccurate – Mozart's death and the commission of the Requiem (which have fuelled much of the public fascination with the composer) were not as mysterious as has been claimed: there was no foul play, Mozart simply died of heart failure. However, the exact nature of this extraordinary composer's character remains elusive.

7 Summary

Over the course of this chapter, you have examined the different factors that have contributed to Mozart's reputation as a great composer, both within his lifetime and since his death. You have considered both his natural talents as a performer and composer and the professional decisions made by Mozart and his father that helped to further his career.

Additionally, you have seen how Mozart responded to the circumstances in which he worked in order to achieve success, in his adoption of the musical genres, instruments and styles that would please his audience. By studying contrasting accounts of his character and life, you have also gained an understanding of how Mozart's reputation has been perpetuated and modified since his death.

While Mozart's achievements were certainly extraordinary, and his fame has endured possibly more than any other composer, the factors that you have encountered here – talent, professional decisions, audience engagement and personal characteristics – can be considered influential for the reputation of any musician.

Later in this module you will encounter other music that will allow you to consider the different circumstances that have influenced musicians' work since Mozart's time. By working through these later units, you will continue to develop the skills in close listening that you have established in this chapter and you will also learn about other concepts that can be applied to all kinds of music.

You should now return to the module website to continue your study of this unit.

References

Anderson, E. (1966) *The letters of Mozart and his family*. London: Macmillan.

Banat, G. (1990) 'Le Chevalier de Saint-Georges, man of music and gentleman-at-arms: the life and times of an eighteenth-century prodigy', *Black Music Research Journal*, 10(2), pp. 177–212.

Deutsch, O.E. (1966) *Mozart: a documentary biography*. London: A. & C. Black.

Eisen, C. (2001) 'Mozart, (Johann Georg) Leopold', in *Grove music online* (2011). DOI: 10.1093/gmo/9781561592630.article.6002278234 (Accessed: 21 October 2017).

Eisen, C. and Sadie, S. (2001) 'Mozart, (Johann Chrysostom) Wolfgang Amadeus', in *Grove music online* (2001). DOI: 10.1093/gmo/9781561592630.article.6002278233 (Accessed: 21 October 2017).

Halliwell, R. (1998) *The Mozart family: four lives in a social context*. Oxford: Clarendon Press.

Irving, J. (2007) 'Sonata', in Eisen, C. and Keefe, S.P. (eds) *The Cambridge Mozart encyclopedia*. Cambridge: Cambridge University Press, pp. 467–75.

Irving, J. (2017) *Mozart's piano concertos*. London: Routledge.

Keefe, S.P. (2011) 'The concertos in aesthetic and stylistic context', in Keefe, S.P. (ed.) *The Cambridge companion to Mozart*. Cambridge: Cambridge University Press, pp. 78–90.

Komlós, K. (2011) 'Mozart the performer', in Keefe, S.P. (ed.) *The Cambridge companion to Mozart*. Cambridge: Cambridge University Press, pp. 213–26.

Link, D. (2011) 'Mozart in Vienna', in Keefe, S.P. (ed.) *The Cambridge companion to Mozart*. Cambridge: Cambridge University Press, pp. 22–34.

Rieger, E. (2001) 'Mozart ['Nannerl'], Maria Anna', in *Grove music online* (2001). DOI: 10.1093/gmo/9781561592630.article.6002278231 (Accessed: 21 October 2017).

Robbins Landon, H.C. (ed.) (1990) *The Mozart compendium*. London: Thames and Hudson.

Schroeder, D. (2011) 'Mozart and late eighteenth-century aesthetics', in Keefe, S.P. (ed.) *The Cambridge companion to Mozart*. Cambridge: Cambridge University Press, pp. 48–58.

Wyn Jones, D. (2011) 'First among equals: Haydn and his fellow composers', in Clark, C. (ed.) *The Cambridge companion to Haydn*. Cambridge: Cambridge University Press, pp. 45–58.

Chapter 5
Mary Wollstonecraft

Alex Barber

Contents

1 Introduction

The people whose reputations you have studied so far are household names. This unit is about someone you may well not have heard of before: the philosopher Mary Wollstonecraft (1759–1797) (Figure 1).

Figure 1 John Opie, *Mary Wollstonecraft*, *c.*1797, oil on canvas, 77 × 64 cm. National Portrait Gallery, London, NPG 1237. © National Portrait Gallery, London.

She was neither a warrior queen nor the mother of a deity, and unlike Mozart's music her writings receive relatively little public exposure. She has been hugely influential, but hers is an influence of ideas rather than of name or personal story.

Wollstonecraft was a notorious figure in her lifetime, both for her views and for her determination to express them; but a scandal that followed her death meant she dropped from public attention almost immediately. This scandal affected both her personal reputation and the reputation of her philosophy. Her ideas, however, shape the social context in which we now live. This chapter attempts to reconnect those ideas to Wollstonecraft, and to a time when they (and she) were both ridiculed and condemned.

What were her ideas? A clue is in the fact that Wollstonecraft is sometimes described as the 'architect' or 'mother' of feminism. This label is potentially misleading, however. For one thing, the word 'feminism' only began to be used in its modern sense a century or so after her death. For another, 'feminism' means different things to different people. Finally, Wollstonecraft was living and writing in a world with different **social norms** to those prevailing today, and in a different intellectual landscape.

A more straightforward way of introducing Wollstonecraft's ideas is to recall a point made in the chapter on Elizabeth I.

Wollstonecraft contrasted with Elizabeth I

Elizabeth I portrayed herself as a warrior queen and saw herself as above other 'weak and feeble' women. Like many powerful women throughout history, she was concerned with safeguarding her own highly vulnerable position rather than improving the situation of women as a whole. Against John Knox's *The First Blast of the Trumpet Against the Monstrous Regiment of Women*, Elizabeth sought to establish herself as an exception and not as an advocate for women more generally (see Chapter 3).

This was not how Wollstonecraft responded to the Knoxes of her own time. Instead of pleading for her personal distinctiveness – distinctive though she certainly was – she decided to challenge their philosophical assumptions.

Wollstonecraft was not the first person to issue such a challenge, but she produced the first developed case against the prevailing notion that 'it is part of the order of nature that the woman obey the man' – these are the words of the Swiss philosopher Jean-Jacques Rousseau (1979 [1762], p. 407). She did so in 1792, in a book called *A Vindication of the Rights of Woman*, a full-blown defence of social equality between the sexes. One of the reputations we will be concerned with in this chapter, then, is that of an idea: social **equality**, and, in particular, equality between the sexes (though, as you will discover, Wollstonecraft saw parallels with other forms of social inequality and condemned it across the board). We will examine the idea of social equality through the prism of her book, its reception at the time, and the factors in her life that shaped her thinking.

To modern readers, *A Vindication of the Rights of Woman* is quite puzzling. Despite its forthright title, Wollstonecraft often comes across as a straightforward misogynist. At various points she says that, unlike typical men, typical women:

> … are 'ridiculous and useless when the short lived bloom of beauty is over'
>
> … resort to 'cunning' and 'random exertions of a sort of instinctive common sense, never brought to the test of reason'
>
> … 'hug their chains and fawn like the spaniel'
>
> … have a 'fondness for pleasure, which takes the place of ambition and those nobler passions that open and enlarge the soul'
>
> … 'seldom [do things] in an orderly manner'
>
> … 'do today what they did yesterday, merely because they did it yesterday'
>
> … are 'like the feathered race, [with] nothing to do but to plume themselves, and stalk with mock-majesty from perch to perch'
>
> … need to become 'more masculine and respectable'
>
> (Wollstonecraft, 2004 [1792], pp. 15–16, 32, 72, 105)

On the face of it, these descriptions of womankind do not signal support for women's rights at all. Spoken in a modern workplace, they would quite possibly contravene equal opportunities legislation. So, one of our tasks in this chapter will be to understand what Wollstonecraft intended when she wrote such things.

Alongside the reputation of her ideas we will also be looking at her own reputation. She was described during her lifetime as a 'hyena in petticoats' and a 'philosophising serpent' (Walpole, 1859 [1792/95]) and, as previously mentioned, a scandal destroyed her reputation after she died. This was a scandal that could only have affected a woman and we will look at it in more detail later in this chapter. Wollstonecraft was very aware that reputational demands for men and women differed. Indeed, she was one of the first to question this 'double standard' (as we would now put it) by highlighting what she saw as its negative impact on both men and women.

This chapter serves as an introduction to philosophy, and Wollstonecraft's book is a work of political philosophy. Like 'feminism', the word 'philosophy' is in common use but has different meanings in different contexts. In the next section I will suggest how you might usefully think of philosophy for the purposes of studying this module.

A monstrous connection?

You may have encountered Wollstonecraft's ideas, perhaps unwittingly, in a very different guise. Nearly 20 years after her death, the novel *Frankenstein* was published by a then anonymous author (Figure 2). The author, as you might know, was in fact Mary Shelley (1797–1851), who was the daughter of Wollstonecraft and William Godwin, also a political philosopher. The portrait of Wollstonecraft in Figure 1 was painted in the early months of Wollstonecraft's pregnancy.

There are many ways of thinking about Shelley's novel and it has invited many different readings. It charts the creation and experiences of a motherless being – the 'creature'. If we see Mary Shelley as identifying with this creature (Wollstonecraft died soon after giving birth to her), we might also see the novel as a creative engagement with some of her mother's views. Our focus in this chapter will be on those views themselves and so the novel is discussed only briefly in Section 6.

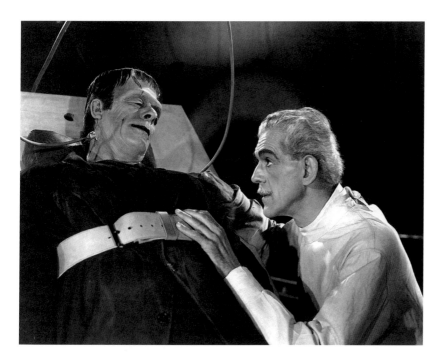

Figure 2 Boris Karloff in the role of Dr Gustav Niemann and Glenn Strange as Frankenstein's Monster in *The House of Frankenstein*, dir. Erle C. Kenton (Universal Studios, 1944). Photo: Moviestore Collection/REX/Shutterstock.

2 Doing philosophy

Philosophy can overlap with nearly any other discipline (including psychology and religious studies, for example), but it has a distinctive history and its own range of questions and methods. The simplest way to appreciate what is distinctive about philosophy is to start doing some, and that is the approach we will take in this module. In the later philosophy chapters in Books 2 and 3, you will look at a discussion of courage by the ancient Greek philosopher Plato, and at accounts of compassion by the German philosopher Schopenhauer. The present chapter is a gentle introduction to the subject via Wollstonecraft's political philosophy.

Doing philosophy will involve you in interpreting and evaluating arguments – and, where appropriate, developing arguments of your own. At the heart of this chapter, then, are Wollstonecraft's arguments, together with the arguments of those she is opposing (these are presented in Section 4).

First, we need to define what an argument is. In philosophy, an **argument** is a reason offered in favour of some claim or opinion. This claim or opinion – the thing being argued for – is called the argument's **conclusion**. The reason being offered in favour of the conclusion should give us grounds for believing it, i.e. for accepting that the conclusion is true. In other words, the argument should supply us with evidence in favour of the conclusion. If it does, then the argument is a good one; if it does not, then the argument is a bad one. As you progress through the module you will learn more about the elements of arguments in philosophy, and about how to tell the difference between good ones and bad ones, but what I have just said is enough for this chapter.

Activity

(Allow around 15 minutes to complete this activity.)

Here is an imaginary example of someone called William presenting an argument:

> *William:* 'I washed up the dishes last night, and all of last week. So tonight, you should do them.'

This is not a very philosophical example, but even here we can distinguish between the argument's conclusion and the reasons William is offering in support of that conclusion. Before reading on, try to answer the following questions:

1 What is the conclusion of the argument?
2 What reason is William offering in support of that conclusion?
3 Is William's argument a good one?

Discussion

1 The conclusion here is stated in the second sentence: the person William is talking to should do the dishes. (The word 'so' is the giveaway here. Conclusions are not always this easy to spot!)
2 The first sentence states William's reasons: recently, he has been doing all the washing up.
3 We cannot tell whether this argument is a good one without more information. For example, perhaps the person William is talking to does all the cooking or is in hospital; or perhaps William didn't really do the dishes all of last week.

One way of arguing for an opinion is to talk up the qualities of someone who holds it, and one way of arguing against that same opinion is to talk that person down. Most domestic disputes take this shape sooner or later ('You are such a moaner, William!'), but in philosophy that is seen as something to avoid. When we evaluate a philosophical position, it should not matter whose position it is; arguments for or against it should stand or fall on their own merits.

Socrates – a philosopher you will meet later in the module – was, by his own description, ugly and cantankerous, but this ought to be irrelevant to our assessment of his philosophy. The mistake of evaluating a piece of philosophy by appealing to irrelevant facts about its author even has a name: the *ad hominem* **fallacy**.

The *ad hominem* fallacy

A **fallacy** is a flawed way of reasoning. Fallacies were categorised quite thoroughly in the middle ages and many have kept their Latin names. *Ad hominem* means 'against the man'.

In philosophy, to commit the *ad hominem* fallacy is to base one's opinions not on the quality of arguments for or against a given view, but on irrelevant personal qualities of the philosopher whose view it is (their sex, for example, or the fact that they are or aren't famous, or that they do or don't seem clever or important, etc.).

Partly in order to avoid committing the *ad hominem* fallacy, most present-day philosophers tend not to concern themselves too much with the biographical details of other philosophers. The quality of the arguments themselves is what matters, and when it comes to accepting or rejecting those arguments the reputation of the philosopher – good or bad – is commonly set to one side. The argument is allowed to float free from its source. While this is the standard approach in philosophy, could it be too simplistic? At the end of Section 5, I will suggest that we may need to rethink the approach a little, particularly when considering Wollstonecraft's philosophy.

We will look at Wollstonecraft in more detail after I make one last point about arguments. In the previous activity, there was someone else in the discussion besides William: the person he was urging to do the dishes. This someone may well disagree with William's conclusion, and be unpersuaded by his reasoning. Philosophical arguments are like this too. For any philosopher arguing in favour of something, there is usually another philosopher arguing for the exact opposite. Wollstonecraft had plenty of opponents in mind when she wrote *A Vindication of the Rights of Woman*. Prominent among them was the most famous philosopher of her era, Jean-Jacques Rousseau (1712–1788). As you may recall from an earlier quote, he believed 'the order of nature' calls for 'the woman to obey the man' (Rousseau, 1979 [1762], p. 407). To understand the significance of Wollstonecraft's decision to criticise Rousseau, we need to know a little more about her life and the intellectual climate of her time.

3 Wollstonecraft's world before 1792: two families

Inequalities of power, wealth and status were still deeply entrenched in Britain at the time of Wollstonecraft's birth in 1759. Her paternal grandfather was part of the emerging manufacturing class, but her immediate family hovered precariously above the poverty surrounding them. Moreover, her father did not inherit the business acumen of his father but instead moved frequently, apparently fleeing bad debts. The young Mary was dragged from east London out to Essex, to Beverley in Yorkshire, then to London again before moving to Laugharne in Carmarthenshire, and then back to London. Her father seems also to have been a violent 'despot' within his family (Godwin, 1798, pp. 7–9).

Wollstonecraft was the second of six siblings to survive childhood. Her elder brother received an inheritance and so freedom from economic anxiety, whereas she spent all but the final years of her life worrying about money and the wellbeing of her younger siblings. When she was old enough she began to teach. (Teaching was one of the few forms of paid employment available to educated young women at the time, as you saw with Mozart's older sister, Nannerl, in the previous chapter.) For a while she was a personal tutor to the daughters of the Viscount Kingsborough in Mitchelstown in County Cork, Ireland. This acquainted her with aristocratic life. On the evidence before her, the hereditary privilege of this (as she saw it) talentless family was not only completely unjust, it damaged the supposed beneficiaries. She thought they led a vacuous life, especially the girls she was charged with educating.

Her negative views of the aristocracy were encouraged by a group of London-based radical thinkers. She had become acquainted with them while working in Newington Green, then a small village north-east of London. This village was coincidentally a kind of refuge for a number of **Dissenters**, a loose affiliation of Protestant Christians who rejected core doctrines of the established churches. Most also rejected existing social hierarchies, and worked hard to reduce or eliminate them. In effect, this group became Wollstonecraft's second family. Her first family remained a source of constant worry and negligible support, but this new one was part of a national network of reformists and helped her find work, supplied her with a loan to run a school in Newington Green, and pulled her thinking in a radical direction.

What did it mean to be a radical? During the eighteenth century, old ideas of authority in its various guises were being challenged in Europe as never before. The **Enlightenment**, a cultural period of around 1670–1800, pitched **radicals** against **conservatives** in many spheres of life. Here are two instances of radical challenges to conservative authority:

Religion – The moral and religious authority of established churches across Europe was called into question. The evidence of the Bible, as interpreted by those with a religious training, was being displaced by appeals to 'natural reason' and 'human sentiment' (roughly: thinking and feeling). These were supposedly possessed by everyone, not just the select few.

Knowledge – The new 'experimental method' (i.e. science) offered a more secure route to knowledge of the physical world than earlier approaches, which tended to be rooted in the authority of tradition and abstract speculation.

The most serious challenge of all was to traditional forms of political authority – or, as Wollstonecraft puts it in her book, to the arbitrary power of tyrants. This phrasing was popular among radical reformists of the time. 'Arbitrary' power meant unjustified political authority, i.e. power rooted in force ('tyranny') rather than reason. Wollstonecraft would have classed Cleopatra and Elizabeth I, for example, as tyrants rather than as great leaders.

Radicals vs conservatives

Much of the debate between radicals (or 'reformists') and conservatives took place in printed pamphlets and monthly journals. These were often polemical in style – that is, they did not pretend to take a neutral stance.

Wollstonecraft kept herself afloat financially by working for the *Analytical Review*, a prominent radical journal. Figure 3 shows a supportive review of her book.

Opposing it were publications such as the *Anti-Jacobin Review and Magazine*. Figure 4 shows three stanzas (XV to XVIII) of a venomous poem about Wollstonecraft published after she had died. The last two lines of XV give the flavour (phrases in square brackets are added to aid interpretation):

> For Mary verily [i.e. truly] would wear the breeches [roughly: trousers]—
> God help poor silly men from such usurping b[itche]—s.

The rest of the poem will make more sense once you have read about the later period in her life in Section 6. The 'William' referred to in the poem was her husband, William Godwin (Mary Shelley's father). You can look more closely at Figures 3 and 4 in the online gallery on the module website.

Many views that were radical in the 1790s are now commonplace, even among present-day conservatives. No one seriously argues today that the vote should be limited to a few wealthy male landowners, for example. Conversely, explicit racism was normal among white people in the eighteenth century, even in Enlightenment circles, but is now widely seen as shameful and regressive.

APPENDIX

TO THE

THIRTEENTH VOLUME

OF THE

ANALYTICAL REVIEW.

ART. I. Wollſtonecraft's *Vindication of the Rights of Woman*.
[*Concluded from Vol. XII. p.* 249.]

IN her fifth chapter our author notices thoſe writers, who have endeavoured to render women objects of pity bordering on contempt. In this bold train Rouſſeau leads the van. His poſition, ' that women ought to be ' weak and paſſive,' is very nobly controverted by Mrs. W. His reflections, ſhe moſt judiciouſly obſerves, were made in a country where the art of pleaſing was moulded into a moſt pernicious vice. With reſpect to his opinion that ' the life of a modeſt woman is a perpetual conflict;' ſhe anſwers, that this very ſyſtem of education, which ſhe is decrying, makes it ſo. Modeſty, temperance, and ſelf-denial, are the ſober offſpring of reaſon; but when ſenſibility is nurtured at the expence of the underſtanding, ſuch weak beings muſt be ſubjected to perpetual conflicts. With reſpect to the tractableneſs which he ſays reſults from the habit of ſubjection, our author eloquently remarks: p. 184.

' The being who patiently endures injuſtice, and ſilently bears inſults, will ſoon become unjuſt, or unable to diſcern right from wrong. Beſides, I deny the fact, this is not the true way to form or meliorate the temper; for, as a ſex, men have better tempers than women, becauſe they are occupied by purſuits that intereſt the head as well as the heart; and the ſteadineſs of the head gives a healthy temperature to the heart. People of ſenſibility have ſeldom good tempers. The formation of the temper is the cool work of reaſon, when, as life advances, ſhe mixes with happy art, jarring elements. I never knew a weak or ignorant perſon who had a good temper, though that conſtitutional good humour, and that docility, which fear ſtamps on the behaviour, often obtain the name. I ſay behaviour, for genuine meekneſs never reached the heart or mind, unleſs as the effect of reflection; and that ſimple reſtraint produces a number of peccant humours in domeſtic life, many ſenſible men will allow, who find ſome of theſe gentle irritable creatures, very troubleſome companions.'

P. 185. ' Of what materials can that heart be compoſed, which can melt when inſulted, and inſtead of revolting at injuſtice, kiſs the

APP. Vol. XIII.   L l   rod!

XIII.

His coat was divers colours, red, white, blue,
And he was riding on a filthy ſwine,
And oft would ope his beaſtly mouth to ſpue,
In that ſame cup, from whence he drank his wine.
Behind him ſat a luſty concubine,
Whom ſtill he kiſs'd with wine-diſtained lip:
Painted ſhe was, and deckt in taudry fine,
Her eye well ſkill'd the wanton wink to tip,
And hand from doting men their gold away to ſlip

XIV.

Next came that curſed ſelon Thomas Paine,
Mounted upon a tiger fierce and fell;
And ſtill a ſhower of blood on him doth rain,
With tears that from the eyes of widow's well;
Loud in his ears the cries of orphans yell;
The axe impending o'er his head alway,
While devils wait to catch his ſoul to hell,
The knave is fill'd with anguiſh and diſmay—
And anxious round he looks, even ſtraws do him affray.

XV.

Then ſaw I mounted on a braying aſs,
William and Mary, ſooth, a couple jolly;
Who married, note ye how it came to paſs,
Although each held that marriage was but folly?—
And ſhe of curſes would diſcharge a volley
If the aſs ſtumbled, leaping pales or ditches:
Her huſband, ſans-culottes, was melancholy,
For Mary verily would wear the breeches—
God help poor ſilly men from ſuch uſurping b———s.

XVI.

Whilom this dame the Rights of Women writ,
That is the title to her book ſhe places,
Exhorting baſhful womankind to quit
All fooliſh modeſty, and coy grimaces;
And name their backſides as it were their faces;
Such licence looſe-tongued liberty adores,
Which adds to female ſpeech exceeding graces;
Lucky the maid that on her volume pores,
A ſcripture, archly fram'd, for propagating w———s.

XVII.

William hath penn'd a waggon-load of ſtuff,
And Mary's life at laſt he needs muſt write,
Thinking her whoredoms were not known enough,
Till fairly printed off in black and white.—
With wondrous glee and pride, this ſimple wight
Her brothel feats of wantonneſs ſets down,
Being her ſpouſe, he tells, with huge delight,
How oft ſhe cuckolded the ſilly clown,
And lent, O lovely piece! herſelf to half the town.

XVIII. Then

Figure 3 (left) *The Analytical Review*, appendix (page 481), vol. 13, issue 4, London, 1792. British Library, London, shelfmark GRC 267.h.10-29. Vol.1-v.20. Photo: © British Library Board/Bridgeman Images.

Figure 4 (right) John Gifford (ed.) *The Anti-Jacobin Review and Magazine*, page 518, vol. 9, issue 38, London, J. Whittle and C. Chapple, 1801. British Library, London, GRC P.P.3596. Photo: © British Library Board/Bridgeman Images.

Appeals to reason over mere tradition were a pervasive feature of Enlightenment debates. This period is sometimes even referred to as the Age of Reason. The so-called 'tyrants' denied that their political authority was 'arbitrary', i.e. unreasonable and unjustified. The most prevalent justification of existing hierarchies – the justification Wollstonecraft and other radicals sought to refute – turned on an assumption of 'natural superiority'. According to this justification, power should lie in the hands of those who were naturally suited to wielding it justly and effectively, since this would be to everyone's benefit. The existing social order ensured this and therefore had to be maintained at all costs. The naturally inferior segments of society should have no political influence beyond supporting and obeying the decisions of their natural betters.

A diverse range of social hierarchies rested on just this kind of justification. The natural superiority of a particular class (the hereditary aristocracy), a particular racial group (white North Europeans) and a particular sex (males), were widely taken for granted. To question this natural superiority too vigorously was therefore to challenge the social order. This was regarded as sedition (i.e. incitement to rebellion), a serious criminal offence at the time. According to conservatives, the radical thinking of Wollstonecraft and her associates, if left unchecked, would cause social collapse – a catastrophe for everyone, not just for the ruling authorities.

Activity

(Allow around 15 minutes to complete this activity.)

The conservatives of Wollstonecraft's time defended traditional forms of authority with philosophical arguments. One such argument was sketched in the two paragraphs you have just read. Let's call it the natural superiority argument.

As you did with the dishwashing argument in the first activity, look back over the preceding two paragraphs and try to identify:

1   The conclusion of the natural superiority argument.

2   The reason offered in favour of this conclusion by those who deploy this argument.

Discussion

1 The conclusion is that the existing social order should be preserved at all costs.

2 The reason offered is that the existing social order benefits everyone, because it keeps political power out of the hands of those not naturally able to make the best decisions.

Today, talk of 'betters' has a slightly comical, old-fashioned feel to it. Phrases such as 'not for the likes of us' are used in jest or ironically. Occasionally, a public figure's hidden snobbery or covert racism is unveiled, and they are scorned. We now live in an egalitarian age, an age that is committed, in theory at least, to social equality (in some loose sense of the term). But how did we get here? By looking at the origins of an idea, especially a political one, we are exposed to the basic arguments for and against it. Exposure to this early history can take us by surprise, and can refresh a topic that may otherwise seem stale and overfamiliar. Examining disputes about equality in the late eighteenth century helps us to understand our own social world as much as it helps us to understand Wollstonecraft's.

As Wollstonecraft began reading the radical thinkers of her era, she came to admire one philosopher in particular: Jean-Jacques Rousseau. His writing on equality and liberty was revolutionary – literally so, in that it helped inspire both the American Revolution of 1775–81 and the French Revolution of 1789–99. This famous opening of his *On the social contract* (*Du contrat social, ou principes du droit politique*, 1762) indicates why:

> Man is born free and everywhere he is in chains. He who believes himself the master of others is no less enslaved than they.
>
> (Rousseau, 1762, p. 3; my translation)

The first sentence here is the best known, but the second captures the sentiment behind Wollstonecraft's contemptuous pity for her aristocratic employers in Ireland: the tyrant is harmed by tyranny too (though not in the same way as the tyrannised are). Dignity and happiness come from the exercise of virtue and reason, not from the rotten fruits of brutish force.

Wollstonecraft belonged to a later generation of writers and thinkers than Rousseau, but they were essentially on the same side politically. So, it was painful for her to discover him defending a hierarchical power relationship in which women were subordinate to men. In his book *Émile, or On Education (Émile, ou De l'éducation)* published later in the same year as his *On the social contract*, Rousseau explains how to educate an ideal citizen, one capable of surviving the corruptions of the real world. Over the first four chapters he addresses an imaginary boy, the 'Émile' of the title. When Wollstonecraft came to read these chapters, she was, by and large, highly sympathetic towards them. (They include claims about religion that led to Rousseau's exile from France. He spent a while in Britain, where the portrait in Figure 5 was painted.) But *Émile* goes horribly wrong for Wollstonecraft in its fifth and final chapter. This is where Rousseau addresses a girl, Sophie, who is Émile's imaginary wife-to-be.

Instead of seeing the power relationship between men and women as yet another example of the tyranny he was so critical of in other contexts, Rousseau reproduced the very views of women that, according to Wollstonecraft, propped up the 'male aristocracy' (2004 [1792], p. 111). Émile is raised to be obedient, first and foremost, to himself (or rather, to his own reason and **sentiments**). Sophie, on the other hand, is advised to be obedient to Émile.

Rousseau justifies this difference in advice by offering what I earlier called a **natural superiority argument**: 'In becoming your husband, Émile has become the head of house. It is for you to obey, just as nature wanted it', he tells Sophie (1979 [1762], p. 478). In 'fulfilling nature's ends', men 'ought to be active and strong' and women 'passive and weak'. He concludes that a 'woman is made to please and to be subjugated' and so 'ought to make herself agreeable to man' (1979 [1762], p. 358).

Wollstonecraft read *Émile* while she was in Ireland in 1787, and these sentences must have struck her as deeply hypocritical. She certainly found him to be 'inconsistent' (Todd, 2003, pp. 114–15). In all other contexts, Rousseau and other radicals rejected assertions of natural superiority as empty and self-serving. Earlier in *Émile*, Rousseau had written of an 'indestructible' natural equality among men (Rousseau, 1979 [1762], p. 236). In *A Vindication of the Rights of Woman*

Wollstonecraft set out to highlight Rousseau's inconsistency. If she was worried that in doing so she would come across as unnatural to those who thought she, as a woman, was 'made to please', she did not show it. Not publicly at least (Figure 6). But in a letter to one of her sisters announcing that she was going to be 'the first of a new genus', i.e. a female professional writer, she immediately added 'I tremble at the attempt' (Todd, 2003, p. 139).

Figure 5 (left) Allan Ramsay, *Jean-Jacques Rousseau*, 1766, oil on canvas, 75 × 65 cm. Scottish National Gallery, Edinburgh. Photo: © National Galleries of Scotland/Bridgeman Images.
Figure 6 (right) John Opie, *Mary Wollstonecraft*, c.1790–91, oil on canvas, 76 × 64 cm. Tate collection, N01167, purchased 1884. © Tate, London 2018.

Figure 7 James Gillray, *Promis'd Horrors of the French Invasion […]*, 1796, coloured engraving. Published by Hannah Humphrey, London. New College, Cambridge. Photo: © and courtesy of the Warden and Scholars of New College, Oxford/Bridgeman Images.

James Gillray's satirical cartoons provided a running commentary of political events of the time. This one imagines the 'Reign of Terror' (*c.*1793–94), the most violent period in the French Revolution, being exported to London. While humorous in tone, the genuine horror of the Terror was cited relentlessly by conservatives against their radical critics. In the centre is the conservative prime minister, William Pitt the Younger, being thrashed by the more reformist MP, Charles James Fox. French revolutionary forces are marching down St James's Street in London between two gentlemen's clubs (White's and Brooks's, both still in existence). Various other recognisable political figures can be seen among the butchery, including the Prince of Wales falling head-first from a balcony.

Figure 7 captures British anxieties about the French Revolution
of 1789. The Revolution exacerbated the antagonism between radicals
and conservatives in other parts of Europe, including Britain. People
either hoped or feared that revolutionary fervour would spread across
the English Channel. Wollstonecraft jumped into this debate in 1790
with her first political publication, a widely read pamphlet called *A
Vindication of the Rights of Men* [underlining is mine, for emphasis]. In
this pamphlet she defended the ideals of the French Revolution against
criticism by a leading Irish and English conservative philosopher and
politician, Edmund Burke (*c*.1729–1797). He is the one being tossed
into the air by an ox in Figure 7.

Her choice of title, with its reference to the rights of 'men', must have
been grating for Wollstonecraft. She was simply following a phrasing
that was commonly used by her fellow radicals, who tended to treat
the rights of women as an afterthought, a joke, or something to ignore
entirely. When her publisher suggested she write a follow-up book to
build on her new-found fame, it was obvious what her title should be.
A Vindication of the Rights of Woman was published in 1792, shortly
after the ongoing revolution in France had brought down the
aristocratic regime.

In the following section, you will be introduced to
Wollstonecraft's and Rousseau's philosophical arguments in their
own words. You should expect to find this part of the chapter a
little slower going than the rest – especially the reading activities.
If you find yourself not understanding something, try reading it
through again more carefully. If that doesn't work, just read on.
You may find that things fall into place anyway.

4 Wollstonecraft's central argument

Wollstonecraft's publisher gave her just a few months to complete *A Vindication of the Rights of Woman* (which I will shorten to *Vindication* from now on). She met this tight deadline but, as she herself soon realised, the rush showed. The book contains repetitions, detours into side issues and a rambling structure. She planned to follow it up with a more polished statement of her position, but her early death in 1797 prevented this. That said, she had been thinking about the topic since her adolescence, and it is easy enough to identify the central and highly original thesis in the book's often vivid passages.

In this section, I will introduce you to the main argument of her book. It was a striking argument at the time and is still provocative today. As you will appreciate from the two previous activities, understanding Wollstonecraft's argument means identifying her conclusion, then identifying the reason or reasons she offers in defence of that conclusion.

The conclusion she defends is that women are not naturally inferior to men. Or to be more precise, her conclusion is that although men have on average greater natural physical strength than women (Wollstonecraft accepted this, even if she thought it was deliberately exaggerated), they were not naturally superior in their **character**. By a person's 'character' she meant their habits, their capacity to reason, their inclinations, their degree of determination, and so on. Wollstonecraft wished to show that, physical strength aside, men's natural superiority over women was every bit as illusory as the natural superiority of aristocrats over the wider populace. The authority of men – their stranglehold on positions of power, and the rights husbands had over their wives – was therefore every bit as illegitimate as aristocratic power.

> ## 'Character' and 'natural'
>
> '**Character**' means something like personality: an individual's
> habits, inclinations, mental abilities and determination, and so forth.
> It was common in Wollstonecraft's time to assume that people from
> different social strata, or different races, or even different nations,
> had naturally different characters. Wollstonecraft questioned an
> equally widespread assumption: that there is a natural 'male
> character' and a natural 'female character'.
>
> '**Natural**' is a slippery word. Rousseau and Wollstonecraft use it in
> relation to character. For them, a natural character trait is one that
> is somehow inborn and inevitable, or at least hard to eradicate.
> There is also a suggestion, in Rousseau's writing at least, that if a
> character trait is natural it is benign, i.e. not something one should
> even want to eradicate.

Before coming to the reasons Wollstonecraft offered in favour of her
conclusion, it is time to confront the puzzle I raised in the
Introduction: her negative descriptions of women. To a modern reader,
these descriptions seem indistinguishable from those of the authors she
was criticising. One of those authors was Rousseau, and in the
activities that follow I will ask you to read both philosophers so you
can appreciate how much they differ beneath this surface similarity.
You will once again find Wollstonecraft describing women's characters
in an extremely negative way. Unlike men, she says, women are
superficial: they are concerned with beauty and with pleasing others
rather than with knowledge and understanding. Where she parts
company from Rousseau is in rejecting his explanation for this
difference in character. Rousseau thought women's character was
'natural' to them, Wollstonecraft argued that it was not.

You may find Rousseau's thought a familiar one. It is common even
today to hear people – including parents – insist that 'boys and girls
are just different'. Perhaps this is something that riles you when you
hear it, or perhaps you think it is basically right. Either way, Rousseau's
claims will not seem entirely alien when you read them in the next
activity.

Activity

(Allow around 30 minutes to complete this activity.)

Reading 5.1 consists of passages from Chapter 5 of *Émile*. (What you will actually be reading is a translation of Rousseau's words being quoted by Wollstonecraft.) In his writing, Rousseau makes various claims about young girls and boys and their differing natures. Read them through and then answer the following questions:

1   According to Rousseau, what character traits do girls have that boys lack?

2   What evidence does Rousseau offer for the naturalness of these traits?

3   What does he conclude about the education of young girls?

Discussion

1   Girls have more of a concern for personal appearance in the eyes of others (the 'art of pleasing'); boys prefer noise and physical activity.

2   Girls choose toys such as mirrors (so they can see how they appear) and dolls (so they can practise dressing), and are reluctant to read and write. These preferences, he implies, indicate that they are destined to care about pleasing others and appearing attractive. A deeper understanding of the world can be left to others.

3   Rousseau concludes that girls should simply be steered towards their true nature, not coerced into acting against it. They should be shown how to sew clothing, for example, and not be forced to read and write.

Because Rousseau sees women's character (e.g. their inclination towards pleasing others and caring a great deal about personal appearance) as natural, he does not see it as flawed and in need of correction. Women's and men's natures are different, he thinks, but these different natures complement one another perfectly. Men's natural character is to be strong and rational, and this fits them out to take decisions on behalf of both; women's natural character is to be weak and submissive, and this fits them out to serve and obey men. Sophie needs to learn to obey Émile in matters of religion and to be sexually alluring. She should be educated only well enough to allow her to be interesting in conversation to her future husband and to provide him with emotional support.

Wollstonecraft agrees with Rousseau in upholding that women's characters are tailored to making them submissive (or 'servile' as she puts it), but she disagrees with him in two crucial respects. First, unlike Rousseau, Wollstonecraft regards women's subservient characters as deeply flawed. Second, she denies that women's characters are a product of nature and hence incapable of being any other way. We will now look at these two points of disagreement in turn.

A theme in Wollstonecraft's negative descriptions of the women of her time is what she saw as their lack of reason. This is why her tone is so harsh: in the 'Age of Reason', reasonableness was prized above nearly every other character trait. The easiest way to appreciate what Wollstonecraft and her contemporaries actually meant by reasonableness is to look at its opposite: unreasonableness. Among other things, an unreasonable person is driven entirely by emotion, lacks purpose, changes their mind easily, is disorderly, needs others to make decisions on their behalf, has a concern for how things appear rather than with how they truly are, and lacks the curiosity needed for an education. According to Wollstonecraft, these negative traits all formed part of the character make-up of a typical woman in the late eighteenth century.

Activity

(Allow around 30 minutes to complete this activity.)

Reading 5.2 consists of a selection of passages from Wollstonecraft's *Vindication* (2004 [1792]) that bring out her low opinion of women's character at the time. You will recognise some passages from the ones listed earlier in this chapter.

Read the passages through once, focusing on answering the questions below. You don't need to understand every aspect of what Wollstonecraft is saying. Grasping the basic point without being sidetracked by details is an important reading skill.

1   What do you think Wollstonecraft means when she talks of the 'sovereignty of beauty' (see the second paragraph of the reading)?

2   As mentioned previously, one way to understand what is meant by 'reason' is to consider its opposites. Which unreasonable negative

character traits is Wollstonecraft highlighting in the third paragraph of the reading?

3   Why is Wollstonecraft so critical of women's (supposed) fear of mice and other 'trifling dangers' in the final two paragraphs of the reading?

Discussion

1   Making the achievement of personal beauty the guiding principle of life; achieving influence via men's approval of ('homage to') their womanly beauty.

2   Inconstancy and unstable behaviour due to excessive feelings and emotions.

3   These exaggerated fears have the effect of making the woman both vulnerable and attractive to men; men step in as protectors, putting women under an obligation to them; women are 'imbeciles' for degrading themselves in this way.

Wollstonecraft thinks the differences between men and women are real, pervasive and harmful to both men and women, but she rejects Rousseau's claim that they are a product of nature:

> Rousseau declares that a woman should [be] made a coquettish slave in order to render her a more alluring object of desire, a sweeter companion to man, whenever he chooses to relax himself. He carries the arguments, which he pretends to draw from the indications of nature, still further, and insinuates that truth and fortitude, the corner stones of all human virtue, shall be cultivated with certain restrictions, because with respect to the female character, obedience is the grand lesson which ought to be impressed with unrelenting rigour.
>
> What nonsense! When will a great man arise with sufficient strength of mind to puff away the fumes which pride and sensuality have thus spread over the subject!
>
> (Wollstonecraft, 2004 [1792], p. 36)

But, you may be asking yourself, what else could explain these supposedly widespread differences other than that they are natural differences, a set of inclinations tied to the sex one is born with?

Wollstonecraft's answer to that question is clever and revolutionary. She suggests that the very belief that differences in character between men and women are 'natural' explains why these differences persist. In other words, she says, there is a self-fulfilling element to these beliefs. If, for example, everyone thinks that girls are more naturally disposed than boys towards caring about their appearance and pleasing others, then girls will be supplied with dolls to dress, with needlework, and so on, while boys will be denied these things. (This, as you saw in Reading 5.1, is exactly what Rousseau proposes.) Unsurprisingly, children will respond to these cues and develop differently. The circle is complete when this difference in outcome is itself treated as evidence of a difference in nature:

> Girls' understanding is neglected, and [they are] forced to sit still, play with dolls, and listen to foolish conversations; the effect of habit *is insisted upon as an undoubted indication of nature.*

> (Wollstonecraft, 2004 [1792], p. 103 [italics added for emphasis])

According to Wollstonecraft, once we stop believing that these differences are natural, we will change the way we treat our children and the differences themselves will disappear.

Nature vs nurture: why does it matter?

This disagreement between Rousseau and Wollstonecraft may seem familiar. In modern terms, it is a disagreement over whether typical **gender** differences (i.e. femininity in women and masculinity in men) are primarily the product of a difference in natural inclination, or are instead more or less wholly nurtured.

Wollstonecraft was the first to give a robust statement and defence of a 'nurture' explanation. The disagreement matters: if women's nature means they are only capable of being cunning and of striving for personal beauty, etc., but never of achieving 'masculine' levels of reason and virtue, there would be no point in educating girls to be reasonable and virtuous. To do so would be like trying to teach a gazelle to play chess.

So far, we have seen two competing explanations of the supposed differences in character between men and women. Rousseau's explanation is that the differences are the product of nature. Wollstonecraft's explanation is that the differences are the product of widespread but false *beliefs about* nature. We have also seen Rousseau's main argument in favour of his preferred explanation: his observations of children. Wollstonecraft does not think Rousseau's observations prove anything, since it could just be that children react differently to different treatment. What we have yet to see is Wollstonecraft's positive argument in favour of her preferred explanation. What reason does she offer for thinking that social factors, not inborn natural differences, are the source of differences between men's and women's characters?

Her argument is simple enough: if Rousseau is right – if girls are indeed naturally inclined to develop into feeble and vain adults – then there would be no need for a system of forced femininity, one that coerces girls and women to behave a certain way. But there is such a system, she insists. She invites her reader to conclude that the differences in character between men and women are therefore not natural at all.

Activity

(Allow around 20 minutes to complete this activity.)

Reading 5.3 presents a further extract from Wollstonecraft's *Vindication* (2004 [1792], pp. 104–5, 109). In this extract, Wollstonecraft uses Rousseau's own words against him. She quotes passages from *Émile* in which he appears to be suggesting that girls and women need to be forced to adopt a feminine character, despite claiming elsewhere that this character is entirely natural to them.

Read the extract and look out for the following phrases (you may want to underline them as you read):

- 'subjected to restraint'
- 'constant and severe restraint'
- 'confinement'
- 'women have, or ought to have, but little liberty'
- 'formed to obey'.

In using phrases like these, Rousseau seems to be making Wollstonecraft's case for her – this, of course, is why she quotes them!

Now answer the following questions:

1   What does Wollstonecraft think Rousseau is revealing in these passages?

2   Would Rousseau have agreed with Wollstonecraft's interpretation of his choice of words, do you think? If not, what would he have said he really meant?

3   In quoting the final paragraph, what is Wollstonecraft implying about girls' speech?

Discussion

1   That girls and women do not have the natural inclinations Rousseau claims they do, since otherwise they would not need to be coerced.

2   He would almost certainly have disagreed. What he took himself to be saying in these passages is not entirely clear, but it is possible that he thought girls and women sometimes fail to recognise what their true nature requires, and so need some external encouragement.

3   That the speech of boys and girls, of men and women, differ because their behaviour is policed differently (e.g. by the different 'severe questions' in the final paragraph) and not because of a difference in their natures (2004 [1792], p. 109).

According to Wollstonecraft this system of forced femininity was maintained into adulthood. In her time, women were praised or condemned using standards that were never used for men, and vice versa. In particular, a character trait that would have been classified as a flaw in a man was regarded as a 'feminine **virtue**' and so commendable in a woman; and vice versa for the 'masculine virtues'. This difference in standards contributes, she said, to women's subordination and damages men in the process. One of the boldest proposals in her book was that the evaluation of a person's character should not be tied to the sex they were born with: 'Virtue has only one eternal standard' (2004 [1792], p. 37).

Activity

(Allow around 35 minutes to complete this activity.)

Reading 5.4 offers further extracts from Wollstonecraft's *Vindication* (2004 [1792], p. 109). In the passages, Wollstonecraft identifies various terms that are reserved for praising women rather than men, and suggests they have a hidden, sinister meaning.

As you read the passages, try to infer what Wollstonecraft believed to be the hidden negative meanings behind the following phrases when used as 'praise' for women.

1 Being soft, delicate, refined (first paragraph)
2 Being deserving of pity (first paragraph)
3 Being beautiful in physical appearance (second to fourth paragraphs)
4 Being gentle; being affectionate (fifth paragraph)
5 Being fearful (sixth paragraph)
6 Being innocent (seventh paragraph)

Discussion

1 Being weak
2 Being an object of contempt
3 Being an object for men's gratification
4 Being an amusing pet for men
5 Being cowardly
6 Being ignorant

In exposing what she sees as the hidden meaning of the terms conventionally used to praise women, Wollstonecraft claims to have exposed one of the primary mechanisms of women's repression. Women who strive after the so-called feminine virtues become men's servants, but women who refuse to do so will be 'hunted out of society as masculine' (2004 [1792], p. 46).

We have covered a lot of ground in this section, so you should not be alarmed if you found it slower going than the earlier sections in this chapter. The following quick summary should help you to understand the broad outline of what you have just read.

Summary of Wollstonecraft's central argument

Wollstonecraft's fellow radicals – her main readership – were familiar with natural superiority arguments, and knew how to respond to them. When she challenged the supposedly 'natural' hierarchy holding between men and women, Wollstonecraft was doing something that would have felt familiar to them.

She drew an analogy between the submissive state of those suffering under aristocratic rule and the subservient state of women. She argued that the natural superiority of male character was as much an illusion as the natural superiority of the aristocratic class.

This led her to disagree with Rousseau in two respects. She agreed with him that there were differences in character between men and women; but unlike him she thought, first, that these differences diminished and damaged women (and men in the process), and second, that the differences were not the product of nature but the product of attitudes such as Rousseau's own.

In Section 6 and in the study materials on the module website, I will mention some possible objections to Wollstonecraft's position. (You may already have reservations of your own. If so, note these down.) But first, let us see how her life changed after the publication of *Vindication*.

5 Wollstonecraft after 1792: fame, revolution, death, scandal, restoration

The publication of *Vindication* secured Wollstonecraft's place in the minds of the educated public. Energised, though also fleeing an awkward infatuation with a married artist, she headed for Paris in late 1792, with the hope that she could help push the anti-aristocratic French Revolution towards recognition of women's rights and not just of men's. Soon after she arrived, however, the Revolution took a horrifying turn (see the box on 'The Terror'). Many of her political allies in Paris were caught and guillotined and the rest fled into exile.

'The Terror'

The Revolution in France had been somewhat violent from the very beginning (see Figure 8), but even its early supporters were stopped in their tracks by the Terror of 1793–94. This amounted to a purge of the more liberal wing of the Revolution ('the Girondists') by hardliners ('the Mountain'). Wollstonecraft herself later wrote an eyewitness account of the Revolution (Wollstonecraft, 1794).

Among the many victims were Olympe de Gouges (1748–1793) and Nicolas de Condorcet (1743–1794). Both had written brief discussions of women's position in society that may have directly or indirectly influenced *Vindication* (Gouges, 2016 [1791]; Condorcet, 2012 [1790]).

La Journeé memorable de Versailles le lundi 5 Octobre 1789 .

Dans cette émeute generale plusieurs Gardes du Corps ont été Maßacrés deux
dentre eux furent Decolés et leurs tetes portées en Triomphe par ce meme peuple
ami de la liberté Nationale

Figure 8 *La Journée memorable de Versailles le lundi 5 Octobre 1789*
['The memorable day: Versailles, Monday 5 October 1789'], produced
in 1789, coloured engraving. Bibliothèque Nationale, Paris.
Photo: © akg-images.

Foreign nationals – except for Americans – were declared enemies, but Wollstonecraft fell under the protection of her new lover, the American businessman Gilbert Imlay (1754–1828), whom she had met in Paris. She fell pregnant by him, but he turned out to be a rogue who disowned her and their child after returning to England and taking up with a younger woman. Wollstonecraft returned too and pretended to be 'Mrs Imlay', but he would not marry her (despite the humiliating begging evident in her letters to him). Ironically, Wollstonecraft was becoming increasingly critical of marriage, at least in the form it took at the time – wives were the legal property of their husbands and divorce was extremely difficult. She saw it as a kind of slavery (2004 [1792], p. 193). But penniless and with a baby, marriage was what she needed, and Imlay refused it. However, this did not stop him asking her to travel to Scandinavia to sort out some of his business interests, which she did, taking with her their newborn daughter, Fanny (Wollstonecraft, 1796).

After two failed suicide attempts, Wollstonecraft put thoughts of Imlay behind her and, with support from her Dissenter friends, began to write again. In 1796 she began a relationship with William Godwin (1756–1836), a prominent English political philosopher and a fellow radical. He too was a critic of marriage, but they married after she became pregnant again. It should have been a happy ending since they were both radical philosophers who advocated a relationship based on mutual respect, reason and friendship rather than romantic love and domination by the husband. Their letters to each other suggest they were not immune to domestic bickering matches (conducted using philosophical reasoning of the highest order), but they were also very affectionate. Their marriage, however, was cut tragically short in 1797 when Wollstonecraft died shortly after giving birth to a second daughter, Mary (who later became Mary Wollstonecraft Shelley, author of the novel *Frankenstein*).

Wollstonecraft's life and reputation had been defined by her womanhood. This is true in one obvious respect: her greatest work is about women and society. In addition, she struggled to achieve financial independence because of her family's preference for her older brother and because public life was essentially a male preserve. Moreover, she desperately sought the love and support of a male partner but was unable to achieve this until the very end of her life; her first political publication (the 1790 pamphlet) had been well received until its female authorship was revealed in the second edition, prompting the suggestion that her ideas were derivative; and she died aged just 38 after contracting an infection during childbirth.

This pattern of being defined by her womanhood continued even after her death. Here we come to the scandal I mentioned in the Introduction to this chapter. After she died, Wollstonecraft's husband, William Godwin, produced a kind of shrine to her in the form of a memoir of her life (Godwin, 1798). This memoir was extremely frank. He seems to have assumed that she, a product of the Enlightenment like him, would have wanted the full truth to be known. What he may not have anticipated, as a man, was the public's vehement reaction to the details of her life being revealed. These included her strong romantic attachment to a married man, her apparent proposal of a *menage à trois* with Imlay and his young lover, her first child being born out of wedlock, and her two subsequent suicide attempts. Wollstonecraft, for all her idealism, was pragmatic about her reputation as a woman, and had done her best to keep much of this hidden during her lifetime.

The ensuing scandal was devastating not only to her personal reputation but to the reputation of her philosophy. *Vindication* was attacked *ad hominem*, with the suggestion that if you accepted the suggestions in *Vindication* you would end up like its shamed author. You have already seen one vicious commentary: the poem in Figure 4. An earlier reviewer in the same journal had suggested that Godwin's memoir of Wollstonecraft was useful in showing 'what it is wise to avoid', and 'illustrates both the sentiments and conduct resulting from such principles as those of Mrs. Wollstonecraft' (Anonymous, 1798, p. 94). The entry for 'Prostitution' in the index for the 1798 volume of the journal contained nothing except 'see Mary Wollstonecraft'. People across the political spectrum spurned Godwin, and by implication condemned Wollstonecraft and her philosophy. The author of *Vindication*, a groundbreaking work that was widely discussed when it first came out, became unmentionable and then unmentioned. The assault on her reputation resulted in her book falling out of print for nearly half a century.

Even Godwin unwittingly damned her with the kind of empty praise Wollstonecraft had said was reserved just for women. In *Memoirs of the Author of 'A Vindication of the Rights of Woman'* (1798), he wrote that the 'strength of her mind lay in intuition. She was often right, by this means only, in matters of speculation'. Twisting the knife without apparently realising it, he condescendingly described the 'errors' in her philosophy as 'comparatively few'. He claimed her philosophy was the 'pure result of feeling and taste'; in 'the strict sense of the term', he suggested, 'she reasoned little'. Somehow she managed to divine the truth, not through force of intellect like him but through 'a kind of witchcraft' (1798, pp. 197–8). Godwin was doing exactly what Wollstonecraft had criticised philosophers for doing. As she had put it six years earlier, 'the portion of rationality granted to woman is, indeed, very scanty' (2004 [1792], p. 68).

Earlier in the chapter, I described a standard approach in philosophy, which is to discount biographical details as irrelevant. On this approach, facts about an author's life and reputation should have no bearing on the evaluation of their arguments. To think otherwise is to commit the *ad hominem* fallacy (see Section 2), but Wollstonecraft's experiences and her posthumous reputation call this approach into question. By paying attention to her life and reputation, her actual philosophy becomes more convincing. For example, the contents of Godwin's memoir of her life, and the hysterical reaction to it, constitute evidence in support of one of her main claims: that women were judged to a different standard than men, in a way that excluded them from rational public discourse.

Wollstonecraft's reputation as a thinker eventually recovered as the women's suffrage movement gained ground, first in North America and then in Europe. However, academic philosophers took longer to admit her into their fold and it was not until the late twentieth century that her work and ideas began to be counted as philosophy and taken seriously. *Vindication* is now recognised, even by those who do not agree with it, as making an enormously important contribution to debates that are still with us to this day.

6 The *Frankenstein* connection

In Section 4 of this chapter, I outlined Wollstonecraft's main argument without making any attempt to evaluate it. (In case you need a quick reminder of what she argued, remember that there is a summary in the box at the end of Section 4.) Yet, there is plenty one might say in response. You will explore two possible criticisms of Wollstonecraft's philosophy after completing this chapter. Another criticism can be found in the novel, *Frankenstein*, which contains one of the more intriguing responses to Wollstonecraft's ideas.

We need to be careful here, though, because Mary Shelley's multifaceted novel can be and has been understood in many different ways. As you read this section, keep in mind that what follows is just one possible interpretation. This is an important caveat: the criticism of Wollstonecraft's position that I extract from the novel is one that is worth raising in its own right. However, whether this is what Shelley really had in mind must be left as an open question.

Shelley's novel was first published in 1818. You may know the basic plot already, either from the book or from one of the many film adaptations (if not, the plot is summarised in the following box). Many interpreters see the novel as a criticism of Enlightenment overconfidence, and especially of the belief that science and reason alone can solve society's problems. Others have suggested that the novel is a metaphor for the enormity of creating life by giving birth.

Frankenstein: plot summary

A young Swiss scientist, Victor Frankenstein, creates life by combining parts of fresh corpses to make one body. On 'a dreary night in November' he infuses the spark of life into his creation, who is never given a name (1818, vol. I, p. 97). His life's project achieved, things go rapidly downhill for Victor. He perceives the creature as hideous and terrifying, and flees from it. The creature is rejected by the rest of society too. When Victor refuses to create a female companion for it, the creature responds by taking bloody revenge on its creator, killing various members of his beloved family, including his future bride, Elizabeth. The creature eventually flees to the frozen Arctic with Victor Frankenstein in desperate pursuit.

Some film adaptations follow this plot reasonably faithfully while others do not. Some, for example, use the name 'Frankenstein' for the creature rather than its creator. Notably, in the novel, we are given two very different perspectives on the same events: Victor's and the creature's.

Shelley wrote the novel when she was 19 and, growing up without her own mother, may well have identified with a creature that asks, 'Who was I? What was I? Whence did I come? What was my destination?' (1818, vol. II, p. 102). As we can see from her journals, Shelley was also reading her mother's work at the time she was writing *Frankenstein* (Feldman and Scott-Kilvert, 1987, p. 97). *Frankenstein* is a novel, not a philosophical work in the usual sense, but it nonetheless resonates with Wollstonecraft's (and Godwin's) radical sympathies, which Shelley largely shared. Here I will mention two apparent connections between *Frankenstein* and *Vindication*. From the second of these connections, we can extract what may have been an implicit criticism of Wollstonecraft's philosophical position.

The first connection has to do with the contrast between Victor's fiancée Elizabeth and his creation. Elizabeth Lavenza is represented by Shelley as the personification of the feminine ideal that Wollstonecraft described as a recipe for servility. Victor's mother describes her as 'the most beautiful child she had ever seen', with a 'gentle and affectionate disposition' (1818, vol. I, p. 45); here is Victor describing her as his childhood friend:

> Elizabeth Lavenza became my playfellow, and, as we grew older, my friend. She was docile and good tempered, yet gay and playful as a summer insect. Although she was lively and animated, her feelings were strong and deep, and her disposition uncommonly affectionate. No one could better enjoy liberty, yet no one could submit with more grace than she did to constraint and caprice. Her [...] hazel eyes, although as lively as a bird's, possessed an attractive softness. Her figure was light and airy; and, though capable of enduring great fatigue, she appeared the most fragile creature in the world. While I admired her understanding and fancy, I loved to tend on her, as I should on a favourite animal; and I never saw so much grace both of person and mind united to so little pretension. Every one adored Elizabeth.
>
> (Shelley, 1818, vol. I, pp. 46–7)

Later, when Victor is departing, '[t]ears gushed from the eyes of Elizabeth' (1818, vol. I, p. 67). In other words, Victor's fiancée embodies the 'feminine virtues' that, according to Wollstonecraft, imprisoned women in a 'gilt cage' (see Reading 5.4).

His creation, on the other hand, with which Shelley herself might well have identified, seems to embody Wollstonecraft's alternative ideal for womankind: rational, more masculine, and entirely devoid of feminine virtues. Instead of being exaggeratedly weak, the creature is gigantically strong. Neither soft nor beautiful, its 'monstrous' appearance provokes revulsion. Its reasoning ability surpasses that of any ordinary human. Instead of remaining sweetly innocent (i.e. ignorant), it obtains a brilliant education after finding and reading some great works of literature. It is brave, not a helpless coward. It incites fear, not pity. And at no point in the novel does anyone treat it as a pet.

The second apparent connection between Shelley's novel and her mother's philosophy has to do with *society's response* to the creature (and so, by implication, to Wollstonecraft's defeminised ideal for womankind). This reaction – of horror, fear, hostility and violence – is the novel's running theme. It is the same reaction any woman at the time could have expected were she to follow this advice from Wollstonecraft:

> [All who view women] with a philosophic[al] eye must [...] wish with me, that they may every day grow more and more masculine.
>
> (Wollstonecraft, 2004 [1792], pp. 12–13)

Shelley gives us a sense of the reaction a 'more masculine' woman – a woman who does not pretend to be weak and helpless and who strives for more than servility and a pleasing appearance to men – could have expected from late eighteenth-century society:

> I had hardly placed my foot within the door, before the children shrieked, and one of the women fainted. The whole village was roused; some fled, some attacked me, until, grievously bruised by stones and many other kinds of missile weapons, I escaped to the open country, and fearfully took refuge in a low hovel.
>
> [...]
>
> Was I, then, a monster, a blot upon the earth, from which all men fled, and whom all men disowned? I cannot describe to you the agony that these reflections inflicted upon me.
>
> (Shelley, 1818, vol. II, pp. 42–3, 80)

This is the creature describing the effects of being hounded by a society that perceives it as 'hideous', 'deformed' and, above all, 'unnatural' (1818, vol II, pp. 101, 141, 111).

This brings us to the criticism of *Vindication* implicit in *Frankenstein* (assuming that we accept the parallels between the two). We can interpret Shelley as commenting on what she saw as the naivety of her mother's suggestion that women should forego beauty and all the other trappings of feminine servility. To follow this suggestion, Shelley seems to be saying, would be to invite the kind of horrific existence the creature experiences. 'Criticism' is perhaps the wrong word for what Shelley is offering here: it is really just a heartfelt dose of realism. It is one thing to know what is wrong with society and another to be able to fix it. As the daughter of Mary Wollstonecraft, Shelley might well have seen herself as a woman who had been encouraged to forego conventional femininity. Her description of the monstrous outcast (Figure 9) could well be seen as a comment on how costly (and pointless) it would have been to follow her mother's advice.

Figure 9 An example of what happens when you violate social norms? Boris Karloff in the role of 'The Monster' in *Bride of Frankenstein*, dir. James Whale (Universal Pictures, 1935). Photo: Universal/Kobal/REX/ Shutterstock.

This is a thought Wollstonecraft herself may have had some sympathy for, given her own experiences. Indeed, she made the same point in her sardonic observation that women 'were made to be loved, and must not aim at respect, lest they should be hunted out of society as masculine' (2004 [1792], p. 46). Even if she was right about the need for social change, demanding that women live according to her principles before that change had occurred was another matter. In one important respect women are like men: they too are only human.

7 Summary

Whether you agree with Wollstonecraft or not, it is astonishing how her arguments anticipate, and give a fresh perspective on, debates that are still alive today. She was the first person to produce a recognisably modern philosophy of gender. But this chapter has not just been about a particular philosopher and a particular philosophical topic, it has also been an introduction to philosophy. Here are three features of the subject you may have spotted yourself in your first encounter with the subject in this module:

- A philosopher's ideas are often shaped by their historical context, but this does not necessarily prevent their philosophy from having present-day significance. Sometimes the original context can be set aside and a philosophical argument considered on its own merits.

- You may have noticed that extracting an argument from a philosophical text is not always easy. This is certainly true when the author uses archaic modes of expression. In addition, philosophers are often engaged in a kind of conversation or debate (Wollstonecraft was responding to Rousseau, for example). To appreciate a philosopher's viewpoint, you often need to figure out what viewpoint they are criticising.

- I hope you have begun to appreciate that a philosophical position can seem persuasive one minute and far more questionable the next. Doing philosophy often involves having the rug pulled out from under your feet by someone presenting a counterargument you hadn't thought of before. You can look forward to experiencing this again in the online portion of the unit, and when you examine Plato's discussion of courage later in the module.

Our engagement with the theme of reputations has been a little different than in other chapters. One explanation for this is that philosophy, by its nature, tries to steer away from personal reputations and to focus instead on the quality of arguments. Yet, by looking at Wollstonecraft and her philosophy we have nonetheless made a number of discoveries about reputations. One is that it can be interesting and illuminating to look at the historical reputation of an idea (gender equality, for example). Another is that it is possible in practice to undermine someone's philosophical contribution (such as Wollstonecraft's) simply by savaging their personal reputation.

Moreover, if Wollstonecraft was right, women were especially vulnerable in this regard. According to her, women were judged to a different standard than men, and the standard they were judged by was calculated to produce servility. She correctly predicted the destruction to her reputation that her refusal to endorse this standard would provoke.

One possible assessment of Wollstonecraft is that, for all her historical importance, she has nothing much to tell us now. You will now have an opportunity to consider what significance her philosophy has, if any, for inhabitants of the twenty-first century.

> You should now return to the module website to continue your study of this unit.

References

Anonymous (1798) 'Review of Godwin (1798)', *Anti-Jacobin Review and Magazine*, 1(1), pp. 94–102.

Condorcet, N. (2012 [1790]) 'On the emancipation of women', in Lukes, S. and Urbinati, N. (eds) *Condorcet: political writings*. Cambridge: Cambridge University Press, pp. 156–62.

Feldman, P.R. and Scott-Kilvert, D. (eds) (1987) *The journals of Mary Shelley, 1814–1844: vol. 1 1814–1822*. Oxford: Clarendon Press.

Godwin, W. (1798) *Memoirs of the author of 'A vindication of the rights of woman'* . London: Joseph Johnson. Reproduced (with original pagination) in Philp, M. (ed.) *Collected novels and memoirs of William Godwin, volume 1*. London: Routledge.

Gouges, O. (2016 [1791]) 'Declaration of the rights of woman and the female citizen', in Warman, C. (ed.) *Tolerance: the beacon of the enlightenment*. Translated by C. Warman. Cambridge: Open Book Publishers, pp. 49–51.

Rousseau, J.-J. (1762) *Du contrat social, ou principes du droit politique*. Amsterdam: Chez Marc Michel Rey.

Rousseau, J.-J. (1979 [1762]) *Émile: or on education*. Edited and translated by Allan Bloom. New York: Basic Books.

Shelley, M. (1818) *Frankenstein: or, the modern prometheus* (3 vols). London: Lackington, Hughes, Harding, Mavor, & Jones.

Todd, J. (ed.) (2003) *The collected letters of Mary Wollstonecraft*. New York: Columbia University Press.

Walpole, H. (1859 [1792/95]) 'Letter to Hannah More, Aug 21 1792' and 'Letter to Hannah More, Jan 24 1795', in Cunningham, P. (ed.) *The letters of Horace Walpole*, vol. 9. London: Richard Bentley.

Wollstonecraft, M. (1790) *A vindication of the rights of men*. London: Joseph Johnson.

Wollstonecraft, M. (1794) *An historical and moral view of the origin and progress of the French Revolution; and the effect it has produced in Europe*. London: Joseph Johnson.

Wollstonecraft, M. (1796) *Letters written during a short residence in Sweden, Norway, and Denmark*. London: Joseph Johnson.

Wollstonecraft, M. (2004 [1792]) *A vindication of the rights of woman*. Edited by Miriam Brody. London: Penguin.

Readings

Reading 5.1 Rousseau on boys' and girls' education

Source: These passages are from an early translation of Jean-Jacques Rousseau's *Émile, or on education* (originally published in French in 1762), as quoted in Wollstonecraft, M. (2004 [1792]) *A vindication of the rights of woman*. Edited by Miriam Brody. London: Penguin, pp. 102–3, 108–9.

Girls are from their earliest infancy fond of dress. Not content with being pretty, they are desirous of being thought so; we see, by all their little airs, that this thought engages their attention; and they are hardly capable of understanding what is said to them, before they are to be governed by talking to them of what people will think of their behaviour. The same motive, however, indiscreetly made use of with boys, has not the same effect: provided they are let pursue their amusements at pleasure, they care very little what people think of them.

[…]

Boys love sports of noise and activity; to beat the drum, to whip the top, and to drag about their little carts: girls, on the other hand, are fonder of things of show and ornament; such as mirrours, trinkets, and dolls: the doll is the peculiar amusement of the females; from whence we see their taste plainly adapted to their destination. The physical part of the art of pleasing lies in dress; and this is all which children are capacitated to cultivate of that art.

[…]

Here then we see a primary propensity firmly established, which you need only to pursue and regulate. The little creature will doubtless be very desirous to know how to dress up her doll, to make its sleeve-knots, its flounces, its head-dress, &c. […] Hence we have a good reason for the first lessons that are usually taught these young females: in which we do not appear to be setting them a task, but obliging them, by instructing them in what is immediately useful to themselves. And, in fact, almost all of them learn with reluctance to read and write;

but very readily apply themselves to the use of their needles. They imagine themselves already grown up, and think with pleasure that such qualifications will enable them to decorate themselves.

[...]

Beauty cannot be acquired by dress, and coquetry is an art not so early and speedily attained. While girls are yet young, however, they are in a capacity to study agreeable gesture, a pleasing modulation of voice, an easy carriage and behaviour; as well as to take the advantage of gracefully adapting their looks and attitudes to time, place and occasion. Their application, therefore, should not be solely confined to the arts of industry and the needle [...]

Reading 5.2 Wollstonecraft's low opinion of womankind

Source: Wollstonecraft, M. (2004 [1792]) *A vindication of the rights of woman*. Edited by Miriam Brody. London: Penguin, pp. 32, 72, 78–9, 80.

To do everything in an orderly manner, is a most important precept, which women [...] seldom attend to with that degree of exactness that men, who from their infancy are broken into method, observe. This negligent kind of guess-work [...] prevents [women from] generalizing matters of fact – so they do to-day, what they did yesterday, merely because they did it yesterday.

[...]

Pleasure is the business of a woman's life, according to the present modification of society, and while it continues to be so, little can be expected from such weak beings. Inheriting [...] the sovereignty of beauty, they have, to maintain their power, resigned the natural rights, which the exercise of reason might have procured them, and chosen rather to be short-lived queens than labour to attain the sober pleasures that arise from equality. Exalted by their inferiority (this sounds like a contradiction), they constantly demand homage as women [...]

[...]

[Because women's] understandings [are] neglected [...], [they] are blown about by every momentary gust of feeling. [...] All their thoughts turn on things calculated to excite emotion; and feeling, when they should reason, their conduct, is unstable, and their opinions are wavering – not the wavering produced by deliberation [...] but by contradictory emotions. By fits and starts they are warm in many pursuits; yet this warmth, never concentrated into perseverance, soon exhausts itself. [...] The passions thus pampered, whilst the judgment is left unformed, what can be expected to ensue? – Undoubtedly, a mixture of madness and folly!

[...]

It would be an endless task to trace the variety of meannesses, cares, and sorrows, into which women are plunged by the prevailing opinion, that they were created rather to feel than reason, and that all the power they obtain, must be obtained by their charms and weakness [...]

Fragile in every sense of the word, they are obliged to look up to man for every comfort. In the most trifling dangers they cling to their support, with parasitical tenacity, piteously demanding succour; and their *natural* protector extends his arm, or lifts up his voice, to guard the lovely trembler – from what? Perhaps the frown of an old cow, or the jump of a mouse; a rat, would be a serious danger. In the name of reason, and even common sense, what can save such beings from contempt; even though they be soft and fair?

These fears, when not affected, may produce some pretty attitudes; but they shew a degree of imbecility which degrades a rational creature in a way women are not aware of [...]

Reading 5.3 Rousseau on coercing girls and women

Source: These passages are from an early translation of Jean-Jacques Rousseau's *Émile, or on education* (originally published in French in 1762), as quoted in Wollstonecraft, M. (2004 [1792]) *A vindication of the rights of woman*. Edited by Miriam Brody. London: Penguin, pp. 104–5, 109.

Girls ought to be [...] early subjected to restraint. This misfortune, if it really be one, is inseparable from their sex; nor do they ever throw it off but to suffer more cruel evils. They must be subject, all their lives, to the most constant and severe restraint, which is that of decorum: it is, therefore, necessary to accustom them early to such confinement, that it may not afterward cost them too dear; and to the suppression of their caprices, that they may the more readily submit to the will of others. If, indeed, they are fond of being always at work, they should be sometimes compelled to lay it aside.

[...]

For the same reason [...] women have, or ought to have, but little liberty; they are apt to indulge themselves excessively in what is allowed them. Addicted in every thing to extremes, they are even more transported at their diversions than boys.

[...]

There results [...] from this habitual restraint a tractableness which women have occasion for during their whole lives, as they constantly remain either under subjection to the men, or to the opinions of mankind; and are never permitted to set themselves above those opinions. The first and most important qualification in a woman is good-nature or sweetness of temper: formed to obey a being so imperfect as man, often full of vices, and always full of faults, she ought to learn betimes even to suffer injustice, and to bear the insults of a husband without complaint; it is not for his sake, but her own, that she should be of a mild disposition.

[...]

The tongues of women are very voluble; they speak earlier, more readily, and more agreeably, than the men; they are accused also of speaking much more: but so it ought to be [...] A man speaks of what he knows, a woman of what pleases her; the one requires knowledge, the other taste; the principal object of a man's discourse should be what is useful, that of a woman's what is agreeable. [...]

We ought not, therefore, to restrain the prattle of girls, in the same manner as we should that of boys, with that severe question; *To what purpose are you talking?* but by another, which is no less difficult to answer, *How will your discourse be received?*

Reading 5.4 Wollstonecraft on praise for women

Source: Wollstonecraft, M. (2004 [1792]) *A Vindication of the Rights of Woman*. Edited by Miriam Brody. London: Penguin, pp. 13–14, 29, 45, 59, 62, 80–1.

My own sex, I hope, will excuse me, if I treat them like rational creatures, instead of flattering their *fascinating* graces, and viewing them as if they were in a state of perpetual childhood, unable to stand alone. I earnestly wish to point out in what true dignity and human happiness consists – I wish to persuade women to endeavour to acquire strength, both of mind and body, and to convince them that the soft phrases, susceptibility of heart, delicacy of sentiment, and refinement of taste, are almost synonymous with epithets of weakness, and that those beings who are only the objects of pity [...] will soon become objects of contempt.

[...]

Women are told from their infancy, and taught by the example of their mothers, that [...] should they be beautiful, every thing else is needless, for, at least, twenty years of their lives.

[...]

Taught from their infancy that beauty is woman's sceptre, the mind shapes itself to the body, and, roaming round its gilt cage, only seeks to adorn its prison.

[...]

[A] pretty woman, as an object of desire, is generally allowed to be so by men of all descriptions; whilst a fine woman, who inspires more sublime emotions by displaying intellectual beauty, may be overlooked or observed with indifference, by those men who find their happiness in the gratification of their appetites.

[...]

[Moralists] have agreed that the tenor of life seems to prove that *man* is prepared by various circumstances for a future state, [but] they constantly concur in advising *woman* only to provide for the present. Gentleness, docility, and a spaniel-like affection are, on this ground, consistently recommended as the cardinal virtues of the sex; and, disregarding the arbitrary economy of nature, one writer has declared that it is masculine for a woman to be melancholy. She was created to be the toy of man, his rattle, and it must jingle in his ears, whenever [...] he chooses to be amused.

[...]

To carry the remark still further, if fear in girls, instead of being cherished, perhaps, created, were treated in the same manner as cowardice in boys, we should quickly see women with more dignified aspects. It is true, they could not then with equal propriety be termed the sweet flowers that smile in the walk of man; but they would be more respectable members of society [...]

[...]

Women are every where in [a] deplorable state; for, in order to preserve their innocence, as ignorance is courteously termed, truth is hidden from them [...]

[...]

Ignorance is a frail base for virtue! Yet, that it is the condition for which woman was organized, has been insisted upon by the writers who have most vehemently argued in favour of the superiority of man; a superiority not in degree, but essence [...]

Chapter 6

Charles Dickens and *A Christmas Carol*

Lynda Prescott and Richard Jones

Contents

1 Introduction

In this chapter, we are concerned with at least two reputations. The first is that of the author Charles Dickens (1812–1870). He made his name as a writer during a period when the novel was not only overtaking poetry as the most dominant literary **genre** but was also becoming immensely popular and reaching an ever-growing readership. Dickens himself was an innovator, experimenting with new approaches to fiction and blending different kinds of writing. Today, 'experimental fiction' is rarely popular, at least initially, but Dickens showed that in Victorian Britain it was possible to write in a daringly different way and at the same time sell a lot of books.

Dickens's immense popularity during his own lifetime was followed by a reputational dip in the decades after his death. This is not an uncommon pattern, but it was especially marked in his case. At least part of the decline could be attributed to the negative way that many literary critics viewed his achievements. For example, when George Henry Lewes, editor of the influential magazine *The Fortnightly Review*, reviewed the first volume of John Forster's *The Life of Charles Dickens* in 1872, he noted the contrast between Dickens's 'immense popularity' with what he called 'critical contempt': 'there probably never was a writer of so vast a popularity', he wrote, 'whose genius was [so] little *appreciated* by the critics' (G.H. Lewes, quoted in Collins, 1971, p. 569).

By the start of the twentieth century, Dickens's fiction was still popular with readers but was considered 'lowbrow' by some critics. However, the critical tide started to turn in the 1930s, and during the last 50 years, an immense flow of academic books and articles has helped to establish his status as a great writer. Indeed, as Lyn Pykett noted in her book, *Charles Dickens*, there is now a 'Dickens industry' (Pykett, 2002, p. 2), which not only includes detailed editorial work but also a mass of different approaches to interpreting and evaluating Dickens's extensive literary output.

Dickens's literary work

To get a sense of the range and quantity of Dickens's writing, you might want to browse through the Chronology included as part of Robert Douglas-Fairhurst's introduction to your set book: see pp. xxxvi–xlviii.

Figure 1 Portrait of Charles Dickens, *c.*1860.
Photo: © Hulton Archive/Getty Images.

The name Charles Dickens is now known all around the English-speaking world, and his works have been translated into numerous other languages. Because so many of his novels have been adapted for stage, film and television, it is possible to become familiar with his work without necessarily reading what he wrote. Currently, Dickens's reputation depends primarily on his achievements as a writer of novels, but during his lifetime his name was also associated with enormous quantities of journalism, essays, political speeches and other forms of non-fictional writing. In this unit, we will be glancing briefly at some non-novelistic aspects of his career to gain a wider sense of what his reputation meant to his contemporaries.

In this chapter, all references to *A Christmas Carol* are to the set book: Charles Dickens, *A Christmas Carol and Other Christmas Books*, edited by Robert Douglas-Fairhurst (Oxford, Oxford University Press, 2006).

The second reputation we are concerned with in this chapter is that of *A Christmas Carol*, the first of Dickens's 'Christmas Books', published in 1843. At under 30,000 words in length, it is usually described as a novella rather than a novel (some of his novels are more than ten times as long!), but it is considered by some readers and critics to be his most perfect work. Literary quality and popularity do not always go hand-in-hand, but in the case of *A Christmas Carol* we have a much-admired literary text that was instantly popular with its first readers and has continued to be read, and adapted, ever since. Indeed, *A Christmas Carol* has now taken so many forms that it has established itself in our collective consciousness and taken on the status of a **myth**. The ghost of Jacob Marley and the Three Spirits he conjures up provide the supernatural elements often present in myths or fairy tales, but *A Christmas Carol* is also a moral **fable**. Through the interventions of the Three Spirits, Scrooge, the miserly businessman, undergoes a total transformation centred on the idea of Christmas as 'a kind, forgiving, charitable, pleasant time [...] when men and women seem by one consent to open their shut-up hearts freely' (p. 12).

This brings us to what we might consider to be another reputation that has been linked to Dickens's work: the reputation that has been acquired by Christmas itself. In 2008, the American historian and fiction writer Les Standiford published a book with the catchy title *The Man Who Invented Christmas: How Charles Dickens's 'A Christmas Carol' Rescued His Career and Revived Our Holiday Spirits.* This provided the basis for a film, *The Man Who Invented Christmas*, released in 2017 and directed by Bharat Nalluri. It is well known that many of the customs and traditions now associated with Christmas originated in the mid nineteenth century, and even if Dickens did not single-handedly 'invent' certain Christmas celebrations, he certainly played a major role in promoting the idea of Christmas as the season of good cheer, fellow feeling and domestic harmony. But as we shall see, what Dickens called the 'magic in the very name of Christmas' (epitomised in *A Christmas Carol*; see Section 7) exists alongside, and acts as a counterweight to, the social and political conflicts that characterised the middle decades of the nineteenth century.

2 Dickens in the limelight

On Saturday 19 March 1870, the front page of *The Penny Illustrated Paper* (a weekly London newspaper) carried a drawing of the audience at St James's Hall on 15 March (Figure 2). The crowd was shown to be looking attentively at a thin, bearded man in a tailcoat standing near the front of the stage behind a small table, with a sheaf of papers in his hand. St James's Hall in London's West End was one of the many imposing venues that had sprung up in British cities during the mid nineteenth century. They were built to provide spaces for musical performances, public dinners and public speaking events of various kinds. The Great Hall at St James's offered seating for 2000 people, and although the drawing in *The Penny Illustrated Paper* could show only a small part of the audience, we know from other sources that not only was the hall completely full on 15 March but large numbers of people were turned away at the doors. The performer they had come to see and hear was Charles Dickens, the most famous writer of his age, and also sometimes an actor, public speaker, and, as at St James's Hall, a professional reader of his own fictional works.

Dickens had given his first public reading more than 16 years earlier in Birmingham Town Hall (another one of those great nineteenth-century venues). It was intended as a fundraiser for the new Birmingham and Midland Institute, a successor to the town's earlier Mechanics' Institute, dedicated to adult education. Advertised in *The Birmingham Journal* as 'CHRISTMAS READINGS BY CHARLES DICKENS, ESQ', there were actually three events, held just after Christmas in 1853. For the first one, on 27 December, Dickens read *A Christmas Carol*, which ten years after its initial publication was still a firm favourite with readers. Two nights later he read another of his 'Christmas Books', *The Cricket on the Hearth*, and then on 30 December there was a second reading of *A Christmas Carol* to an audience composed, at Dickens's request, of members of the working class, with ticket prices reduced to sixpence.

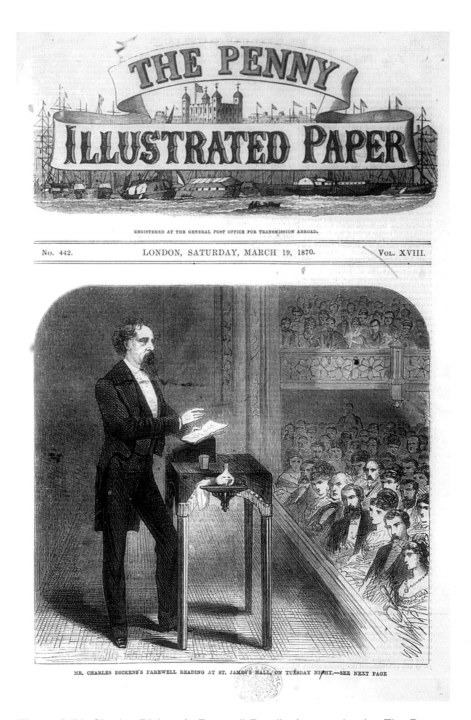

Figure 2 'Mr Charles Dickens's Farewell Reading' engraving in *The Penny Illustrated Paper*, London, 1870. British Library, London. Photo: © British Library Board. All Rights Reserved/Bridgeman Images.

Over the next four years, Dickens gave numerous other public readings for charitable causes, then in 1858 he turned professional, effectively developing his readings into a second career, which was even more profitable than being the country's most popular writer. He read to huge audiences not just in London but in towns and cities all around the British Isles, usually travelling from place to place on the expanding railway network. Between December 1867 and April 1868 he gave 75 readings in the United States, an immensely lucrative tour that allowed him to bank nearly £19,000 (over two million pounds in today's value) when he returned to London.

Activity

(Allow around 10 minutes to complete this activity.)

Pause and reflect on this brief account of Dickens as a performer of his own works. Did you find anything in this account surprising? How does it fit (or is it hard to fit) with your previous ideas about Dickens, and even your idea of what a 'writer' is?

Discussion

If you had previously known Dickens simply as a writer of (mostly very long) novels, the idea of him having a profitable second career as a public performer might have been unexpected, but you can probably view this in the broader context of writing as a financially precarious occupation – even now, when copyright law offers more protection to writers than it did in the mid nineteenth century.

If you were already familiar with this part of Dickens's biography, you may have been reflecting on some of the historical detail in the account, such as the fact that public speaking (oratory) was an important part of nineteenth-century life. This is worth bearing in mind when we come to look at the voice of the narrator of A Christmas Carol in more detail.

3 *A Christmas Carol* in the limelight

A Christmas Carol was one of the most frequently performed works in Dickens's public readings. Popular with both British and American audiences, between 1853 and 1870 he gave no fewer than 127 readings of this work. It formed the first part of what was to be his very last public reading (depicted in Figure 2), where it was followed by a comic extract, *The Trial from Pickwick*, from an earlier serialised novel, *The Pickwick Papers* (1836–37); this was a favourite combination. At the end of the St James's Hall 'farewell' performance, the audience called Dickens back to the stage several times, and he spoke to them directly about his sadness at retiring from his public readings:

> In this hall, and in many kindred places, I have had the honour of presenting my own cherished ideas before you, for your recognition; and in closely observing your reception of them, have enjoyed an amount of artistic delight and instruction which, perhaps is given to few men to know.
>
> (Andrews, 2006, pp. 265–6)

The end of his speech was tinged with allusions to the theatre and the magic it can create: 'From these garish lights I vanish now for evermore, with a heartfelt, grateful, respectful, and affectionate farewell' (Andrews, 2006, p. 266).

Although Dickens was only 58 years old, his health was breaking down; his friends and family were convinced that the strenuous physical demands of his reading tours had hastened his decline, and indeed at that final performance his doctor ordered Dickens's son Charley to sit close to the stage, ready to lead him off if he broke down. Less than three months later, on 9 June 1870, Dickens died as the result of a stroke. At his own request, his funeral was quiet and simple, albeit in Westminster Abbey's Poets' Corner. It was followed by extensive public mourning, on both sides of the Atlantic. His American friend, the poet Henry Wadsworth Longfellow, wrote to Dickens's family that news of his death 'filled all our hearts with the deepest sorrow. In truth I may say it is a universal grief [...] And surely no author was ever so widely beloved and lamented as Dickens'. Indeed, said Longfellow, 'Dickens was so full of life that it did not seem possible he could die' (Hilen, 1982, p. 354).

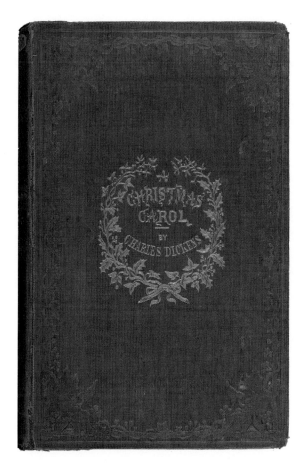

Figure 3 Front cover of the first edition of
Charles Dickens, *A Christmas Carol*, London,
1843. British Library, London, shelfmark:
Dex.293.(1.) Photo: © British Library Board.
All Rights Reserved/Bridgeman Images.

In a sense, Longfellow was right. A century and a half after his death,
Dickens's name is still widely recognised and his novels and stories
continue to attract new readers and new treatments. Some of the
(nearly) 1000 fictional characters he created have taken on a life of
their own: many people who have never read Dickens's work will
nonetheless recognise references to the starving orphan Oliver Twist,
the withered, jilted bride Miss Havisham, or the curmudgeonly miser
Ebenezer Scrooge. It is the vitality of Dickens's characters that partly
accounts for his enduring reputation as a writer, but the power of his
fictional **narratives** is also a significant factor. Like Shakespeare's plays,
they lend themselves to continual reinterpretation or reinvention. *A
Christmas Carol* is a prime example. Within weeks of its publication,

'pirated' versions of the text (such as *A Christmas Ghost Story, Reoriginated from the original by Charles Dickens*) appeared on the market, and several unauthorised theatrical versions were also staged.

However, Dickens was happy to collaborate on authorised dramatisations, notably with Edward Stirling, an assiduous adapter of Dickens's work for the theatre. If you had gone to London's Adelphi Theatre to see Stirling's *A Christmas Carol; or, Past, Present and Future*, Dickens's work would have literally been in the limelight, as bright illumination from calcium light had become part of the technical repertoire that enhanced the great expansion of theatres in Victorian towns and cities. But the story of *A Christmas Carol* has continued in the metaphorical limelight of public attention long after electric lighting replaced gaslight and limelight in theatres. It has lent itself easily to numerous screen versions, including the much acclaimed *The Muppet Christmas Carol* (1992) with Michael Caine as Scrooge, and has morphed into newer print genres such as the graphic novel, with Lee Bermajo's *Batman: Noël* (2011). Your understanding of *A Christmas Carol*'s reputation may well derive from one or more of such reimaginings of Dickens's story.

Activity

(Allow around 4 hours to complete this activity.)

If you have not yet read *A Christmas Carol*, you should now read the text all the way through and then return to this chapter. This will probably take three to four hours, but aim to find a reading pace that is both comfortable and enjoyable.

As you will discover, the study of literature involves thinking about what we do when we read. Each person's reading experience is unique and depends on a whole host of factors, including our own individual reading history and the present context within which we are reading. Right now you may be conscious that you are reading a literary work for study purposes, something very far from Dickens's intentions in writing it. (Indeed, the idea of 'English Literature' as a subject for university study scarcely existed in Dickens's day.)

So before you launch into *A Christmas Carol*'s 'Stave I' – a word which, like 'carol' has musical associations but here functions rather like 'chapter' – pause for a moment over the work's full title: *A Christmas Carol in Prose. Being a Ghost Story of Christmas*. You might have encountered the term 'prose' before, mainly in the context of formal study (and in opposition to poetry or verse), so it may strike you as being a technical literary term. However, Dickens was probably using it to contrast with his use of 'carol' (a seasonal song) and to steer his reader's expectations towards the popular (prose) genre of a ghost story.

One more thing to think about before you embark on your reading is the collection of expectations and assumptions you may be bringing to *A Christmas Carol*, especially if, like most of us, you have previously encountered the story in another form. Try to recall some of the impressions the version you have already experienced left with you, and then as you read through the text, try to be aware of how the impressions created by reading Dickens's text differ from those recollections.

4 Narrating

If you had been in the audience at one of Dickens's public readings, you would have been in no doubt about who was telling you the story: there in front of you would have been the author himself, speaking words that he had written and was now reading aloud. But Dickens would also have been *performing* for his audience, dramatising his characters so that the voice of Scrooge would sound different from the tones of his nephew, and different again from the voices of the ghostly apparitions. As a young man, before he established himself as a writer, Dickens had wanted to become an actor, and throughout his adult life he retained his love of the theatre and frequently took part in amateur theatricals. One of the reasons his public readings were so popular was because he was, by most accounts, a very good actor, capable of bringing all kinds of characters to life. But, of course, there are key differences between drama written for the stage and a story written for readers, such as *A Christmas Carol* in its original form.

In the theatre, the words spoken by the characters on the stage are all-important – they carry the action, along with gesture, movement, and so on. When we read a prose story on the page, the words spoken by the characters (which usually appear in quotation marks as direct speech or dialogue) are still important, but the verbal texture of the story includes other elements that drive the story forward. We have already used the term 'narrative' to refer to this kind of storytelling: it is not quite the same as 'story', which in the most basic sense is a sequence of events, but when we talk about a narrative we're also saying something about *how* a story is told. We've used the term 'narrator', too: sometimes this refers to a person (who may also be a character in the story we're reading) and sometimes to a kind of disembodied voice through which the story is told. Crucially, the **narrative voice** gives us a perspective on the story, or, in literary terms, a point of view.

The heading of this section, 'Narrating', is a reminder that, when we read a prose story, we are not only engaging with a story and a storyteller but are also concerned with the process of storytelling. This is something that unfolds through time (reading time), can be dynamic and changeable, and can have an effect on us as readers. Leaving behind our imaginary position as members of the audience at one of Dickens's readings, we are now back in the real-life position as readers of *A Christmas Carol*, but what difference does that make to our idea of who is telling us the story? To answer this question, we will now look more closely at the opening sentences.

Activity

(Allow around 10 minutes to complete this activity.)

Reread the first paragraph of *A Christmas Carol* on p. 9 of the set book. As you do, imagine reading it aloud (or actually try doing so!) and think about the kind of tone that would suit the language being used. Choose two or three words or phrases to try to pin down this tone.

Discussion

In trying to describe the tone of the opening paragraph, you have been attempting some literary analysis. Even though there is no single right answer, there are likely to be some common elements, even in differing responses. For example, a very short and direct sentence like 'There is no doubt whatever about that' is likely to make a similar impression on most readers, along the lines of 'here is someone quite sure of themselves'. Short sentences often create an emphatic effect, and that seems to be the case here.

The emphasis is redoubled in the next, longer sentence, which piles up the evidence of the burial register with a list of signatories, all sounding very official and impersonal (until we get to the next sentence and the chief mourner is named). So, any descriptive words you might have chosen that put the narrator's voice at the decisive, firm, factual, assertive end of the spectrum would be well supported by the text. It would be very hard to argue that this narrator is vague or uncertain.

However, having just decided that the narrator's voice is firm and assertive, we should go back to consider the very first sentence: 'Marley was dead, to begin with.' This sentence is also short and quite emphatic, but how did you interpret 'to begin with'? Is this just a reference to a story beginning, or does it suggest, rather disturbingly, that once the beginning of the story is over Marley might no longer be dead? After all, this is a ghost story, so the idea of the dead coming back to some form of life is likely to be on the reader's mind. But it seems as if the narrator of *A Christmas Carol* is determined to have some verbal fun before satisfying our curiosity on this score.

Activity

(Allow around 10 minutes to complete this activity.)

Read on through the third paragraph on p. 9, from 'Mind!' to '[...] dead as a door-nail'. Do you notice any difference in the narrator's language?

Discussion

That colloquial exclamation 'Mind!' at the start of the paragraph does seem to signal a change, especially as it appears to be addressed very directly to the reader. The change thereafter involves frequent use of words like 'I', 'me', 'my', 'myself', and the reader is explicitly brought into the (rather one-sided) conversation with 'You will therefore permit me [...]'. Possibly you picked out other changes in this paragraph, but for the moment we will focus on the way that in this third paragraph the narrator becomes a person, an 'I'.

Narrators who write about themselves (by using 'I') are not unusual. A few years after writing *A Christmas Carol*, Dickens began drafting an autobiographical piece of writing that worked its way into his longest novel, *David Copperfield*, published serially in 1849–50. The first chapter of this novel has the striking title: 'I am born', and the first sentence is no less striking: 'Whether I shall turn out to be the hero of my own life, or whether that station will be held by anybody else, these pages must show' (Dickens, 1999 [1849–50], p. 1). *David Copperfield* is a work of fiction, but in it Dickens draws directly on experiences from his own life, especially his childhood, so there is an autobiographical flavour to the novel. The technical term for narratives, fictional or otherwise, that are told from the point of view of a narrator recounting their own experiences is known as being written in the **first person** (this term comes from the grammatical description for the personal pronouns 'I' and 'we'). Dickens's autobiographical fragment – which was not published until after his death – is a first-person narrative, and so is the novel *David Copperfield*.

Novels written in the first person were less common in Dickens's day than they are now. More usually, the narrators of nineteenth-century novels use the grammatical third person, referring to 'he', 'she', or 'they'. Quite often these narrators can tell us what characters are thinking and feeling, and can anticipate events in the story that have yet to happen; this kind of narrator is called 'omniscient' or all-knowing. It is often tempting to think of an omniscient narrator's voice as being that of the author, especially if the narrator expresses views or attitudes that we know, from other sources, to be close to the author's heart. To explore this relationship between author and narrator a little further, a brief excursion into literary and social history may be helpful.

In Britain (the first industrialised nation), the middle decades of the nineteenth century were marked by immense and disruptive social change. Many writers used the formats of prose fiction – short stories, novellas, but especially full-length novels – as a means of informing readers about these rapid changes in the world around them, with a view to bringing about reform. During the 1830s and early 1840s, a spate of 'industrial novels' introduced middle-class readers to the harsh lives of factory workers, including children labouring in largely unregulated manufacturing industries. Although mostly forgotten now, these fictional works paved the way for later 'social-problem' novels that helped to shape the reputations of major writers of the time such as Elizabeth Gaskell (1810–1865), Charles Kingsley (1819–1875), the Prime Minister Benjamin Disraeli (1804–1881), George Eliot (1819–1880) and others. These novelists were able to make the literary conventions of **realism** do much of their work for them, describing the physical details of everyday life through precise, factual language. For example, in *Mary Barton: A Tale of Manchester Life* (1848), the author Elizabeth Gaskell sometimes adopts what might be described as a documentary approach to representing the hardships endured by her working-class characters.

Activity

(Allow around 20 minutes to complete this activity.)

Read this short passage from the novel *Mary Barton* in which two Manchester workmen, Jem Wilson and John Barton, go to visit a sick colleague.

As you read, consider how Gaskell's choice of words steers the reader towards viewing this as a factual account. Try to pick out some of the ways she does this.

On the way Wilson said Davenport was a good fellow [...] that his children were too young to work, but not too young to be cold and hungry; that they had sunk lower and lower, and pawned thing after thing, and that now they lived in a cellar in Berry Street, off Store Street [...] [Berry Street] was unpaved; and down the middle a gutter forced its way, every now and then forming pools in the holes with which the street abounded. Never was the old Edinburgh cry of 'Gardez l'eau' more necessary than in this street. As they passed, women from their doors tossed household slops of every description into the gutter; they ran into the next pool, which overflowed and stagnated. Heaps of ashes were the stepping-stones, on which the passer-by, who cared in the least for cleanliness, took care not to put his foot. Our friends were not dainty, but even they picked their way till they got to some steps leading down into a small area, where a person standing would have his head about one foot below the level of the street, and might at the same time, without the least motion of his body, touch the window of the cellar and the damp muddy wall right opposite. You went down one step even from the foul area into the cellar in which a family of human beings lived. It was very dark inside. The window-panes were many of them broken and stuffed with rags, which was reason enough for the dusky light that pervaded the place even at mid-day.

(Gaskell, 1970 [1848], pp. 97–8)

Discussion

We could begin with the names of the characters. Wilson, Barton and Davenport are presumably fictional characters (though you might have noticed how ordinary, and therefore probable, these names sound in comparison with Scrooge, Cratchit or Fezziwig from *A Christmas Carol*). We also have some names of places, Berry Street and Store Street: these can still be found on street maps of central Manchester, near a branch of the Ashton Canal. The use of these real-life names contributes to the impression that we are being presented with a real (not fictional) account.

In addition, the narrator's description of Davenport's cellar is detailed and precise, and in fact remarkably similar to accounts in official reports that were beginning to appear during this period. You might also have noticed the restraint in phrases such as 'the cellar in which a family of human beings lived'. The narrator clearly implies that this cellar is totally unfit for human habitation, but refrains from the comparisons with animal habitats that many contemporary commentators used to strengthen their condemnation of such slums, along with adjectives such as 'revolting' or 'repulsive'. In fact, Gaskell's narrator is quite sparing with adjectives, adding to the unobtrusive quality of the narrative voice.

If you are wondering about the French term 'Gardez l'eau', this means 'beware of the water'. It's more usually written in English, or Scots, as 'Gardyloo' – so the use of the formal term helps to further the impression of objectivity. It was indeed associated with the unsanitary tenements of Edinburgh, where legislation – the 'Nastiness Act' (1749) – limited the disposal of waste from the windows of upper storeys to certain hours of the night. In contrast to Edinburgh's tall and overcrowded tenements, in Manchester's working-class districts the poorest families, like Davenport's, tended to be driven below ground into what became notorious cellar dwellings (subsequently prohibited by a Local Act of 1853).

Even a short extract like this one from *Mary Barton* indicates how the nineteenth-century realist novel could address acute social problems in an authentic-seeming style. Dickens was a great admirer of Gaskell and enlisted her as a regular contributor to his weekly magazine *Household Words* (1850–59), whose aim was 'the raising up of those that are down, and the general improvement of our social condition' (Storey et al., 1988, p. 22). In fact, the first part of another story by Gaskell set in Manchester, *Lizzie Leigh*, appeared in the opening number of *Household Words*. By this period, Dickens's own reputation, both as a writer and as a public figure involved in numerous societies and charities working to improve conditions for the poor and dispossessed, was very much in tune with the reformist purposes of writers like Gaskell.

However, though their aims may have been similar, the literary methods of Gaskell and Dickens were very different. Dickens is certainly capable of detailed realism, every bit as hard-hitting as Gaskell's, but his fiction never remains within the bounds of a single kind of writing for long. Readers of his novels and shorter fictions find themselves switching between what we might call different **modes**: grotesque, dramatic, sentimental, satiric, as well as realist and, above all, comic – often in rapid succession. Similarly, Dickens's narrators are seldom unobtrusive, and as we can see in *A Christmas Carol*, the narrative voice encompasses a wide range of moods and tones. Whereas Gaskell's narrator in *Mary Barton* can be quite closely identified with the voice of the sympathetic author, the narrator of *A Christmas Carol* has such a protean, dynamic character that the author-narrator link is stretched to the point of vanishing.

The fact that *A Christmas Carol* declares itself to be a ghost story removes it even further from the demands of realism, including the requirement for a steady and consistent narrative voice. Looking at p. 10 of *A Christmas Carol*, we can see examples of how the narrator switches from one mood to another in the space of a few paragraphs. The narrative voice initially has an oratorical note with the exclamation: 'Oh! But he was a tight-fisted hand at the grindstone'. This is quickly followed by the kind of exuberant piling-up effects that Robert Douglas-Fairhurst draws attention to in the Introduction to your set book: 'No warmth could warm, no wintry weather chill him. No wind that blew was bitterer than he, no falling snow was more intent upon its purpose, no pelting rain less open to entreaty' (see pp. ix–x). Then just a few lines later, the narrator switches tack again with the conventional fairy-tale phrase 'Once upon a time', like a fresh start, with a fresh voice.

Although the narrator often strikes a comic or satirical note, there is also scope for something more poetic. As we see at the end of Stave I, when the ghost of Jacob Marley leaves Scrooge's room:

> Scrooge followed to the window: desperate in his curiosity. He looked out.
>
> The air was filled with phantoms, wandering hither and thither in restless haste, and moaning as they went [...]
>
> Whether these creatures faded into mist, or mist enshrouded them, he could not tell. But they and their spirit voices faded together; and the night became as it had been when he walked home.

> (2006, p. 26)

After the departure of Marley's Ghost, Scrooge goes to sleep then wakes at the beginning of Stave II, unsure whether he has been dreaming or not. We know from the Stave II title, as well as from

Marley's message, that the first of the Three Spirits will be appearing, so for the final activity in this section we will look more closely at the narrator's role in drawing the reader into this new phase of the tale.

Activity

(Allow around 10 minutes to complete this activity.)

Reread the three paragraphs from near the top of p. 28, from 'The hour itself' to '[...] at your elbow.' What do you think are the most striking features of this short passage?

Discussion

One of the most surprising things for the reader must be to have the narrator enacting the role of 'unearthly visitor' in alarming proximity ('at your elbow'). This dramatic turn has been heralded by the phrase 'I tell you' a few lines earlier, a phrase that has no function other than to remind us that we are in the presence of a narrator who wants to make us share Scrooge's sudden shock.

In this example, the narrator's voice seems to belong less to a written text and more to an oral tradition of storytelling, with the storyteller and listeners clustered together in the same physical space. The conventions of this storytelling situation, whether actual or merely represented on the printed page, were closely associated with a very popular nineteenth-century literary genre, the ghost story.

5 Ghosts

The loose, episodic structure of Dickens's first novel, *The Pickwick Papers*, published in monthly parts, includes a number of embedded tales, including several ghost stories such as the Christmas-themed 'Story of the Goblins Who Stole a Sexton'. Throughout his writing career, Dickens maintained his enthusiasm for ghostly tales: one of his later short stories, 'The Signalman' (1866), still appears in numerous anthologies of ghost stories and has been filmed for TV. But despite his interest in psychic phenomena of all kinds, Dickens was on the whole quite sceptical. In 1848 he wrote a long and critical review of Catherine Crowe's book *The Night Side of Nature; or Ghosts and Ghost Seers*, proposing 'a few obvious heads of objection that may be ranged against the ghosts' (Slater, 1996, p. 82).

Dickens was even more sceptical about spiritualism, which became immensely popular during the second half of the nineteenth century, and in 1859 he became embroiled in a controversial exchange with a prominent supporter of spiritualism, William Howitt. What really seems to have fired Dickens's imagination, though, is the purely literary potential of the ghost story, whether as a distinct form or as an unnerving component in other fictional works. In particular, he popularised the idea of ghost stories being told at Christmas, ideally round a roaring fire. With its Three Spirits, it is easy to see how *A Christmas Carol* fits within this tradition, even though it is far more than just a 'Ghost Story of Christmas'. In this section, we will explore the way that Dickens presents each of the Three Spirits who appear in Staves II, III and IV, treating them as characters in their own right.

As you will have noticed from your reading of *A Christmas Carol*, the Ghosts of Christmas Past, Christmas Present and Christmas Yet to Come are distinguished not only by the time they belong to but also by their appearance and behaviour, including their entrances and exits. In contrast to the ghost of Jacob Marley (a tortured and transparent spectre, clanking conventional chains), the Three Spirits are as highly individualised as the novella's human characters.

Activity

(Allow around 20 minutes to complete this activity.)

Continue your rereading of the first part of Stave II from the point where we left it in the previous activity ('[...] I am standing in the spirit at your elbow') through to the bottom of p. 28 ('[...] distinct and clear as ever'). Think about how this description of Scrooge's first 'unearthly visitor' differs from the introduction of Marley's Ghost on p. 19 (three paragraphs from 'The same face [...]' to '[...] fought against his senses').

Discussion

The differences between Marley's Ghost and the Ghost of Christmas Past begin from the fact that Marley was, within the fictional terms of the story, a real person whom Scrooge had known and who had, alarmingly, returned from the dead. As such, Marley's Ghost shares some of the stock characteristics of ghosts in fiction: although his figure is transparent it is still recognisable, and his 'death-cold eyes' exert a 'chilling influence'.

Compare this with Scrooge's first impressions of the 'unearthly visitor' who draws back his bed curtains as the neighbouring church clock strikes one. It certainly is a 'strange figure', described in terms of contradictory qualities. It is proportioned like a child but has the white hair of an old man (the only hint of gender); it carries a 'wintry emblem' of fresh green holly, while its dress is trimmed with summer flowers; and it gives out light but also carries its own, rather comical, extinguisher. Most strangely of all, the figure is constantly changing: 'now a thing with one arm, now with one leg, now with twenty legs, now a pair of legs without a head', and so on.

In the description of the first of the Three Spirits, Dickens takes us even further away from the realms of realism, with a shape-changing figure who goes on to transport Scrooge through the solid walls of his house, through space and time, to experience some of the Christmas scenes from his past as an observer. We will shortly look in more detail at the first scene in which Scrooge re-encounters his lonely childhood self, but for now we will focus on the Christmas 'domestic ball' presided over by the benevolent Mr and Mrs Fezziwig. This involves music, dancing, games, copious eating and drinking, and above all a welcome for everyone, from the three Miss Fezziwigs to 'all the young men and women employed in the business', the household servants and 'the girl from next door but one' (p. 35).

In this festive scene, Dickens gives us a city version of the country Christmas at Dingley Dell that he describes in Chapter 28 of *The Pickwick Papers*, but there is more than sheer jollity involved in the scene the Ghost of Christmas Past conjures up, as Scrooge slips back again into an awareness of his former self. The Ghost nudges him into reflecting on the gratitude he had felt towards Fezziwig, which had nothing to do with how much or how little money was spent on the festivities. Prompted again by the Spirit's glance, Scrooge's latter self comments: 'I should like to be able to say a word or two to my clerk just now. That's all' (p. 37).

Appropriately, the second stage of what the Ghost of Christmas Past calls Scrooge's 'reclamation' (p. 29) is mainly focused on his clerk, Bob Cratchit, and his family. However, the second Spirit who conducts Scrooge on the next stage of his journey has an entirely different appearance and demeanour from the insubstantial Ghost of Christmas Past.

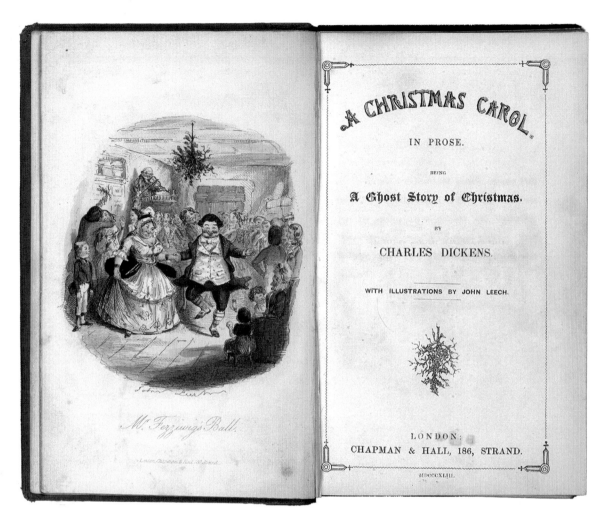

Figure 4 Title page and frontispiece (John Leech, 'Mr Fezziwig's Ball) of Charles Dickens, *A Christmas Carol*, London, 1843. British Library, London, shelfmark: Dex.293.(1.) Photo: © British Library Board. All Rights Reserved/Bridgeman Images.

Figure 5 John Leech, 'Scrooge's Third Visitor' in the first edition of Charles Dickens, *A Christmas Carol*, London, 1843. British Library, London, shelfmark: Dex.293.(1.) Photo: © British Library Board. All Rights Reserved/Bridgeman Images.
Figure 6 Robert Seymour, 'Old Christmas', in Thomas K. Hervey's, *The Book of Christmas*, London, 1837 (first published 1836). British Library, London, shelfmark:12355.aa.36. Photo: © British Library Board. All Rights Reserved/Bridgeman Images.

Activity

(Allow around 10 minutes to complete this activity.)

Compare Figure 5 (John Leech's depiction of the Ghost of Christmas Present in the 1843 edition of *A Christmas Carol*) with Figure 6 (Robert Seymour's illustration entitled 'Old Christmas' in Thomas K. Hervey's *The Book of Christmas* from 1836). What similarities are there?

Discussion

The most obvious similarity is that both illustrations depict men with beards! You may also have noticed their jovial expressions, the holly wreaths, and the loose, flowing robes (the caption to Seymour's illustration mentions Old Christmas being clad in a 'furry pall'). Food and drink are also prominent in both.

Thomas K. Hervey's *The Book of Christmas* (first published in 1836 and quickly reprinted) was very influential, and Dickens was almost certainly familiar with it, because its artist, Robert Seymour, was also the illustrator for Dickens's *The Pickwick Papers*. Actually, *The Pickwick Papers* had begun not as a novel but as a series of 'comic scenes' written to accompany Seymour's drawings. In the rapidly expanding book market of the early nineteenth century, illustrations were a key element, thanks to technical advances in image reproduction. Throughout his career, Dickens worked with many successful artists, beginning with the well-known George Cruikshank, illustrator of his first published collection of written pieces, *Sketches by Boz* (1836), and later *Oliver Twist* (1838). So Dickens's reputation as a writer was closely entwined with those of the artists he worked with. In the case of *A Christmas Carol*, which Dickens published at his own expense (hoping to make a larger profit that way), he kept a particularly sharp eye on the visual elements. You can read more about this in your set book, in Robert Douglas-Fairhurst's 'Note on the illustrations' (p. xxxi).

In depicting the Ghost of Christmas Present, Dickens was probably drawing on traditional visual **personifications** of what we now think of as Father Christmas. However, while comparing Leech's figure with Seymour's, you might also have noticed that Seymour's Old Christmas is depicted outdoors, riding on a goat through a snowy landscape – very different from the bright, warm room in which Dickens's Ghost of Christmas Present first appears. Showing Old Christmas with a goat reflects the fact that the first part of Hervey's book discusses the complex origins of the Christmas festival, including Scandinavian folk tales around the celebration known as Yule, honouring the god Thor whose carriage is pulled through the sky by two magical goats. In contrast, the scenes involving Dickens's Ghost of Christmas Present raise Christian associations, not least when Bob Cratchit recounts his son Tiny Tim's reference to the healing miracles performed by Jesus, remembering 'upon Christmas Day, who made lame beggars walk, and blind men see' (p. 50).

If the Ghost of Christmas Present seems in some ways a fairly familiar and solid figure, the last of the Spirits, who appears in Stave IV, takes the reader back into the realms of imagination, this time with darker overtones.

Activity

(Allow around 20 minutes to complete this activity.)

Reread the opening of Stave IV, from 'The Phantom slowly [...]' (p. 63) to '[...] carried him along' (p. 64). What are the main differences between the third Spirit (the Ghost of Christmas Yet to Come) and the previous two?

Discussion

Scrooge does not have to wait for the Ghost of Christmas Yet to Come: it advances towards him as soon as the Ghost of Christmas Present has vanished, bringing its own atmosphere of 'gloom and misery'. Like the Ghost of Christmas Past, this phantom is insubstantial, but whereas the first Spirit was associated with light, this one is difficult to separate 'from the darkness by which it was surrounded'. Unlike the cheery, genial Ghost of Christmas Present, this ghost of the future induces fear and 'a vague uncertain horror' in Scrooge. Most chillingly, perhaps, this ghost does not speak, but uses a single pointing hand to communicate.

In the presence of this silent phantom, Scrooge is forced to become ever more vocal, hazarding answers to his own questions, which brings him inexorably to contemplate his own, unmourned death. In contrast, the Ghost takes Scrooge once again to the Cratchits' house, now without Tiny Tim, to witness the family's tender and heartfelt mourning. Although the Ghost still does not speak, the narrator interprets the meaning of this second death for both Scrooge and the reader: 'Spirit of Tiny Tim, thy childish essence was from God!' (p. 74).

6 Children

The Three Spirits announced by Jacob Marley are sent to work on Scrooge at a very personal level. When Scrooge asks The Ghost of Christmas Past whether 'Past' means 'Long Past', the Spirit is very definite: 'No. Your Past.' The Spirit also leaves Scrooge in no doubt about the purpose of his visit: 'Your reclamation [...] Take heed!' (p. 29). Therefore, it is no surprise that this Spirit's first task is to lead Scrooge to the places he remembers from his boyhood, but the happiness of seeing these remembered places quickly gives way to other emotions as Scrooge, and the reader, enter a dilapidated school and come upon 'a solitary child, neglected by his friends' (p. 31). Scrooge sits down on a bench in the old schoolroom near the lonely boy, and cries at the sight of his younger self. At this point, the reader glimpses the beginnings of a history that have led to Scrooge becoming 'hard and sharp as flint [...]; secret, and self-contained, and solitary as an oyster' (p. 10), but more importantly, Scrooge's long-hardened heart is touched and he weeps for the boy he used to be.

The psychological significance of this moment is bolstered by the ghostly appearance of fictional characters, beginning with Ali Baba who appears outside the schoolroom window, 'wonderfully real and distinct to look at' (p. 31), just as the young Scrooge had conjured him up in his solitary imaginings. The present-day Scrooge we met at the opening of *A Christmas Carol* would have had no time for such fancies, but, as is often the case in Dickens's writing, playfulness and imagination are closely linked with the development of human sympathy. Tellingly, Scrooge's excitement at remembering the 'wonderfully real' tales that had brightened his lonely childhood leads not only to 'pity for his former self' (p. 32) but to regret at having roughly turned away the boy who had come carol-singing at his present-day door the night before. The old man's 'reclamation' thus begins with recognition of his younger, imaginative self and quickly shifts to sympathy for the unfortunate young carol-singer.

A focus on children and the importance of childhood is not unique to *A Christmas Carol* but runs throughout Dickens's writing. It is tempting to think of this as a personal preoccupation: the autobiographical fragment mentioned in Section 4 is in fact an emotional recollection of his own sufferings as a 12-year-old child labourer in one of London's unsavoury factories while his father was imprisoned for bankruptcy. But in fact, as the following extract from an essay on 'Fictions of childhood' (2001) by the American academic Robert Newsom makes clear, this was a preoccupation that Dickens shared with the Romantic poets of an earlier generation, which came to have considerable influence on society:

> Dickens is conventionally credited with having imported into a central role in the novel the figure of the innocent child – often suffering and orphaned, abandoned, or simply neglected – from Romantic poetry, where it (and its healthier and happier siblings) had been celebrated, notably if esoterically, by William Blake and, far more popularly, by William Wordsworth. Since a growing concern with children was itself a central feature of the evolving ethos of the middle class throughout the nineteenth century, especially in Britain and the United States, it is an interesting albeit impossible speculation to imagine what might have happened to our ideas of the family had Dickens opted for a career as an actor, say, instead of that as a novelist – much less what the fictions of Emily and Charlotte Brontë, George Eliot, Robert Louis Stevenson, Henry James, Mark Twain, Lewis Carroll, Rudyard Kipling, James Joyce, among many others, would have been like without the example of Dickens before them. Impossible though the speculation may be to complete, it seems clear that Dickens has, via such characters as Oliver Twist, Little Nell, Tiny Tim, Paul Dombey, and a host of others, made an enormous difference in the way our culture thinks about children.
>
> (Newsom, 2001, p. 92)

Activity

(Allow around 30 minutes to complete this activity.)

Reread the account of the Cratchits' Christmas in Stave III, from 'Then up rose Mrs. Cratchit [...]' (p. 49) to '[...] and especially on Tiny Tim, until the last' (p. 54), and think about why Scrooge's interest in Tiny Tim is stirred.

As you read the passage, try to keep the spotlight of your attention on Tiny Tim, registering how his importance in the family is revealed.

Discussion

As we saw in Stave II, Scrooge is already reflecting on his relationship with Bob Cratchit (to whom he has been a far less considerate employer than Fezziwig was to Scrooge's younger self), and now he sees Bob with his family, including the vulnerable but much-loved son Tiny Tim, whose 'withered little hand' he holds.

Tiny Tim becomes the embodiment of 'the Poor', whose plight the hard-hearted Scrooge had dismissed at the opening of A Christmas Carol (pp. 13–14) in words that the Ghost now taunts him with: 'If he be like to die, he had better do it, and decrease the surplus population' (p. 52). We know that the process of 'reclamation' begun by the Ghost of Christmas Past is really working now, as Scrooge is 'overcome with penitence and grief' at the thought of poor, crippled Tiny Tim dying.

During the months before he wrote *A Christmas Carol*, Dickens had reason to become especially concerned with the situation of real-life children in Britain in the 1840s. He had read the shocking parliamentary report on child labour published in 1842. The *Report of the Children's Employment Commission* recorded, in appalling detail, the conditions under which children as young as four worked in Britain's mines and factories.

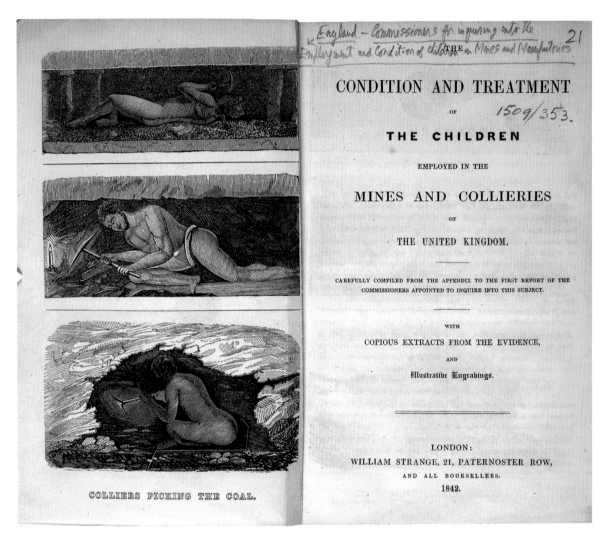

Figure 7 Title page and frontispiece ('Colliers Picking The Coal') of *The Condition and Treatment of the Children […]*, London, William Strange, 1842. British Library, London, shelfmark: 1509/353. Photo: © British Library Board. All Rights Reserved/Bridgeman Images.

When playwright David Edgar adapted *A Christmas Carol* for the Royal Shakespeare Company in 2017, he made this report the starting point for his play, which opens with 31-year-old Dickens and his close friend John Forster arguing about Dickens's plans for a Christmas book:

JOHN: For *Christmas*?

CHARLES: Yes.

JOHN: You cannot be serious.

CHARLES: I have never been more serious.

JOHN: But for Christmas…

CHARLES (waving the report): Have you read this?

JOHN: I don't need to read it.

CHARLES: It's entitled 'The Physical and Moral Condition of the Children' – that's the *children*…

JOHN: It's a government report.

CHARLES: '…and Young Persons Employed in Mines and Manufactures…'

JOHN: Dickens. You of all people cannot produce a tract…

CHARLES: I shall call it 'An Appeal to the People of England…'

JOHN: … based on a government report…

CHARLES: '… on behalf of the Poor Man's Child.'

JOHN: … and claim that it's a Christmas book, by you.

CHARLES: I am a radical, campaigning writer. I fight for social justice. Why dress it up as entertainment?

(Edgar, 2017, pp. 9–10)

In starting the play this way, we can see how Edgar is interested in engaging or challenging some of the preconceptions that his audience might bring to Dickens or *A Christmas Carol*. In case Charles's final question is one that you are asking yourself, you should know that John later urges him to 'do what you do best. And write it as a story. Which will echo down the ages.' (Edgar, 2017, p. 11). In fact, in July 1842, Dickens did write an impassioned letter to the influential liberal newspaper, *The Morning Chronicle*, supporting a parliamentary bill to restrict the employment of children working underground. The report on child labour was not the only evidence goading Dickens into action on behalf of 'the Poor Man's Child'. He had recently made the first of several visits to one of London's 'Ragged Schools' which, supported by various charities, attempted to provide shelter, food and some rudimentary education for street children.

Activity

(Allow around 30 minutes to complete this activity.)

Turn to the 'Introduction to *A Christmas Carol*' in your set book and read the first paragraph of the section entitled 'The dire neglect of soul and body' (pp. xv–xvi).

Then reread the section in Stave III of *A Christmas Carol*, which describes the children 'Ignorance' and 'Want', from 'Much they saw [...]' (p. 60) to '[...] The bell struck twelve' (p. 63).

What effect do you think the fictional context of *A Christmas Carol* has on this representation of the two 'wolfish' children?

Discussion

The Ghost of Christmas Present shows Scrooge numerous scenes of the 'blessings' accompanying the Christmas spirit, ending with a children's Twelfth Night party, so when the two 'wretched, abject, frightful, hideous, miserable' children are uncovered under the third Ghost's robe, the contrast is all the more shocking.

The personification, as children, of the abstract qualities of 'ignorance' and 'want' is matched by the Ghost addressing Scrooge as 'Man!' Scrooge is both the callous individual who has been happy to consign such children to prisons and workhouses, and also the representative of a society that condones such terrible consequences for the young and vulnerable.

In Stave III, Dickens has shown us the young Cratchits, including Tiny Tim, enjoying their Christmas dinner together, as well as the allegorical children, Ignorance and Want, whose plight would be shocking at any season. This conjunction links Dickens's concern for poor and neglected children with what the French critic Louis Cazamian has referred to as a 'philosophie de *Noël*' (Ledger, 2011, p. 183).

7 'A magic in the very name of Christmas'

All through his writing life, Dickens had been drawn to Christmas and its celebration as representing the values of benevolence, good fellowship and forgiveness. One of his earliest published pieces was 'Christmas Festivities', which appeared in *Bell's Life in London* on 27 December 1835. This was then reprinted the following year under the title 'A Christmas Dinner' in his collection of journalistic pieces, *Sketches by Boz*:

> Who can be insensible to the outpourings of good feeling, and the honest interchange of affectionate attachment, which abound at this season of the year! A Christmas family party! We know nothing in nature more delightful! There seems a magic in the very name of Christmas. Petty jealousies and discords are forgotten; social feelings are awakened, in bosoms to which they have long been strangers
>
> (Slater, 1994, p. 217)

The 'magic' of Christmas is part of the transformation that, in *A Christmas Carol*, turns Scrooge from a hard-faced and unfeeling miser into a compassionate benefactor. Throughout Dickens's writings, both fictional and non-fictional, belief in the possibility of regeneration and moral growth is a central theme. We can trace religious underpinnings of this philosophy in his writings, but Dickens was also very critical of the religious hypocrisy he observed in Victorian society, and his positive references to Christianity centre on the importance of doing good rather than doctrine. His enthusiasm for Christmas, as we can see in the quotation from 'Christmas Festivities', is compatible with secular values, even though going to church (as Bob Cratchit and Tiny Tim do in *A Christmas Carol*) might also be mentioned as a minor element.

So what of the claim that Dickens 'invented' Christmas? As we saw from our earlier references to Thomas K. Hervey's *The Book of Christmas* (1836), Dickens's contemporaries were keenly interested in the history of Christmas festivities. However, the 'traditional' Victorian Christmas also had a markedly commercial character. The social historian Judith Flanders, author of *Christmas: A Biography* (2017), draws attention to this element in an article on the British Library's *Discovering Literature: Romantics and Victorians* website:

> Whatever writers like Dickens said about the traditional Christmas at home, in reality, Christmas was always a commercial proposition. Christmas games and pastimes were promoted and marketed by magazines; Christmas music was the product of commercial enterprises selling sheet-music; food was processed and transported by new industrial processes; presents at Christmas were a novelty promoted by retailers.
>
> (Flanders, 2014)

Although Dickens played a key part in the development of seasonal book-buying and selling, the idea of publishing books specifically for Christmas was not entirely new. In the rapidly expanding Victorian literary marketplace, there were already annuals and gift books, such as *The Keepsake* (a very successful illustrated annual containing short stories by well-known writers printed between 1828 and 1857) published in time for Christmas and New Year gift-giving. However, Dickens's 'Christmas Books' were more modestly priced and aimed to reach a wide readership.

Activity

(Allow around 10 minutes to complete this activity.)

In the Introduction to your set book, read Robert Douglas-Fairhurst's brief account of how *A Christmas Carol* was produced for the Christmas market, from 'The *Carol* took Dickens [...]' (p. xix) to '[...] an unprecedented success' (p. xx).

Notice how Douglas-Fairhurst links the author's perspective on the finished work with details of the book as a physical object and seasonal merchandise.

When we read *A Christmas Carol*, or watch one of its many adaptations, it is easy to transpose our cultural assumptions about Christmas traditions onto a work that seems to encapsulate so many of them. However, the crucial historical dimension in literary studies helps us to unpick these assumptions, which in turn may open the way to a different kind of reading pleasure.

8 Summary

Figure 8 Charles Dickens's grave at Westminster Abbey.
Photo: copyright: Dean and Chapter of Westminster.

Thinking about the reputation of Dickens and *A Christmas Carol* has allowed us to bring a great deal of hindsight to the subject. But, as well as considering what the writer and the text signify to us now, we have also attempted to broaden our understanding of Dickens as a major figure in his own time. In addition, we have looked more closely at some of the contemporary circumstances around the composition, publication and reception of his work. In doing so, we briefly explored the way that Dickens responded and contributed to traditions around Christmas in Victorian Britain. This notion of tradition – as a set of values or practices that develop over time – will be explored further in the second book of the module, *Traditions*. For now, we might just note how Dickens's reputation became caught up in it.

Throughout the chapter, you have been paying close attention to Dickens's words and the way in which he drew upon different kinds of writing in his work. The close study of language in this chapter should enhance your awareness of how the language of any written text, not just one classed as 'literature', works on a reader.

You should now return to the module website to continue your study of this unit.

References

Andrews, M. (2006) *Charles Dickens and his performing selves: Dickens and the public readings.* Oxford: Oxford University Press.

Collins, P. (ed.) (1971) *Dickens: the critical heritage.* London: Routledge and Kegan Paul.

Dickens, C. (1999 [1849–50]) *David Copperfield.* Edited by Nina Burgis. Oxford: Oxford University Press.

Dickens, C. (2006) *A Christmas Carol and other Christmas books.* Edited by Robert Douglas-Fairhurst. Oxford: Oxford University Press.

Edgar, D. (2017) *A Christmas Carol (RSC stage version).* London: Nick Hern Books.

Flanders, J. (2014) 'Victorian Christmas', *British Library*, 15 May. Available at: https://www.bl.uk/romantics-and-victorians/articles/victorian-christmas (Accessed: 11 November 2018).

Hilen, A. (ed.) (1982) *The letters of Henry Wadsworth Longfellow, vol. v, 1866–1874.* Cambridge, Mass. and London, England: Belknap Press.

Ledger, S. (2011) 'Christmas', in Ledger, S. and Furneaux, H. (eds) *Charles Dickens in context.* Cambridge: Cambridge University Press, p. 183.

Newsom, R. (2001) 'Fictions of childhood', in Jordan, J.O. (ed.) *The Cambridge companion to Charles Dickens.* Cambridge: Cambridge University Press, pp. 178–85.

Pykett, L. (2002) *Charles Dickens.* Basingstoke: Palgrave Macmillan.

Slater, M. (ed.) (1994) *Dickens' journalism, volume 1: sketches by Boz and other early papers, 1833–39.* London: J.M. Dent.

Slater, M. (ed.) (1996) *Dickens' journalism, volume 2: 'the amusements of the people' and other papers: reports, essays and reviews 1834–51.* London: J.M. Dent.

Standiford, L. (2008) *The man who invented Christmas: how Charles Dickens's 'A Christmas Carol' rescued his career and revived our holiday spirits.* New York: Crown Publishers.

Storey, G., Tillotson, K. and Burgis, N. (eds) (1988) *The pilgrim edition of the letters of Charles Dickens, vol. 6, 1850–1852.* Oxford: Clarendon Press.

Chapter 7
Van Gogh

Kim Woods with Renate Dohmen

Contents

1 Introduction

In this chapter we will be exploring one of the most famous artists of all time, Vincent van Gogh (1853–1890). Some of you will already be familiar with his paintings and his reputation; even if you cannot place the name, you might recognise his work. Those of you who don't know of him yet are in some ways the lucky ones, as you can now experience his work for yourselves and make up your own mind, unburdened by the weight of reputation and the misconceptions that the name Van Gogh brings with it.

When it came to art, Van Gogh was a late starter. Although he had sketched in the past and had sometimes included drawings in his letters, he only decided to become an artist at the age of 27 in 1880 (after failed careers as an art dealer and evangelist). Apart from brief periods of training in Antwerp and Paris, he was essentially self-taught, relying initially on the drawing course published by the art dealership Goupil & Cie, where his younger brother, Theo, worked all his life. Vincent also worked there for some time, but by 1882 he had turned to oil painting.

His career as a painter lasted a mere eight years before he died by his own hand in July 1890 (or was accidentally shot, as a later, fiercely contested theory has it; see Naifeh and White Smith, 2011, pp. 869–86). A fast worker and hugely prolific, he produced over 800 paintings, sometimes painting one a day. Although virtually none of them sold during his lifetime, today his work fetches notoriously high prices. In 1987, one version of his painting *Sunflowers* was celebrated as the first modern work of art to fetch a multimillion dollar price.

Introducing Vincent

Often, Van Gogh is referred to by his forename 'Vincent'. Using an artist's forename is a bit overfamiliar for academic writing, but in his case there is some justification. Using Van Gogh's first name can serve to distinguish him from his art dealer brother Theo, who was invariably known by the same surname (this chapter refers to his brother as 'Theo', and Vincent van Gogh as 'Van Gogh' to avoid confusion).

'Vincent' is also much easier for non-Dutch speakers to say than the guttural 'Van Gogh', and that may also have played a part. Interestingly, Van Gogh himself chose to sign his paintings as 'Vincent'.

You might also notice that Van Gogh is spelled with a lower case 'v' when it is used together with his forename: Vincent van Gogh.

From the mid twentieth century, and even before, Van Gogh has captured the imagination not only of art lovers but also the public. He has been celebrated in films, including *Lust for Life* (1956) and, more recently, the painted, animated film *Loving Vincent* (2017) and *At Eternity's Gate* (2018); in at least one song, *Vincent (Starry Starry Night)*, based on the 1889 painting *Starry Night* (Figure 1; song by Don Maclean (1971)); in numerous types of merchandise from umbrellas to tea towels; and in countless biographies, books and articles. In this chapter, we will be trying to understand the grounds for Van Gogh's reputation, but we will also be questioning and challenging it, using a mixture of evidence including Van Gogh's own letters, the insights of some twentieth and twenty-first-century scholars and, of course, his paintings.

Figure 1 Vincent van Gogh, *Starry Night*, 1889, oil on canvas, 74 × 92 cm. The Museum of Modern Art, New York, acquired through the Lillie P. Bliss Bequest. Acc. n.: 472.1941. © 2018. Digital image, The Museum of Modern Art, New York/Scala, Florence.

2 Viewing Van Gogh

The first theme that we shall be exploring is artistic recognition. Why was Van Gogh so unable to establish a reputation during his lifetime? How does his approach compare with that of his more recognised contemporaries, and what were the innovative aspects of his work that contemporaries found difficult to come to terms with?

2.1 *Sunflowers*

Van Gogh's sunflower paintings are perhaps the most famous of all his works of art. He did six, five of which survive. The one shown in Figure 2 is in the National Gallery in London. It is one of the most visited pictures in the gallery and tourists can regularly be found having their photograph taken in front of it.

Activity

(Allow around 30 minutes to complete this activity.)

Look carefully at Figure 2. In your opinion, what do you think are the most important aspects of the painting? What do you think are the least important?

You may remember the list of criteria from the first activity on the module website. In a similar way, use the following prompts to help you decide:

- pattern and shape
- a sense of three-dimensional objects and space
- accurate plant forms
- colour
- symmetry
- brushwork and texture
- meaning.

Figure 2 Vincent van Gogh, *Sunflowers*, 1888, oil on canvas, 92 × 73 cm.
The National Gallery, London, bought, 1924. Acc. n.: NG3863. © 2018. The
National Gallery, London/Scala, Florence.

Discussion

The sense of three-dimensional space seems to me to be the least important: the vase looks quite flat or two-dimensional, and it does not really give a sense of being placed on the surface of a receding table. All the other elements in *Sunflowers* have a role to play (we will look into this in more detail shortly), but I would choose colour, closely followed by brushwork, as the most important aspects of the painting.

The painting itself is a celebration of yellow, with only accents of green and a narrow strip of blue marking the edge of the table and the vase. Yellow is generally a bright colour, and the light yellow background used here creates a sense of vibrancy and brilliance. To me, this seems to be the basis of the picture.

The subject of the painting is clearly recognisable as sunflowers (it is known that Van Gogh painted them from life), but their shapes are somewhat exaggerated. The 15 flowers, not 14 as sometimes described, have been arranged roughly symmetrically. The arrangement of forms and objects within the painting is called the **composition**. The spiky shapes of the flowers at the edges of the bunch in the vase contrast with the soft, rounded shapes of the six flowers in the centre, but it is worth noting that despite the irregular appearance of the flowers, the composition is in fact quite carefully balanced.

Another element to consider is **texture**, which is achieved partly by the **brushwork**. Instead of applying paint in one consistent way – regular small brushstrokes, for example – Van Gogh varied the brushstrokes to evoke the different textures of the flowers. The paint is densely applied in the sunflowers down the middle, so thick in places that it actually casts a shadow on the canvas. This is not the case with the sunflowers round the edges. This combination of dense, varied brushwork and exaggerated shapes creates a vitality and excitement far beyond what might initially be expected from the depiction of a simple vase of flowers.

The particular shades of yellow used in the central and peripheral flowers are also varied, standing out against the lighter background. This contrast in **tone** (between the light background and darker flowers) creates the illusion of bringing the vase and its contents towards the viewer, creating a sense of immediacy and involvement. As the flowers are the subject of the painting, we might expect them to be 'spotlit' against a darker background, so this reversal is unusual and is one of the features that makes the picture so effective and unique.

Figure 3 Paul Gauguin, *Vincent van Gogh Painting Sunflowers*, 1888, oil on canvas, 73 × 91 cm. Van Gogh Museum, Amsterdam, obj. no. s0225V1962. Photo: © Van Gogh Museum, Amsterdam/Bridgeman Images.

Sunflowers are grown near Arles in the South of France, where Van Gogh settled in 1888. Three of his sunflower pictures, including the National Gallery version in Figure 2, were painted in August 1888 to decorate the walls of the room where Van Gogh's friend, the painter Paul Gauguin (1848–1903), was to stay when he came to work with Van Gogh at his house later that year. Gauguin was clearly impressed with them and later asked to have one for himself. Sunflowers became a kind of personal attribute for Van Gogh, as he remarked in January 1889 (referring to French artist contemporaries), 'You know that Jeannin has the peony, Quost has the hollyhock, but I have the sunflower, in a way' (Jansen et al., 2009 [Letter 741]). When Gauguin decided to paint a portrait of Van Gogh, he chose to paint him working on one of the versions of *Sunflowers* (Figure 3). Van Gogh painted further sunflower pictures during and after Gauguin's visit. In

January 1889, he completed copies of two of them, one presumably intended for Gauguin. Two copies of the National Gallery picture survive, each replica slightly different. This suggests that the sunflower pictures were a source of fascination for Van Gogh and had a particular significance for him.

As we shall see in the following section, Van Gogh was familiar with a wide range of art, including what we might call the 'Old Masters' (work by famous artists of the past, in particular from the thirteenth to the seventeenth centuries). The fact that he grew up in a clergy household in the Netherlands and became an evangelist himself for a brief period also meant that he was closely familiar with religious associations. Therefore, it is not far-fetched to suggest that meaning might be invested in Van Gogh's sunflower pictures, not just through the emotion they record and evoke but also through their associations. Famously, the sunflower head moves during the day to follow the progress of the sun, and it was perhaps this that prompted the artist to declare to his sister in 1890 that his sunflowers symbolised gratitude.

The painting *Sunflowers* bristles with character. Twenty-first-century viewers have been conditioned by exposure to painters like Van Gogh, so it is perhaps easy for us to be open-minded about his work and see its value. An audience expecting photographic accuracy or a conventional flower painting might be perplexed by this painting, or even alarmed by it. As previously mentioned, Van Gogh did not gain recognition for his work during his lifetime – it was mainly his brother Theo and a few artist friends like Gauguin who could see its importance. The reason for this is that his work went against the grain of conventional viewing habits in the nineteenth century, and it is important to understand how and why this was.

2.2 Academic art and the Impressionists

Establishing the reactions that relatively ordinary viewers had about
Van Gogh's work (as opposed to the views of professional critics or
those involved in the art world) is difficult because of the lack of
records available, but we do have the testimony of two women. Van
Gogh's own sister Elisabeth, who was neither close to her brother nor
particularly knowledgeable about art, admitted that 'it was a long time
before I could comprehend Vincent van Gogh's art' (Gogh, 1913,
p. 55). After the 1908 exhibition of his work in Amsterdam she
realised that, 'In his colour lies the great secret of the strong
individuality of his art' (1913, p. 36). Katherine Dreier, the translator of
Elisabeth's recollections of her brother, saw Van Gogh's work at the
1912 Cologne exhibition of modern art and found it 'vibrant with life'
(1913, p. xvi). She commented that through drawing in colour Van
Gogh advanced on the achievements of the group of nineteenth-
century artists known as the Impressionists (discussed below). Dreier
also offered an insight into how contemporary viewers reacted to Van
Gogh's work: 'They come to pictures with preconceived ideas of what
they wish to see, and if the exhibition is along other lines, they
condemn.' (1913, p. xxi). Two questions arise out of these remarks:
first, what was distinctive about Van Gogh's use of colour; and second,
what did the art-viewing public expect to see instead?

European academies of art, and the French Academy in particular,
considered the accurate representation of figures and space to be much
more important than colour. Colour was deemed secondary because,
according to the conventions of the time, it was thought to appeal
primarily to the senses rather than to the mind. Van Gogh inverted
these priorities of what we call academic art, but he was by no means
the first artist to do so. One of Van Gogh's great artistic heroes, the
celebrated French painter Eugène Delacroix (1798–1863), was also
renowned for his unorthodox approach to painting that defied
academic conventions.

Delacroix's challenge to academic art

Delacroix's 1830 picture *Liberty Leading the People* (Figure 4) shows an allegorical female figure, personifying liberty, emerging through the smoke of gunfire, leading a throng of rebels. The colour scheme revolves around the red, white and blue of the French flag, the 'tricolour'. The figures are slightly simplified and suggested rather than described in full three-dimensional detail. The composition is dynamic and dramatic, with the people depicted moving relentlessly forward. The subject is a patriotic one and shows the so-called 'July Revolution' of 1830, in which the populace of Paris overthrew the repressive King Charles X in favour of Louis Philippe. It is classed as a 'history painting', which at the time was considered the highest form of art by European academies of art. History paintings do not usually show an event from contemporary history like this one, and are expected to depict scenes that are grand, noble, and demonstrate exemplary human behaviour by figures such as emperors or kings, usually with plenty of gravitas. Delacroix, in contrast, presents everyday people who participated in the uprising: a street urchin with pistols, an artisan with a sabre, a more prosperous citizen in a top hat. However, their presentation in contemporary dress in poses that were indecorous challenged academic conventions, as did the visible brushwork. His picture was painted shortly after the event and was bought by the state the following year only to be locked away from view, as it was considered politically too challenging by a government fearful of uprisings. Interestingly, for all that he admired Delacroix's colour, Van Gogh never tackled heroic subjects like this.

During the nineteenth century, the traditions of **academic art** emphasised accuracy in representing lifelike shapes and forms as well as a convincingly illusionistic three-dimensional space. This is what a viewer of conventional tastes would expect to see. In academic pictures, it is as if we are looking through the surface of the painting into a plausible world that the artist has conjured up through paint.

Figure 4 Eugène Delacroix, *Liberty Leading the People*, 1830, oil on canvas, 360 × 225 cm. Musée du Louvre, Paris. Photo: © akg-images.

Crucially, to produce this kind of illusionistic accuracy, individual brushstrokes were uniform; not usually visible but carefully blended. In the mid nineteenth century, artists began to challenge these conventions. If you look closely at Delacroix's painting (Figure 4) you will see that he does not present a smooth surface finish. Even though he presents a historic subject, the heroic figures look rather undignified. Following in the footsteps of earlier rebels such as Delacroix, the Impressionists also challenged these conventions and created work that showed visible brushmarks with brighter colours than was the norm. They also made a point of leaving the studio and painting '*en plein air*' (French for 'outdoors').

Like the Impressionists, Van Gogh disliked the meticulous academic approach and had little success in mastering it. In July 1885 he declared, 'My assertion is simply this – that drawing a figure academically correctly – that an even, reasoned brushstroke have little – at least less than is generally thought – to do with the needs – the urgent needs – of the present day in the field of painting' (Jansen et al., 2009 [Letter 514]). This does not mean that Van Gogh thought drawing was unimportant – far from it. The crucial point to grasp is the difference between drawing that aimed for anatomical or spatial accuracy and drawing that sought to capture character or essence, as Van Gogh did. In the case of *Sunflowers*, he surely succeeded.

Van Gogh met some of the Impressionists and saw their work while living in Paris in 1886–87. These connections were made mainly through his brother Theo, who ran the Paris Montmartre branch of the art dealers Boussod, Valadon & Cie (formerly Goupil & Cie) from 1886, where he dedicated a small exhibition space to Impressionist painting. Although this became a meeting place for contemporary artists and collectors, pictures fetched low prices (if they sold at all), even though the Impressionists Claude Monet and Edgar Degas had established some renown. It was not until after the death of the Van Gogh brothers that the Impressionists Camille Pissarro or Alfred Sisley, for example, attained any real recognition, which may be hard to imagine today when their work is so celebrated (Rewald, 1986, pp. 14–15, 82).

Van Gogh had already worked directly from nature long before he encountered Impressionist practice. In a letter of July 1885, he contrasts the sterility of working in a studio with working outdoors, with all the risks of flies, dust and sand getting in the paint, then scraping the wet picture on hedges on the way home (Jansen et al., 2009 [Letter 515]). In June 1888, he described to his artist friend, Émile Bernard (1868–1941), his method of anchoring the legs of his easel into the ground so that it would not blow away when painting outside during the mistral (a ferocious wind characteristic of the South of France) (Jansen et al., 2009 [Letter 628]).

In his letters, Van Gogh repeatedly stresses how important it was to him to maintain a direct connection with nature. Nevertheless, he distanced himself from Impressionist aims. In August 1888 he declared, 'Because instead of trying to render exactly what I have before my eyes, I use colour more arbitrarily in order to express myself forcefully' (Jansen et al., 2009 [Letter 663]). He sought to convey his own distinctive and imaginative vision of nature through an exaggerated use of colour, a feature that is characteristic of Post-Impressionist art.

Figure 5 Vincent van Gogh, *Willows at Sunset*, 1888, oil on canvas, 42 × 38 cm. Kröller-Müller Museum, Otterlo, Netherlands. Photo: © akg-images.

Activity

(Allow around 10 minutes to complete this activity.)

Look closely at Van Gogh's *Willows at Sunset* (Figure 5) and the Impressionist Monet's painting *Impression, Sunrise* (Figure 6). What would you say are the main similarities and differences? Take some time to jot down your ideas.

Discussion

Both paintings explore the effects of the sun, which is setting over the horizon in *Willows at Sunset* and rising in Monet's painting. However, in Van Gogh's *Willows at Sunset*, the yellow sky and the reddish earth tones with yellow accents in the grass are not colours we would normally associate with a sunset. In contrast, Monet's colour is more believable, though pared down to shades of blue, violet and orange.

Another similarity is that they have both been simplified down to essentials. Van Gogh's sun is a disc with rays, almost as a child might paint it, and the pollarded willows are simplified to skeletal forms silhouetted against the hot sunset. Monet's chimneys and the surface of the water are suggested rather than described in detail, while the boat stands out darkly in the foreground like Van Gogh's willows, adding contrast in tone.

Van Gogh's grass, trees and sunrays are depicted through the direction, shape and colour of the brushstrokes. This is presumably the kind of technique Katherine Dreier was referring to when she used the term 'drawing in colour' in relation to Van Gogh's work in 1913. Monet's brushstrokes are also clearly visible; notice, for example, the use of single brushmarks to indicate the surface of the water, which are less defined when compared to Van Gogh's painting.

Another difference is Van Gogh's use of colour. The sky is hardly ever as yellow as shown in the painting, nor is the grass at sunset likely to have such a reddish earth tone. He is clearly taking some artistic license with his choice of colours. In contrast, Monet's painting captures the effect of a sunrise as seen through fog or mist, but heightens the colour contrasts and the red of the sun, especially its reflection on the surface of the water.

Figure 6 Claude Monet, *Impression, Soleil Levant* (Impression, Sunrise), 1872, oil on canvas, 48 × 63 cm. Musée Marmottan, Paris. Photo: © akg-images/Erich Lessing.

Monet's painting, *Impression, Sunrise*, is an early work that does not yet display all the characteristics of Impressionist art – but it is the painting which gave a name to the movement. One of the main differences between this painting and Van Gogh's painting concerns colour theory. Following scientific research into colour perception, which organised colours on a circle, the Impressionists believed that a colour is at its most vibrant when placed next to its opposite, or 'complementary', colour on this colour wheel. This scheme, for example, pairs the colours red, blue and yellow with their opposites green, orange and violet. Monet's painting is structured according to these principles, as the orange of the sun is contrasted with violet and blue – a technique that was developed more systematically in his later work. If you look closely, you will see that Van Gogh is also using complementary colours. The blue line on the horizon is providing a contrast to the expanse of yellow sky, and the result is indeed 'vibrant with life', to quote Dreier once again. However, this choice of blue is more arbitrary than the choice of Monet's colours. When the sky is lit up by the sun, there is no such straight band of light blue on the horizon.

Van Gogh may not have learned his approach to nature from the Impressionists, but his encounter with their work in Paris was crucial in transforming his use of colour. Inspired by their method, Van Gogh turned to using bright and pure colours applied with marked brushstrokes, adapting the techniques of the Impressionists in his own way, as you have seen in *Willows at Sunset*. He also explored and sometimes used complementary colours, but never with the kind of consistency and commitment shown by the Impressionists. As we have seen, Van Gogh could also abandon the accurate **local colour** of the world altogether: the sky might be yellow or green, or the soil purple and yellow (see, for example, Figure 20). Though important, the connection between his work and nature was an indirect one. If the art world was barely ready for the Impressionists in the 1880s, it was certainly not ready for him.

3 Pursuing success

'Achieving FAME is something like when smoking, sticking your cigar in your mouth by the lighted end' (Jansen et al., 2009 [Letter 673]). This was Van Gogh's ironic, borrowed, quote on the futility of pursuing artistic fame, included in a letter to Theo in September 1888. The quote shows the impossibility of attaining fame (you cannot have both ends of a cigar in your mouth at the same time) and the danger of pursuing it (burning your mouth on the lit end). In another letter dated September 1888, he returned to this humorous image as a warning against departing from his artistic goals in a bid to win favour: 'we're far too much smokers to put the cigar in our mouth the wrong way round' (Jansen et al., 2009 [Letter 683]). The message is clear: there is no compromise. If the world is not ready for this kind of art, the only thing to do is stick to your resolve until it is.

Famously, Van Gogh sold virtually nothing during his lifetime: just one or two paintings and a few drawings. He was painfully aware of this failure, but on paper at least he remained confident that this would change, as stated in his letter of July 1882: 'As for the commercial value of my work, I have no pretensions other than that I would be very surprised if in time my work doesn't sell as well as that of others' (Jansen et al., 2009 [Letter 252]). Six years later in October 1888, he still expressed confidence that he could recoup the expenses of his work over the years, but feared that if he did 'the hardship of producing paintings will, however, have taken my entire life, and it will seem to me that I haven't lived' (Jansen et al., 2009 [Letter 712]). As a result, money worries pervade Van Gogh's letters.

There is a romantic stereotype of artists 'starving in garrets' awaiting recognition from an uncomprehending public, which they receive only after death. In Van Gogh's case, he was not literally left to starve, but he remained poor and never attained recognition in his lifetime. As Theo observed in a letter to their mother, it was only once his brother was dead that he began to receive attention: 'Life was such a burden to him; but now, as often happens, everybody is full of praise for his talents' (Roskill, 2008, p. 85). In fact, Theo was premature in his judgement, as it was not really until the first two decades of the twentieth century that a series of exhibitions really began to bring Van Gogh's paintings into the spotlight (Költzsch and De Leeuw, 1990, pp. 42–4). In his case, at least, recognition was hard won.

Mythologising creative talent

The phrase 'genius starving in a garret' comes from a poem of 1795 by a little-known poet called Mary Robinson. Initially associated with unrecognised writers, the theme was introduced to art through the picture of the suicide of the poet Thomas Chatterton, painted in 1856 by English artist Henry Wallis, and now in Tate Britain in London. Here the poet breathes his last in his miserable attic room (Figure 7).

Figure 7 Henry Wallis, *Chatterton*, 1856, oil on canvas, 62 × 93 cm. Tate, London, bequeathed by Charles Gent Clement 1889, N01685. Photo: © Tate, London 2018.

3.1 The art market

Achieving artistic success in France in the 1880s entailed not only appealing to a buying public but also navigating the art market. Van Gogh himself worked for Goupil & Cie in their The Hague, London and Paris branches from 1869 to 1876 and, as previously mentioned, his brother Theo worked in the art trade all his life. Theo did send his brother money, but finding a market for Van Gogh's work was an ongoing problem. In 1884, Van Gogh even accused Theo of not trying to sell his pictures and insisted that he needed a business contract whereby he turned over to Theo most of his output in return for a basic living allowance. There were precedents for such an agreement between artist and dealer. Van Gogh's hero, the painter Jean-François Millet (1814–1875), received art materials and money from his friend and biographer Alfred Sensier in return for artwork that Sensier then sold (Herbert, 1976, p. 23). Van Gogh himself mentioned this very arrangement in a rather bitter exchange of letters with his brother. Art dealer Paul Durand-Ruel had paid a monthly allowance to some of the Impressionist painters, Monet among them, in return for exclusive rights to their work (Rewald, 1986, p. 20). Unfortunately, unlike these two business arrangements, there was no possible profit in it for Theo, as Van Gogh's pictures never sold.

Despite not changing his artistic methods to better suit the market, Van Gogh was not a naïve artist working with no thought to commercial success. He understood the art market, but felt only criticism for its practices, tastes and dealers, parodying their activities, in his letter dated June 1888, as selling 'the right sort of paintings in the right sort of place to the right sort of gentleman' (Jansen et al., 2009 [Letter 620]). The sorry truth was that neither Van Gogh with his significant artistic contacts, nor his brother with his insider knowledge, could break through and make sales in a market dominated by a buying public that expected art to reflect the rules of academic art.

One fundamental criticism that Van Gogh had was that the art world just wanted a kind of cultivated painting that was out of touch with the real world. In January 1885, he wrote: 'If the critics or connoisseurs were more familiar with nature, their judgement would be better than now, when it's the routine to live only among paintings and to compare them with one another' (Jansen et al., 2009 [Letter 480]). Van Gogh resisted the temptation to gear his approach to public taste in order to make a sale. In a letter of March 1882, he comments:

> Believe me that in artistic matters the words hold true: Honesty is the best policy. Better to put a bit more effort into serious study than being stylish to win over the public. Occasionally, in times of worry, I've longed to be stylish, but on second thoughts I say no – just let me be myself – and express severe, rough, yet true things with rough workmanship. I won't run after the art lovers or dealers, let those who are interested come to me.
>
> (Jansen et al., 2009 [Letter 210])

By the 1880s, Van Gogh classed himself as a painter of peasant and rural life and distanced himself from the 'chic' art acceptable to the bourgeois **salon** (as cultural gatherings of the well-to-do middle classes were called). During this period, he was living with his family in Nuenen in the Netherlands, taking the opportunity to paint the rural surroundings. He also repudiated **bourgeois** life and the social distinctions that it sought to maintain, a source of contention with his parents who, he claimed in December 1883 (probably unfairly), showed the same reluctance about having him in their home 'as there would be about having a large, shaggy dog in the house' (Jansen et al., 2009 [Letter 413]). In taking this kind of stance, Van Gogh was aligning himself with an artistic tradition that, likewise, was not interested in 'chic'.

3.2 The peasant painter

The origins of Van Gogh's self-identification as a peasant painter may partly be traced to his heritage, for there was a strong tradition of Dutch peasant paintings in the seventeenth century. He also embraced more modern ideas about the dignity of ordinary people and had particular admiration for Millet, recently deceased. In February 1884, Van Gogh wrote to Theo: 'to me *Millet*, not Manet, is that essential modern painter who opened the horizon to many' (Jansen et al., 2009 [Letter 428]). The new horizon included the rural poor.

This painting of *The Sower* (Figure 8) is one of several versions that Millet made around 1850. The peasant is captured late at work, sowing seed while the sun sets. The subject matter has connotations of the Parable of the Sower, which, in the Christian New Testament, addresses the theme of receptivity to God. Millet might indeed have intended such religious connotations since he saw godliness and virtue in physical labour and in working the land (notice, for example, the bright light on the horizon, which lights up the sower from behind, dignifying the man's labour and suggesting a spiritual dimension to the simplicity of rural life). In all other respects, however, Millet's painting delivers a visual challenge, defying the academic conventions of his time. The picture space is almost entirely filled with the figure of a rough working man, an unlikely subject to grace the drawing room of the kind of individual with the money to buy it. The rhythm of the pose conveys dignity, but there is little concession to beauty: the mouth of the man is slack, wide and slightly open; his clothes are plain; and his face is hidden in shadow, casting him more as a type than as an identifiable individual. There is also no poetic landscape to soften the theme of hard manual work, just a bare ploughed field and the crows gathering to sabotage the labour of sowing. Millet's technique is equally radical, using thick, broad brushstrokes to capture the figure through the essentials of pose and gesture, rather than blended, academic brushwork to record detailed forms. This is not a comfortable, nostalgic picture of country life, but a record of hard graft.

Figure 8 Jean-François Millet, *The Sower*, 1850, oil on canvas, 107 × 83 cm. Museum of Fine Arts, Boston, gift of Quincy Adams Shaw. Photo: © akg-images.

Jean-François Millet

Unusually for an artist, Millet himself came from farming stock and concentrated on rural themes familiar to him. His unidealised focus on the rural poor was initially highly challenging to an art world that privileged 'noble' themes. Millet also had republican friends, and his art was associated with social radicalism.

However, from around 1865 his work attained acceptability, mainly on the strength of its religious connotations, and by the 1880s (not long after his death in 1875) Millet's controversial origins had been shed. Instead, he accumulated a mythical posthumous reputation, propagated particularly by his biographer Sensier, as a simple-living, deeply pious man of the land who identified with the peasants he painted (Van Tilborgh, 1998, pp. 16–18, 39–40). His paintings fetched increasingly high prices, which, as some commentators did not fail to point out, were markedly at odds with the poverty and labour depicted in his work (Thomson, 2010, p. 41).

Van Gogh read Sensier's biography of Millet in spring 1882, a year after it was published. He was well acquainted with Millet's work through photographs and engravings, and was living in Paris with his brother in 1887 when the great retrospective of Millet's work was held there at the École des Beaux-Arts. There are very few letters surviving from his stay in Paris to cast light on Van Gogh's activities, but in view of his admiration for Millet, it seems likely that he went to see it. It is impossible to understand Van Gogh's art, particularly his early work, without appreciating the degree to which he modelled himself on the myth of Millet in both art and lifestyle. Yet unlike Millet, Van Gogh was hampered by his bourgeois upbringing, which he actively sought to repudiate.

Famously, Sensier reported that Millet was content to wear peasant 'sabots' or clogs, and included a drawing of them as a kind of signature of the artist. One of the most famous paintings of Van Gogh's earlier years, *Shoes* (Figure 9), is thought to have been his own version of Millet's sabots. Here, Van Gogh substitutes the clogs for a pair of battered working boots to signify himself as a simple working man.

Figure 9 Vincent van Gogh, *Shoes*, 1886, oil on canvas, 38 × 45 cm. Van Gogh Museum, Amsterdam, obj. no. s0011V1962. Photo: © Van Gogh Museum, Amsterdam/Bridgeman Images.

In adopting the Millet myth of a peasant painter, Van Gogh was further departing from the artistic fashions of his own day, for during the 1870s and 1880s, radical artists in Paris tended to choose fashionable themes of urban life for their subject matter. And even though Van Gogh no longer described himself as a painter of peasants by the late 1880s, he continued to draw on Millet all his life and, for example, made many direct copies from the prints of Millet's work during his illness in 1889. *The Sower* (Figure 10) was among them. As you read on, take a careful look at it. Van Gogh has reproduced the composition faithfully, but supplied his own colour scheme and vision of the countryside. Gone are the shadows and the crows, the redemptive light is more subdued and the brushwork is much more marked. However, like Millet's work, Van Gogh's painting also emphasises a sense of harmony with nature and the rejection of academic conventions.

Figure 10 Vincent van Gogh, *The Sower (after Millet)*, 1890, oil on canvas, 64 × 55 cm. Kröller-Müller Museum, Otterlo, the Netherlands. Photo: Coll. Kröller-Müller Museum, Otterlo.

Arguably, Van Gogh came closest to capturing the realities of rural peasant life in his first major painting, *The Potato Eaters*, completed in 1885 (Figure 11). This was a serious, meticulously planned painting, for which he did numerous preparatory studies from life. This would be the normal way of preparing a grand 'history painting', and *The Potato Eaters* may be seen as a kind of modern take on this tradition. It shows peasants in a dark rural cottage, eating a simple dinner of potatoes around the table.

Figure 11 Vincent van Gogh, *The Potato Eaters*, 1885, oil on canvas, 82 × 114 cm. Van Gogh Museum, Amsterdam, obj. no. s0005V1962. Photo: © Van Gogh Museum, Amsterdam/Bridgeman Images.

Activity

(Allow around 10 minutes to complete this activity.)

Take a good look at Figure 11 and make a note of your reactions to it. Remember to pay attention to the features that you encountered earlier, including composition, use of colour, light and brushwork.

Discussion

You might have found that you associated the cramped space depicted and the lack of colour with a sense of gloom or melancholy; or you might have found it to be a homely scene of simple comforts.

Looking closely suggests that the composition is carefully arranged and creates an overall balance between the figures: the two eaters either

side of the woman turning her back towards the viewer visually balance each other, creating an overall sense of harmony. Earthy colours dominate the image. The dark room is lit by the oil lamp hanging from the ceiling, which bathes the stark faces of the peasants and the dish of potatoes on the table in light. The brushwork is rough and marked, especially in the hands and faces of the peasants, emphasising their coarseness.

In April 1885, when the *The Potato Eaters* was painted, Van Gogh was hardly a beginner, so the perceived lack of finish in the figures and the restricted sense of space were no accident. What is remarkable about this painting is its deliberate lack of refinement. There is also none of the athletic rhythm of pose that we identified in Millet's *The Sower*. Moreover, Van Gogh made no attempt to inject the kind of picturesque sentiment that might make the work acceptable in a bourgeois drawing room. Nor can it be seen as an exercise in nostalgia for a simpler rural life, as peasant paintings so often were, though it might be possible to argue that Van Gogh later travelled to the South of France with exactly that hope. This is an uncomfortable work technically and in its stark subject matter, but its radicalism lies in this very discomfort.

3.3 The social critic

Figure 12 Vincent van Gogh, *The Potato Eaters*, 1885, lithograph,
27 × 32 cm. Rijksmuseum, Amsterdam, RP-P-1912-609.

Van Gogh's views on society appear to have been formed more by
socially concerned literature than current affairs. He is known to have
read the English writers Charles Dickens and George Eliot, pen name
of Mary Anne Evans (1819–1880), as well as the French novelist Émile
Zola (1840–1902), all of whom addressed the plight of the ordinary
working person. In addition to the novels he read and his own
experience of the realities of rural poverty, Van Gogh took inspiration
from magazines containing images intended to raise sympathy for the
poor, such as the English publication *The Graphic*. In January 1882,
while living in The Hague in the Netherlands, Van Gogh enthused to
his brother about the woodcut illustrations in *The Graphic*, which
confirmed his aspiration to produce work 'that is realistic and yet done
with sentiment' (Jansen et al., 2009 [Letter 199]). Van Gogh's aim at
this time was to produce an art of, and for, ordinary people, and at
one stage he was evidently considering trying to become an illustrator,
though this came to nothing. He did, however, produce a **lithograph**

of *The Potato Eaters* (Figure 12). You will notice that the composition has been reversed in the printing process, which is normal.

An English illustration was the inspiration behind one of Van Gogh's most famous paintings, later titled *Van Gogh's Chair*, produced in Arles in the South of France in 1888 (Figure 14). The idea of a chair standing in for an identifiable individual appears to have come from a print produced by the British artist Luke Fildes, which was included in the edition of *The Graphic* immediately after the death of Charles Dickens in 1870 (Figure 13). It shows Dickens's chair pulled out in readiness for the great author to sit down at his desk, which, poignantly, he would never do again.

Figure 13 Samuel Luke Fildes, *The Empty Chair, Gad's Hill — Ninth of June, 1870*, engraving in *The Graphic*, 1870. Photo: © Illustrated London News Ltd/Mary Evans Picture Library.

Van Gogh's own painting of a chair (Figure 14) was done years later and is very different, but it conveys his own identity in much the same way. The chair itself is a cheap, rustic piece of furniture of the sort we know the artist chose for his house in Arles and which appealed to his austere lifestyle. The pipe and tobacco are attributes of Van Gogh himself, and in a way so are the vivid colour and brushwork. The signature 'Vincent' on the onion box behind is scarcely necessary.

As we have seen, Van Gogh's work of the mid 1880s displays social concern together with a deliberately unrefined technique. His approach was profoundly informed by the artists he admired, particularly

Delacroix, Millet and English illustrators, and he came to command respect within a circle of artist friends that included Gauguin and Bernard as well as some of the Impressionists. Art dealers and the buying public, however, showed no interest in his work during his lifetime, although posthumously he came to epitomise the 'mad genius', a conception that fuelled his meteoric rise to fame.

Figure 14 Vincent van Gogh, *Van Gogh's Chair*, 1888, oil on canvas, 93 × 74 cm. The National Gallery, London. Photo: © The National Gallery/ Bridgeman Images.

4 Genius and madness

In the 1972 book and TV broadcast *Ways of Seeing*, art critic and writer John Berger reproduced this landscape *Wheatfield with Crows* by Van Gogh (Figure 15).

Figure 15 Vincent van Gogh, *Wheatfield with Crows*, 1890, oil on canvas, 51 × 103 cm. Van Gogh Museum, Amsterdam, obj. no. s0149V1962. Photo: © Van Gogh Museum, Amsterdam/Bridgeman Images.

Activity

(Allow around 15 minutes to complete this activity.)

Before we explore this painting further, look very carefully at how Figure 15 is executed and write a description of it, basing your approach on the kind of close observation that you did in the first activity of this chapter. Think about composition, colour, light and brushwork, as well as what the painting actually depicts.

Try looking at the image from a normal reading distance, then place it further away to see how the picture appears at a longer distance. Remember, you can also look more closely at this painting in the online gallery on the module website, or, if you have one, try using a magnifying glass on this printed version.

Discussion

This painting is wider than it is high and therefore in landscape format (if it were the other way round, its format would be 'portrait'). It presents a network of rectangular brushstrokes. The wheat is depicted more through colour than form, though if viewed from a distance there is some sense of the wheat stalks in the foreground and the choppy heads of wheat above.

The gold of the wheat contrasts with the complementary blue of the sky, while the reddish-brown path is contrasted with the complementary green verge, creating great colour intensity and atmosphere.

The crows are presented as simplified black silhouettes against the sky and the field. The black brushstrokes in the sky seem at first glance to evoke a storm brewing, but there are a couple of little white clouds on the horizon. You might also notice that there are no shadows depicted despite the bright light, which again shows that Van Gogh goes beyond the observation of nature.

In *Ways of Seeing*, Berger added the following caption to this picture: 'this is the last picture that Van Gogh painted before he killed himself', commenting, 'it is hard to define exactly how the words change the image but undoubtedly they have' (Berger, 1972, p. 28). How does Berger's caption change the way that you look at this painting? Which questions might you ask that you would not have thought to ask beforehand? For example, do those black crows and the blackening sky now offer a sense of foreboding rather than atmosphere? Does the colour seem unnaturally intense, perhaps even unbalanced? Does the brushwork maybe seem frantic rather than rapid and deft?

Van Gogh's final painting was actually a view of tree roots, which was left unfinished on the day he died and hence does look rather jumbled and incoherent. *Wheatfield with Crows* was finished a little earlier. Knowledge of Van Gogh's assumed death by suicide prompts us to look not only artistically but also biographically, on the assumption that the artist's state of mind will be reflected in his painting. On one level, this is not unreasonable: some of us may have had the experience of returning to some work that we did when we were tired, ill or anxious and thought that it was not up to our usual standard. Here, though, we are going one step further and looking at Van Gogh's work psychobiographically, searching for signs of the mental disturbance that we know he suffered from during his life.

Genius and madness

The idea of artistic genius is a concept that has a particular and controversial history. You have already seen, in the unit on Mozart, how genius can be connected with notions of the divine, demonic and even the childlike. The idea that 'genius' is a type of madness can be traced back to the ancient Greek philosopher Plato, who believed that poets and prophets could be possessed by divine inspiration (*Phaedrus*, 245a). Plato's pupil, Aristotle, went on to link those of above average ability with 'melancholy' (*Problems*, p. 277). These ideas became widespread over time and began to be associated with artists. You will be able to listen to a discussion about the notion of the 'artistic genius', and how this might affect our understanding of Van Gogh's work, when you return to the module website at the end of this chapter.

There is no doubt that Van Gogh had a difficult and troubled character, even allowing for the effects of the overwork and physical austerity that accompanied his interpretation of artistic vocation. His final breakdown was of a completely different order, however. It began with a night-time confrontation with Gauguin in December 1888, following which Van Gogh cut off part of his own ear and delivered it to one of the women at the local brothel. He tried initially to pass the ear incident off as 'a simple artist's bout of craziness' in a letter of January 1889 (Jansen et al., 2009 [Letter 732]), referring perhaps to the stereotype of artistic talent and madness. Later, however, he recognised that the severity of his situation was of a quite different order. He was hospitalised and then transferred to the mental institution Saint-Paul-de-Mausole in nearby Saint-Rémy as a voluntary patient, recognising that he could no longer manage alone. He suffered recurring attacks of acute mental disturbance, but in between episodes he was lucid and could explain his own condition to the doctor on his admission to Saint-Paul-de-Mausole. In May 1890 he moved closer to Paris, to Auvers-sur-Oise, where he was supervised by Dr Gachet (a doctor specialising in mental disorders and an amateur artist) until his death in July. Between attacks, but not during them, Van Gogh's drive to paint remained unabated and this last period of his life was extraordinarily productive.

In the light of significant advances in our understanding of mental health, how should Van Gogh's so-called 'madness' be understood, and how did it affect his art, if at all? There has been much debate about the nature of Van Gogh's illness. Initially, he was thought to suffer from temporal lobe epilepsy, for several members of his family were epileptic, including his aunt. Other possible diagnoses include bipolar disorder, a kind of psychosis (cycloid), borderline personality disorder, and the effects of syphilis and alcohol. Crucially, any of these mental health conditions would be exacerbated by obsessive working habits and self-neglect. Writing after Van Gogh's alleged suicide, his former friend and fellow artist Anton van Rappard saw the artist's mental breakdown as the result of pushing himself too hard: 'Whoever has witnessed this wrestling, struggling and sorrowful existence could not but feel sympathy for the man who demanded so much of himself, that it ruined body and mind' (Roskill, 2008, p. 53).

In June 1889, Van Gogh wrote to his brother of his own feelings of failure, not because of his illness but because what he had managed to do did not match up to his intentions: 'I still have remorse, and enormously when I think of my work, so little in harmony with what I'd have wished to do' (Jansen et al., 2009 [Letter 777]). Although this might be seen merely as the negative reaction of a sick man, it was written at a time of lucidity and shows clearly the demands he made on himself. Van Gogh's ferocious commitment to his work, writing in July 1890 that 'I still love art and life very much' (Jansen et al., 2009 [Letter 896]), shows that he was by no means defeated by a troubled mental state. Although unable to paint during periods of poor mental health, he continued to do so as soon as he had recovered. This suggests that Van Gogh practised his art despite his psychological condition not because of it.

Figure 16 Vincent van Gogh, *Self-Portrait with Bandaged Ear*, 1889, oil on canvas, 61 × 50 cm. The Courtauld Gallery, London, P.1948.SC.175. Bequest by Samuel Courtauld 1948. © The Samuel Courtauld Trust, The Courtauld Gallery, London.

Van Gogh painted *Self-Portrait with Bandaged Ear* (Figure 16) shortly after he had cut off a part of his ear. It records his appearance dispassionately, while still wearing a bandage, and shows the same variety of colour and rich, thick brushwork as with his other work of this period. Nevertheless, there may be an element of autobiographical sadness. The canvas on the easel in the background is not yet painted, as if waiting for the artist to start afresh, as indeed Van Gogh declared he needed to after his attack. The Japanese print in the background, apart from being a personal possession, is also a poignant reminder of his utopian dreams about the new life he had hoped to start in the South of France, a place he had always associated with a mythical Japan. Based on the many Japanese prints Van Gogh had collected, studied and also copied, he imagined Japan as a simple, primitive civilisation and a beautiful, sun-filled harmonious world characterised by cheerful colours.

His hopes of bringing together a group of artists, living and working in the South of France, had been dashed by the hasty departure of Gauguin after the ear episode. The self-portrait, therefore, suggests a taking stock, and was not necessarily done as an experiment or as practice (though it is true that he lacked other models at the time). The meaning invested in it suggests an autobiographical approach, but one that is thoughtful and self-aware.

Although Van Gogh's art may not be seen as arising out of his illness, he frequently claimed to have invested his work with particular emotions. As early as July 1882, he explained to his brother that, 'Whether in figures or in landscapes, I would like to express not something sentimentally melancholic but deep sorrow' (Jansen et al., 2009 [Letter 249]). In September 1888, he declared of a painting entitled *The Night Café*: 'I have tried to express the terrible human passions with the red and green' (Jansen et al., 2009 [Letter 676]). In July 1890, referring to his three paintings of wheat fields (of which *Wheatfield with Crows* was one), he described himself as 'knowing clearly what I wanted', adding that 'I made a point of trying to express sadness, extreme loneliness' (Jansen et al., 2009 [Letter 898]).

Figure 17 Vincent van Gogh, *Wheatfields with Reaper*, 1889, oil on canvas, 73 × 93 cm. Van Gogh Museum, Amsterdam, obj. no. s0049V1962. Photo: © Van Gogh Museum, Amsterdam/Bridgeman Images.

Despite these insights, it would be a mistake to see gloom and anguish in all of Van Gogh's later works. For example, in September 1889, he painted two versions of *Wheatfields with Reaper* (Figure 17) from his hospital room in Saint-Rémy, explaining:

> I then saw the image of death in it, in this sense that humanity would be the wheat being reaped. So if you like it's the opposite of that Sower I tried before. But in this death [is] nothing sad, it takes place in broad daylight with a sun that floods everything with a light of fine gold […] I myself find that funny, that I saw it like that through the iron bars of a cell.
>
> (Jansen et al., 2009 [Letter 800])

So, through the effect of his pictures, it seems that Van Gogh also wanted to convey positive emotions. He articulated this in a letter of September 1888:

> And in a painting I'd like to say something consoling, like a piece of music. I'd like to paint men or women with that *je ne sais quoi* of the eternal, of which the halo used to be the symbol, and which we try to achieve through the radiance itself, through the vibrancy of our colorations.
>
> (Jansen et al., 2009 [Letter 673])

This casts a different light on his intentions – far from producing work expressive of a psychological state, he wanted his art to make people feel better.

5 Van Gogh's letters and his artistic identity

As you have probably gathered from the references in this chapter, Van Gogh was a prolific letter writer. Most of his letters were to his brother Theo, whose support he really valued, but occasionally Van Gogh also wrote to fellow artists, such as his friends Gauguin and Bernard. Theo kept every single one of Van Gogh's letters, no doubt primarily for private reasons, but conceivably also as a record of his brother's artistic progress and development, and these letters were published by Theo's widow in 1913 (Theo died just six months after his brother in 1891). They are a vital primary source and have been much read for the unique insight they offer into the workings of Van Gogh's mind.

Even though Van Gogh often represented himself as somewhat uncouth and a simple man (for example, his identification as a peasant painter), he was in fact far from a naïve, instinctive artist. He was highly articulate, well read, well connected, particularly knowledgeable about literature and religion, and was able to read and speak both French and English as well as his native Dutch. He mentions many authors in his letters, including Dickens, whose work he read avidly in English as well as in Dutch translation. Through working for an art dealer in The Hague, Paris and London, Van Gogh also had exposure to a very wide range of artists, whom he mentions frequently and appreciatively in his letters. In this final section of this chapter, we will be taking the opportunity to read between the lines to see what Van Gogh's writing reveals about his activities, artistic ideas and aspirations as an artist.

Letters are usually regarded as private, and so ethical objections are sometimes made about reading them. In Van Gogh's time, letters of famous people were sometimes published, including those of his artistic hero Delacroix (Roskill, 2008, p. 11). In addition, Delacroix kept a journal that was also later published. As might be expected of an intelligent and reflective individual, Van Gogh's frequent and lengthy letters constituted a kind of journal in which he articulated his approach to his work and his own perceived artistic persona as well as everyday matters. We know that Van Gogh read Sensier's biography of Millet, but whether the eventual publication of his own letters might have occurred to him is impossible to say. At the very least, the models of Delacroix's written accounts and Millet's biography must surely have informed the way Van Gogh explored his chosen vocation in his own writing.

Activity

(Allow around 40 minutes to complete this activity.)

Reading 7.1 reproduces one of Van Gogh's letters to Theo, written in April 1885 from his parents' house in Nuenen. Although the letter may seem quite long, it is actually one of his shorter ones.

Read through the letter quickly to get a general idea of what it is about. Then go back and read it again more slowly. Do not worry if you do not know who some of the people referred to are, but use the notes to help you.

Now answer the following questions:

1 How do you think the fact that Van Gogh is writing to his brother affects what he says or does not say?
2 What kind of self-image of the artist emerges in this letter?
3 What does the letter tell us about Van Gogh's artistic aims and practices?

Discussion

1 Theo is an informed reader who can be relied upon to keep up with his brother's comments about art and artists. But Van Gogh may be treading a little carefully on the subject of money, as Theo financially supported him and had just sent an extremely generous sum. In the letter, he is certainly justifying his lack of success to his brother as well as his expenditure of buying a lithographic stone. He also lets his brother know that he is relying on his moral support to keep him going. This would put emotional pressure on Theo to keep supporting him. In predicting that the year will be grim financially, perhaps Van Gogh intended to forewarn Theo and secure further support.

2 The artist presents himself as a painter of peasant life, who is at odds with the bourgeois lifestyle of his family and of the art world, taking Millet as his role model. He states that to be a 'genuine' peasant painter one needs to immerse oneself in peasant life, and repudiate any aspiration to luxury, pointing out that this is what he is doing. He also states that his artist acquaintances do not agree with him. This presents him as taking a different and more 'authentic' approach that does not follow artistic fashion and defies conventions. He says that it is no use expecting public approval, which adds

further emphasis to his self-identity as an artistic outsider. It also justifies his lack of recognition to his brother who pays him.

3   Van Gogh lets us know that he is working very intensively, limited only by the drying time of the oil paint. He speaks of also producing a lithographic print, watercolours and drawings. He does not seem hopeful that the magazine *Le Chat Noir* would take his work and states that he is going to produce his own print anyway.

It is important to note that Van Gogh's letters contain evidence of self-fashioning – the deliberate construction of a particular kind of self-image (Pollock and Orton, 1978, p. 7). For example, it was in his letters that Van Gogh identified himself firmly as a peasant painter like his hero Millet, an image he also cultivated through his dress, his behaviour and some of his self-portraits. Despite the appearance of ties and hats in the portraits done in Paris, Van Gogh more commonly represented himself in the clothes of a working man (Zemel, 1997). His 1888 *Self-Portrait as a Painter* (Figure 18) shows him as a working artist. It serves as a kind of manifesto of his artistic approach.

Unconventionality was another aspect of Van Gogh's artistic self-image: 'We cannot change the fact of his being eccentric', his father remarked in 1884 (Roskill, 2008, p. 59). Theo seemingly agrees in 1889 by writing 'He has long since broken with what is called convention' (Roskill, 2008, pp. 77–8). Van Gogh's abandonment of bourgeois comforts, his austere lifestyle, self-neglect and fervent devotion to his work were conscious decisions. From 1880, Theo provided his brother's living expenses and paid for his art materials. It has been calculated that, in 1888, he received substantially more money than the postman Joseph Roulin, whom he befriended in Arles and who had to support a family of five. Yet poverty and exertion were ways in which Van Gogh defined himself and his art.

Figure 18 Vincent van Gogh, *Self-Portrait as a Painter*, 1888, oil on canvas, 65 × 50 cm. Van Gogh Museum, Amsterdam, obj. no. s0022V1962. Photo: © akg-images.

For love not money

The idea of working for love not money has a particular history. For example, in antiquity, poetry was considered to be a 'liberal' art – one that was associated with the mind. Painting and sculpture were viewed as 'mechanical' arts because they involved manual labour. In antiquity, liberal arts were considered to have a higher status because they pertained to those who were considered to be free citizens. They were also thought to be 'free' in the sense that they were not associated with the production of mundane objects of daily use.

However, in the fifteenth and sixteenth centuries in Europe, the visual arts began to be seen as a 'liberal' activity. Of course, artists still engaged in manual work – and still got paid for it – but it became important for them to be seen to be motivated by high-minded factors. Even today, we might frown on an artist who is 'just in it for the money'.

The artist Gauguin, who shared a house with Van Gogh in Arles for a couple of months in 1888, painted a self-portrait specifically to exchange with Van Gogh. As you can see in Figure 19, it includes a simulated portrait in profile in the top right-hand corner of the painter Émile Bernard, who was both Van Gogh's and Gauguin's friend. The portrait draws the three artists together as comrades in art (De Leeuw, 1997, p. 411).

Figure 19 Paul Gauguin, *Self-Portrait with Portrait of Émile Bernard (Les Misérables)*, 1888, oil on canvas, 45 × 50 cm. Van Gogh Museum, Amsterdam, obj. no. s0224V1962. Photo: © akg-images.

Van Gogh clearly admired Gauguin and his work. When he invited Gauguin to stay with him in Arles, he had had high hopes that their friendship would develop into a fruitful working relationship and a productive artistic exchange of ideas. However, it was not to be. The two soon parted company over a fundamental disagreement about what they understood an artist to be. Gauguin disputed the concept of 'truth to nature' altogether, in favour of the free-ranging, innate imagination of the artist as 'genius', while Van Gogh subscribed to a principle similar to the one proposed by the novelist Émile Zola of 'nature seen through a temperament' (quoted in Dorra, 1994 [1865], p. 319). In other words, he recorded what he saw in his own individual way, as he saw it, observing nature from his point of view.

In a letter of June 1888, Van Gogh writes:

> I must warn you that everyone will find that I work too quickly. Don't you believe a word of it. Isn't it the emotion, the sincerity of our feeling for nature, that leads us and – if these emotions are sometimes so strong that we work – without feeling that we're working – when sometimes the brushstrokes come in a sequence and in relation one to another like the words in a speech or a letter – then we have to remember that it hasn't always been like that, and that in the future there will also be quite a few heavy days without inspiration. So we have to strike while the iron's hot and lay aside the bars we forge.
>
> (Jansen et al., 2009 [Letter 631])

The persona arising out of Van Gogh's own writing is that of a self-aware, well-informed, articulate and reflective individual, relying not on his belief in innate talent but on hard work and integrity.

Summary

In the mid 1880s, Van Gogh described himself as a painter of peasants, painting ordinary people in a radical, unidealised way that demonstrated deep sympathy. By 1888 (two years before his death), his art had radically changed and reveals a highly subjective response to Southern France, which for him had taken on a mythical dimension of the kind of happy, sun-filled world of the Japan of his imagination (as seen in Figure 20). His technique evolved from the dark colour and deliberately unrefined character of *The Potato Eaters* to the vibrant colour and deftness of his later work, between 1888 and 1890. How his mental condition affected his art is difficult to quantify, but it is clear that he worked in spite of it rather than because of it.

Figure 20 Vincent van Gogh, *The Sower*, 1888, oil on canvas, 73 × 92 cm. Foundation E. G. Bührle Collection, Zürich.

That the art world now places indiscriminate value on anything by Van Gogh is testament to his change in fortune. It also demonstrates how cultures of taste and what it means to be an artist changes over time. While we now take the myth of the 'mad genius' and of the artist as cultural outsider for granted, in Van Gogh's time, the predominant understanding of the artist was as an establishment figure linked to the art academy. These shifts in meaning are reflected in the reaction of the art market to his work, which ignored him during his lifetime and profited from him after his death.

You should now return to the module website to continue your study of this unit.

References

Aristotle. (2011) *Problems, Volume II: books 20–38. Rhetoric to Alexander.* Edited and translated by Robert Mayhew and David C. Mirhady. Loeb Classical Library 317. London: Harvard University Press.

Berger, J. (1972) *Ways of seeing.* London: Penguin.

Dorra, H. (1994) *Symbolist art theories: a critical anthology.* Berkeley, Calif.: University of California Press, pp. 318–19 [Note 1].

Herbert, R.L. (1976) *Jean-François Millet.* Exhibition held at the Hayward Gallery, London 22 January–7 March 1976 [Exhibition catalogue].

Gogh, E. du Quesne van (1913) *Personal recollections of Vincent van Gogh.* Translated by K.S. Dreier. London: Constable & Co.

Jansen, L., Luijten, H. and Bakker, N. (eds) (2009) *Vincent van Gogh – the letters.* Amsterdam and The Hague: Van Gogh Museum and Huygens. Available at: http://vangoghletters.org (Accessed: 10 February 2019).

Költzsch, G.-W. and Leeuw, R. de (eds) (1990) *Vincent van Gogh and the modern movement, 1890–1914.* Museum Folkwang Essen, Van Gogh Museum Amsterdam. Freren: Luca.

Leeuw, R. de (ed.) (1997) *The letters of Vincent van Gogh.* Translated by A. Pomerans. London: Penguin.

Naifeh, S. and White Smith, G. (2011) *Van Gogh: the life.* New York: Random House.

Plato (1925) 'Phaedrus', in *Plato in twelve volumes*, vol. 9. Translated by H.N. Fowler. London: William Heinemann Ltd. Available at: http://data.perseus.org/citations/urn:cts:greekLit:tlg0059.tlg012.perseus-eng1:245a (Accessed: 5 February 2019).

Pollock, G. and Orton, F. (1978) *Vincent van Gogh: artist of his time.* Oxford: Phaidon.

Rewald, J. (1986) *Studies in post-impressionism.* Edited by Irene Gordon and Frances Weitzenhoffer. New York: H.N. Abrams.

Roskill, M. (ed.) (2008) *The letters of Vincent van Gogh.* New York: Touchstone.

Thomson, B. (ed.) (2010) *Gauguin: maker of myth.* Exhibition held at Tate Modern, London 2010–2011 [Exhibition catalogue].

Tilborgh, L. van (1998) *Millet, Van Gogh.* Translated by F. Everaars. Paris: Editions de la Réunion des Musées Nationaux.

Zemel, C.M. (1997) *Van Gogh's progress: utopia, modernity and late-nineteenth-century art.* Berkeley, Calif.: University of California Press.

Readings

Reading 7.1 Vincent to Theo van Gogh, 13 April 1885

Source: Leeuw, R. de (ed.) (1997) *The letters of Vincent van Gogh*. Translated by A. Pomerans. London: Penguin, pp. 284–7. Underlining reproduced from Van Gogh's original letter.
(Note: this letter appears, in a slightly different translation, as Letter 493 in Jansen, Luijten and Bakker's online edition of Van Gogh's letters (2009). The online edition includes a facsimile of the sketch (of *The Potato Eaters*) that Van Gogh encloses with the letter.)

[*c*.13 April 1885]

My dear Theo,

Many thanks for your regist. letter of yesterday & the enclosure. I am writing at once in reply & enclose a small sketch, based more closely on my last study than the one before. I haven't been able to get as far with it as I would have liked. I worked on it continually for 3 days from morning to night, and by Saturday night the paint had begun to get into a state which prevented further work until it had dried out completely.

I went to Eindhoven today to order a small stone, as this is to become the first of a series of lithographs, on which I intend to start again. When you were here I asked you about the costs of reproduction by the G. & Cie process. I think you said it would be 100 frs. Well, the old, now so little thought of, ordinary lithographic process is quite a lot cheaper – <u>especially in Eindhoven, perhaps</u>. I get the use of the stone, graining, paper, & the printing of 50 copies for <u>3 guilders</u>.

Anyway, I intend to do a series of subjects from peasant life – les paysans chez eux.[1]

---

[1]   Peasants at home.

Today I went for a splendid walk for a few hours with an acquaintance of mine whose first watercolour of a figure I showed you.

I don't say that the scenery isn't <u>even more</u> stirring and more dramatic, say in Brittany, in Katwijk or in the Borinage – yes indeed, but even so, the heath and the villages here are <u>very</u> beautiful as well, and once there, I find an inexhaustible source of subjects from peasant life – and the only thing that matters is to get down to it, to work.

I've a great mind to do some watercolours & drawings again as well – and when I'm in my studio, I'll be able to make time for that in the evenings.

I was <u>tremendously</u> pleased that you sent me the 100 frs. As I said, it was absolutely essential that I pay several things off – and that was on my mind. Not that people were bothering me for it, but I knew they needed the money. And that is why I wrote that I might have to keep something back when the estate is settled.[2] But that won't be necessary now – although I can tell you that this year is bound to be very grim. But I keep thinking of what Millet said, 'Je ne veux point supprimer la souffrance, car souvent c'est elle, qui faits s'exprimer le plus énergiquement les artistes.'[3]

I think I'll be moving by 1 May – although I'm getting on well of course with Mother and our sisters, I can still see and sense it is pour le mieux[4] this way – since in the long run it would hardly be feasible to live together. Which I can put down neither to them personally nor to myself personally so much as to the incompatibility of the ideas of people who seek to maintain a certain social standing and a painter of peasant life who gives the matter no thought.

When I say that I am a painter of peasant life, that is a fact, and it will become increasingly apparent to you in the future that I feel at ease as one. It was not for nothing that I spent so many evenings musing by the fire in their homes with the miners and the peat cutters and the weavers & the peasants – unless I was working too hard for that.

By continually observing peasant life, at all hours of the day, I have become so involved in it that I rarely think of anything else.

---

[2] Pastor Theodorus van Gogh had unexpectedly died of a heart attack on 26 March 1885.
[3] I would never do away with suffering, for it is often what makes artists express themselves most forcefully.
[4] For the best.

You write that the public attitude – that is, indifference to Millet's work, as you have just had occasion to observe at the exhibition – is not encouraging, either for artists or for those who have to sell paintings. I quite agree – but Millet himself felt & knew this – and on reading Sensier I was very struck by something he said at the beginning of his career, which I don't remember <u>word for word</u>, only the purport of it, namely, 'that (i.e. that indifference) would be bad enough if I had need of fine shoes and the life of a gentleman, but – puisque j'y vais en sabots – je m'en tirerai'.[5] And so it turned out.

What I hope never to forget is that 'il s'agit d'y aller en sabots', [6] that is, being content with the kind of food, drink, clothes and sleeping arrangements with which peasants are content.

That is what Millet did and indeed <u>he wanted nothing else</u> – and to my mind this means that he set an example to painters <u>as a human being</u>, which Israëls and Mauve, for instance, who live rather luxurious lives, have not, and I repeat, Millet is <u>father Millet</u>, that is, counsellor and mentor <u>in everything</u> to the younger painters. Most of <u>those whom I know</u>, but then I don't know all that many, would not subscribe to this view. For my part, I do, and fully believe in what he says.

I'm talking at some length about this dictum of Millet's because you write that when <u>city-dwellers</u> paint peasants, their figures, <u>splendidly</u> done though they may be, cannot but remind one of the faubourgs[7] of Paris. I used to have the same impression too (although in my opinion B. Lepage's woman digging potatoes is certainly no exception), but isn't this because the painters have so often failed to immerse themselves <u>personally</u> in peasant life? Millet said on another occasion, Dans l'art il faut y metre sa peau.[8]

De Groux – this is one of his qualities – painted <u>peasants</u> properly. (And they, the State, demanded historical pictures from him! Which he also did well, but how much better he was when he was allowed to be <u>himself</u>.) It will always be a shame and disgrace that De Groux is not yet as fully appreciated by the Belgians as he deserves. De Groux is one of the <u>best Millet-like masters</u>. But although he neither was'nor is acknowledged by the public at large, and although, like Daumier and Tassaert, he remains in obscurity, there are people, <u>Mellery</u>, for example, to name but one, who are working along his lines again today.

[5] As I go about in clogs, I'll manage.
[6] What matters is going about in clogs.
[7] Suburbs.
[8] One has to put one's all into art.

I saw something by Mellery recently in an illustrated paper, a bargee's family in the little cabin of their boat – husband, wife, children – round a table.

As far as popular support is concerned – years ago I read something on the subject in Renan which I have always remembered and which I shall always continue to believe – that anyone who wishes to accomplish something good or useful must not count on or seek the approval or appreciation of the general public, but, on the contrary, must expect only a very few warm hearts to sympathize and go along with him – and then only perhaps.

If you come across the 'Chat noir' people, you might show them this small sketch to be going on with, but I can do a better one if they like, for this one was done in a great rush and is simply meant to give you a clearer idea of the effect and the composition than the first one. Regards & thanks, with a handshake,

Ever Yours,
Vincent

You needn't tell the 'Chat noir' that I also intend to make a lith. of this subject for myself. That lith. won't be for publication, anyway, but is entirely a private affair. For that matter, I don't much care if they don't want to have it – because I shall certainly make lithographs myself of whatever I want to have lithographed.

Conclusion

Richard Jones

In this book, you have studied people who, for different reasons, have retained the power to speak to us – and, in varying ways, to influence our lives. They have spoken to us through their reputations. When you move on to the next book, you will continue to think about the ways in which the past gives shape to the present, by exploring the idea of 'traditions'.

It may surprise you to learn how much you have accomplished at this point in the module. The following list is offered as a summary of some of the learning outcomes you have met so far. Of course, it is not meant to be definitive. You will be able to make your own list. (You might also want to review the learning outcomes for the module on the module website.)

- You have been introduced to the subject areas of Art History, Classical Studies, English Literature, History, Music, Philosophy and Religious Studies.

- You have worked with different kinds of evidence.

- You have been introduced to the distinction between primary and secondary sources.

- You have encountered the way that works of art take particular forms, such as sonatas, prose fiction and landscape painting.

- You have practised skills of close analysis in relation to written texts, visual sources and music.

- You have identified the steps of an argument within a piece of writing.

- You have explored how works of art, documents or practices are created and encountered in particular contexts.

- You have noticed some of the assumptions that we might bring to our study of different cultures and periods.

Now that you have reached the end of the book, you might like to return to some of the questions that we asked at the beginning. Why are some people remembered and some forgotten? Why are people remembered for some things and not for others? What bearing does a reputation have on the person who is said to have it? What does a reputation tell us about those who are willing to believe in it? Take some time to review these questions. Even if you are still not sure about your answers, you might well find that your attitude to them has changed. Here, at the end of this book, you will probably have a clearer sense of what you need to do to answer them.

Glossary

academic art   art produced according to the conventions of the art academy, which emulated ancient classical art and emphasised truth to life.

***ad hominem* fallacy**   the **fallacy** of arguing for or against a claim by invoking the personal traits of someone who embraces or rejects that claim. (Literally: the fallacy of arguing 'to the man'.)

allegro   in music, performed in a cheerful or lively way.

apocrypha   texts that are closely related to but were not included in the **Hebrew Bible** or in the Old or New Testament of the **Christian Bible.**

argument   a reason offered in favour of some claim or opinion. The thing being argued for is the argument's **conclusion.**

BCE   stands for 'before common era' and is equivalent to BC.

bourgeois   relating to well-to-do middle classes, who usually are associated with materialistic values and conventional attitudes.

brushwork   the way a painter applies paint to a surface. It is typically characterised by the size, **texture**, and precision of the strokes.

canonical gospels   the Gospels according to Matthew, Mark, Luke and John. These texts are the best-known sources of information about Jesus' life and his sayings, chosen by the leadership of the Christian Church to be included in the New Testament of the **Christian Bible** (as opposed to the apocryphal gospels; see **apocrypha**).

CE   stands for 'common era' and is equivalent to AD.

character   a person's inclinations, habits, abilities, patterns of behaviour, etc. (See also: **virtue**.)

Christian Bible   a collection of ancient scriptures regarded as authoritative by Christian churches. It consists of the Old Testament, which is closely related to the **Hebrew Bible**, and the New Testament, which deals explicitly with Christianity and includes the **canonical gospels**.

composition   the way in which the visual elements of a work of art are arranged, especially in relationship to one another.

conclusion   what one is arguing for when one presents an **argument**.

conservative   someone who wishes to maintain existing traditions in religious practice, social relations, cultural traditions, forms of knowledge, etc. (Compare: **radical**.)

Dissenter   a Christian who rejects state-sponsored and hierarchical forms of the religion. The Dissenting movement in Britain was at its height in the seventeenth to nineteenth centuries and took many subtly different forms.

doctrine   a belief or idea (or set of beliefs or ideas) that is identified and formally declared as an officially recognised teaching by the Church leadership.

dogma   in the Roman Catholic Church, a dogma is a **doctrine** that the Church leadership officially declares to be an essential part of the Catholic faith.

dynamics   the intensity of volume with which sounds are expressed.

ecumenism   the aim of bringing together and developing closer relationships between the different branches of the Christian Church.

Enlightenment   a cultural movement that came to dominate European intellectual life from around 1670 to 1800. Enlightenment values often traded on a radical appeal to reason, and invoked the classical period, when similar values were thought to have held sway. (It was sometimes called the Age of Reason.)

equality   while most would say they are in favour of social equality in some sense, the phrase can mean different things, including: equality before the law, equality of opportunity, equality of quality of life.

fable   a short fictional tale (often, though not necessarily, featuring animals) that conveys a moral or political lesson.

fallacy   a way of arguing that is flawed in some way. The different ways of arguing badly have often retained their Latin names (see e.g. *ad hominem* **fallacy**.)

first person   in first-person **narrative**, the narrator presents events from his or her own point of view, using the terms 'I' or (less often) 'we'.

gender   in academic usage, masculinity and femininity (genders) are contrasted with maleness and femaleness (sexes). A person's gender includes any characteristics that result from adoption of the social norms their society associates with their sex. A person's sex does not include these social elements. The assumption that there can be just two genders is itself a **social norm** that has been increasingly questioned.

genre   a form or category of art, music or literature. Genre sometimes refers to high-level distinctions (for example, between poetry, prose and drama) and sometimes to other subdivisions (for example, differentiating between the prose fictional forms of novel, novella and short story).

Hebrew Bible   a collection of ancient Jewish scriptures. It is divided into three sections: Torah (Law), Nevi'im (Prophets) and Ketuvim (Writings).

Hellenistic   a period of history, usually seen as lasting from the death of Alexander the Great (323 BCE) to the death of Cleopatra VII (30 BCE).

icon   a devotional painting, particularly in **Orthodox** Christianity.

lithograph   a print made using lithography, a printing process that uses a flat stone or metal plate upon which the image areas are worked using a greasy substance that the printing ink will adhere to, while the non-image areas are ink-repellent.

local colour   the true colour of an object or a surface as seen in typical daylight, rather than its colour as seen through atmosphere or interpreted by the taste or imagination of the artist.

Messiah   from the Hebrew word for 'anointed one', this title relates to prophecies in the **Hebrew Bible** (or Old Testament) predicting the arrival of a leader, liberator or saviour who will initiate a golden age. In Christian thought, it is believed that Jesus is the Messiah, which is why he is often referred to as 'Christ' (from *christos*, the Greek word for 'anointed one').

mode   whereas **genre** implies something about the form of a literary or artistic work, 'mode' is less specific, indicating mood or manner. Examples might be 'comic', 'didactic', 'grotesque', 'satiric', etc.

monotheistic   relating to the belief that there is only one God; from Greek *mono*, meaning 'one', and *theos*, meaning 'God'.

myth   in literary terms, myth is usually a positive term. Rather than suggesting a false or invented story, it often refers to a story or **narrative**, which, even if it is fictitious, conveys deeper truths about how a society or cultural group expresses its shared views about fundamental aspects of life.

narrative   an account, which could be true or fictitious, of an event or connected sequence of events.

narrative voice   the process of telling a story (or narrative). The events that make up the story might be described as the 'what' of the **narrative**, and the 'narrative voice' as the 'how'.

natural   this word does not always have a straightforward meaning, but it is often used to suggest that something is inborn, inevitable and benign.

natural superiority argument   an argument that seeks to justify the power one group (e.g. men, aristocrats, white people) has over another group (women, the masses, non-white people) by claiming that the first group is naturally better qualified to wield power.

Orthodox   a branch of Christianity that originated, during the ninth to fifteenth centuries (and beyond), in the gradual estrangement of the Church of Rome in the West and the Church of Constantinople in the East. A formal split occurred in the eleventh century.

personification   a figure of speech in which abstract ideas, things, or animals are represented as human.

pitch   the degree of highness or lowness of a sound.

polemic   a strong spoken or written attack on someone or something.

primary source   in historical studies, a document (or other evidence) created at the time being studied. In literary studies, a primary source is the work being studied (rather than critical writings about the work).

Protestant   a branch of Christianity with roots in the reforms of the Roman Catholic Church in Europe during the sixteenth century.

pulse   the beat underlying a piece of music.

Qur'an   the principal Muslim scripture. The Qur'an is divided into 113 individual numbered sections referred to as *suras*. Each *sura* contains numbered verses called *ayas*.

radical   someone who advocates breaking with some fundamental aspect of an existing tradition. Sometimes called a reformist. (Compare: **conservative**.)

range   the extent of an instrument or voice, from its lowest **pitch** to its highest.

realism   a **mode** of writing that appears to render actual life as authentically as possible. It depends on literary conventions such as close, accurate description and largely unobtrusive methods of narration. A secondary meaning of realism relates to subject matter that is everyday and unheroic.

relic   an item kept as an object of reverence. This can include body parts or belongings of saints or venerated people (such as drops of breast milk from the Virgin Mary, the blood of Thomas Becket or the Veil of the Virgin).

relief sculptures   sculptures that project out from a solid background (e.g. a wall) of the same material.

Roman Catholicism   a branch of Christianity that recognises the authority and leadership of the Pope. The word 'Catholic' comes from the Greek term for 'universal'; 'Roman' claims a continuation with the Church founded by St Peter in Rome.

salon   commonly refers to exhibitions (salons) organised by the academy, which until the nineteenth century was the only venue in which artists could exhibit their work. On a smaller scale, the term also refers to a cultural gathering in private **bourgeois** houses.

secondary source   in historical studies, a document (or other evidence) created after the period being studied, offering an interpretation of it. In literary studies, a secondary source is a work of criticism about a text being studied.

sentiments   now somewhat archaic; the closest modern equivalents are 'emotions' or 'feelings'.

social norm   an opinion, widespread in a particular society at a particular time, about how people should behave.

solo   in music, performed alone (Italian for 'alone').

tempo   the speed at which a piece of music should be played, i.e. the speed of the **pulse**.

texture   the surface quality or 'feel' of an object: its smoothness, roughness, softness, etc.

timbre   the character of the musical sound of an instrument or voice.

tone   in art, tone refers to the lightness or darkness of a particular colour.

trill   a musical embellishment consisting of rapid alternation between the main note and the adjacent note.

tutti   in music, performed together (Italian for 'all').

verism   a style of portraiture which aims at an exaggeratedly realistic depiction, usually in order to project the gravity and authority of the subject.

virtue   a desirable **character** trait (e.g. honesty); the opposite of a virtue is a vice, an unwelcome character trait (e.g. lack of resolution).

Acknowledgements

Grateful acknowledgement is made to the following sources:

Chapter 1

Extracts from Plutarch: from *THE MAKERS OF ROME* by Plutarch, translated by Ian Scott-Kilvert (Penguin Books, 1965). Copyright © Ian Scott-Kilvert, 1965. Reproduced by permission of Penguin Books Ltd.

Chapter 2

Page 89: Blumberg, A. (2016), 'Why Catholics And Muslims Alike Come To Pray At This Shrine To Mary', 25th May 2016, Huffpost, www.huffingtonpost.co.uk.

Readings 2.1 and 2.2: New Revised Standard Version Bible: Anglicized Edition, copyright © 1989, 1995 National Council of the Churches of Christ in the United States of America. Used by permission. All rights reserved worldwide.

Reading 2.3: From: The Quran: An Encyclopaedia, Leaman, O. ed. Copyright 2006 Routledge, reproduced by permission of Taylor & Francis Books UK.

Reading 2.4: 'Summary Statement on Feminist Mariology', Singapore Conference, in King, U. (ed), Feminist Theology from the Third World. Copyright © 1994 SPCK. Reproduced with permission of the Licensor through PLSClear and used by permission of Wipf and Stock Publishers. www.wipfandstock.com

Chapter 7

Reading 7.1: van Gogh, V. (1996), The Letters of Vincent van Gogh, in Pomerans, A. (trans.), Penguin Classics. Translation Copyright © Sdu Publishers, 1996

Index